Mountain Biking
Wyoming

Amber Travsky

FALCON®

HELENA, MONTANA

A FALCON GUIDE ®

Falcon® Publishing is continually expanding its list of recreation guidebooks. All books include detailed descriptions, accurate maps, and all the information necessary for enjoyable trips. You can order extra copies of this book and get information and prices for other Falcon® guidebooks by writing Falcon, P.O. Box 1718, Helena, MT 59624 or calling toll free 1-800-582-2665. Also, please ask for a free copy of our current catalog. Visit our website at www.FalconOutdoors.com or contact us by e-mail at falcon@falcon.com.

1 2 3 4 5 6 7 8 9 0 MG 04 03 02 01 00 99

All photos by Amber Travsky unless otherwise noted.

Library of Congress Cataloging-in-Publication Data

Travsky, Amber, 1955-
  Mountain biking Wyoming/by Amber Travsky.
      p.   cm.
  ISBN 1-56044-805-9 (pbk.)
      1. All terrain cycling—Wyoming—Guidebooks. 2. Wyoming—Guidebooks.
  I. Title.
  GV1045.5.W8T73   1999   98-50260
  796.6'3'09787—dc21   CIP

CAUTION

Outdoor recreational activities are by their very nature potentially hazardous. All participants in such activities must assume the responsibility for their own actions and safety. The information contained in this guidebook cannot replace sound judgment and good decision-making skills, which help reduce risk exposure, nor does the scope of this book allow for disclosure of all the potential hazards and risks involved in such activities.

Learn as much as possible about the outdoor recreational activities in which you participate, prepare for the unexpected, and be cautious. The reward will be a safer and more enjoyable experience.

♻ Text pages printed on recycled paper.

This book is dedicated to:
Rich, for his encouragement and support
and Darth, the wonder dog, for his ever-willing sprit.

Contents

Acknowledgments

When I began this project, I was quite naive about the time and effort it would entail. I originally thought I could intersperse the riding with my wildlife consulting projects and cover the state in a relaxed fashion. As the project progressed, it became increasingly obvious that I had to get more serious about researching the bike routes. Eventually, I loaded up my truck and headed out across Wyoming, exploring and discovering those hidden places that make this state such a treasure.

For several months, I pedaled, carried, and pushed my bike from the arid Bighorn Basin to the alpine peaks of the Snowy Range Mountains. During my travels, old friends all across the state offered encouragement and warm showers as I pulled into their driveways, muddy and smiling. Lively conversation over a cold brew was a welcome diversion after spending so many days, even weeks, alone on the trails.

My large family of six brothers and sisters, as well as my dad, continued to offer encouragement. Their envy was occasionally evident, as I relayed stories of biking past the Tetons and camping in the Sierra Madres. Their envy was less apparent when I told of getting my truck hopelessly mired in mud or of taking a nasty endo over my bike handlebars.

To thank each and every person would be impossible and I am sure I'd forget a few. But the support of so many friends and relatives has contributed to the enjoyment of this adventure and I thank them all.

For most of the routes in this book, my faithful canine companion, Darth Vader, accompanied me. This Australian shepherd made the miles much less lonely. But, my heart was always yearning, to some extent, for home. I cannot fully express the thanks to my husband, Rich, for his support and encouragement through the course of this project. Traveling and exploring is great fun, but there is no place like home.

Map Legend

Interstate	(00)	Campground	▲
US Highway	(00)	Cabins/Buildings	▪
State or Other Principal Road	(00) (000)	Peak	9,782 ft.
National Park Route	(00)	Hill	
Interstate Highway	⟹	Elevation	9,782 ft. ✕
Paved Road	⟹	Gate	•—•
Gravel Road	⟹	Mine Site	⚒
Unimproved Road	======⟹	Overlook/Point of Interest	◻
Trailhead	◯	National Forest/Park Boundary	
Main Trail(s) /Route(s)	— — —		
Alternate/Secondary Trail(s)/Route(s)	– · – · –	Map Orientation	N
Parking Area	Ⓟ		
River/Creek	～	Scale	0 0.5 1 Miles
Spring	⚲		
One Way Road	*One Way*		

Statewide Locator Map

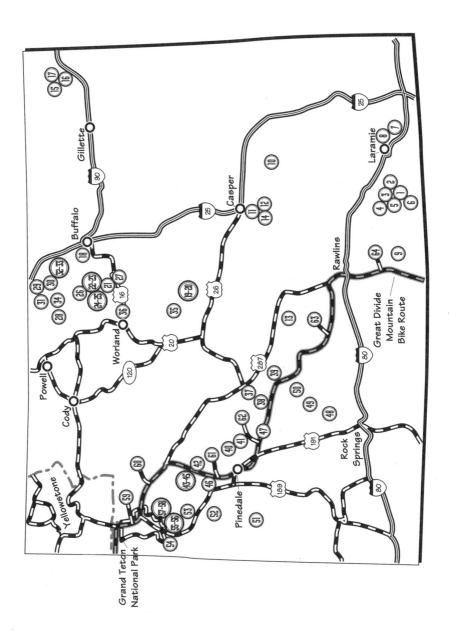

Preface

I got my first bike when I was 8 years old. It was a single-speed mutt my dad had pieced together from garage sale parts. It meant freedom. That first solo ride around the block opened the world to me.

When I was 12, I saved my babysitting money to purchase my first ten-speed. I gazed at its bright red finish with pride. I pedaled all around town and even ventured to the base of the nearby mountains. The world was a safer place back then and my mom and dad just waved as I headed out, never holding me back from my expeditions.

A few years ago I worked with a woman who was mean and nasty; she had a very negative view of the world. I found out she had never, in her 50-plus years of life, ridden a bicycle. If, when she was 12 years old, she had glided through the neighborhood on her own red ten-speed, I'm sure she'd be a happier person today.

My love of the bicycle has never wavered. A decade ago I discovered road touring and have since pedaled much of the Rocky Mountain West and even a portion of Siberia. Then the mountain bike came onto the scene. As a wildlife biologist, I was comfortable in the backcountry, having tracked elk in isolated wilderness and pronghorn across remote prairie land. My love of the backcountry and my passion for cycling created a perfect match with the mountain bike.

As a biologist, I have traveled much of Wyoming's backcountry. On the Red Desert, I rappelled down climbing ropes into prairie falcon nests to band the young birds; I used a tranquilizer gun to radio-collar elk in the Bighorns; I hiked steep cliffs to record the daily activities of bighorn sheep near the Hole-in-the-Wall country. Wyoming is an amazing state and the most spectacular scenery is miles from the interstates and paved highways. Mountain biking gravel backroads, rough doubletracks, and singletrack hiking trails is a great way to explore these out-of-the-way areas.

Mountain biking brings out the kid in me. I've coated my bike, my legs, my arms, and even my face in chocolate-colored mud in my quest to pedal the state. I like that a lot. I stopped for a shower at a friend's house in Pinedale and she just laughed at the mess. Whether it's splashing through mudholes, buzzing down a dirt road, or even bike hiking up a rocky slope, mountain biking gives me the same sense of freedom I had as a 10-year-old.

In the course of researching the rides for this book, I was told on several occasions, "Oh, you can't bike that trail. It's too rough." Or "You wouldn't want to bike that. Why, I even have trouble using my ATV on that trail." There was the woman fishing who watched me ford a river. When I got over to her bank, she said, "Well, I'll be.... It just never occurred to me that a person would try bicycling this trail." I laughed and told her, "A bike can go anywhere. It's only a matter of how much a person is willing to push and carry."

There are over 30 million acres of public land in Wyoming. Even excluding the wilderness areas where bicycles aren't allowed, a person will never run out of new trails, new vistas, and undiscovered hideaways. The rides in this book run the gamut from smooth gravel roads suitable for a ride with the kids, to steep and rocky crag country where passage is gained only by picking up the bike and hiking. From the "gnarly" to the "gentle," this book includes them all. Get out, get active, and explore this wonderful state.

Introduction

Wyoming is big. Really big. It covers over 97,000 square miles, with nearly half of that under federal ownership. It is home to less than a half million people, making it the least populated state in the nation. The pronghorn outnumber the people in this state. This vastness and lack of populated areas make Wyoming a mountain biker's paradise.

That's not to say you can pedal anywhere and everywhere. In some areas, private landowners are especially protective of their property. Access restrictions exist even on some federal lands; most notable is the exclusion of mountain bikes from all federally designated wilderness areas. Knowing where you are as you bike is important, not only in respecting private property rights, but also for safety reasons.

How can you know where to ride? With all that open space and federal land, it's hard to know where to go. Unexpected terrain changes can transform an easy ride into a vertical challenge. A good, easy-to-follow trail can disappear when it enters an open meadow. An obvious trail can deadend at a salt lick, revealing that it was actually a cattle trail and not a biking trail at all.

The ride descriptions in this book will help you select a ride that meets your purposes. Are you looking for a ride that your novice friends will enjoy? Maybe a gut buster that sends the heart racing or a technical ride that requires full concentration and balancing finesse? This book will help you find your way, keep you on track, and add to the enjoyment of your ride.

To enjoy mountain biking in Wyoming, you need to be aware of some of the unique situations and problems that could arise. Being prepared for the unexpected in weather while being aware of general direction-finding techniques can help ensure a safe and pleasurable outing.

WYOMING CONDITIONS

Weather

The fundamental rule in Wyoming is to be prepared for anything. Natives jokingly remind visitors if they don't like the weather, just wait. It will change in five minutes. A sunny blue sky can give way to a hailstorm in a half hour. Snow has been reported in the high country every month of the year. Be prepared.

Summer temperatures in the mountains can reach into the upper 80s during the day, while dropping to the 40s and 50s at night. In contrast, temperatures well into the 90s and 100s can develop on the eastern plains and within the Bighorn Basin. The high desert regions of the Red Desert and the Great Divide Basin are especially unpredictable. The open sagebrush prairie leads one to expect warmer temperatures, but these desert areas range in elevation from 7,000 to 9,000 feet. It can get chilly even in August.

For those not accustomed to Wyoming weather, the seasonal changes can provide the greatest surprises. Actually, it's not the changes, but their timing. Residents joke, "There are two seasons in Wyoming—winter, and the Fourth of July."

Mountain biking in Wyoming is possible throughout the year for those willing to wear extra clothing and brave the wind and cold. Hardcore riders equip their bikes with studded tires or tire chains. The majority of mountain bikers begin their pedaling season in the spring, pedaling the lower elevations until snow leaves the high country. Often, snowdrifts linger at elevations above 9,500 feet until early July.

Spring can be especially unpredictable, with calm winds and warm temperatures one day, changing to cold sleet and snow the next. As temperatures rise frozen roads thaw and turn into paths of mud and gumbo.

Summer is especially pleasant in the mountains, where temperatures rarely exceed the 80s. In contrast, the eastern prairies and Bighorn Badlands have temperatures that often reach 100 degrees F. Summer daily weather patterns typically begin with clear skies and calm winds. As the day progresses, storm clouds may develop into afternoon and evening rain showers accompanied by thunder and lightning.

Fall has the most predictable weather, as Indian summer extends into September and October with crisp mornings, mild daytime temperatures, and chilly evenings. This is a great time to be in the woods, but take extra precautions during the hunting season. Wear a hunter orange vest and avoid biking into areas when you hear shooting.

Heat and Sun

Blue skies are common in Wyoming. But the low humidity and high intensity of the sun require special precautions.

Keep well hydrated. The low humidity may keep you from visibly sweating, but that doesn't mean you aren't losing water. Don't wait until you're thirsty to start drinking; your sense of thirst lags behind your real need for water. Fully hydrate before and after the ride. When on the bike, drink at least every 15 minutes and at least a pint an hour, even if you don't feel thirsty. The use of a water bladder is a smart alternative where you can regularly sip water instead of having to reach for a water bottle.

Wyoming's high altitude makes the sun more intense. Use a sunscreen. Wear a shirt that is light colored, lightweight, and has long sleeves that you can roll down or up.

Clothing Considerations

As mentioned, Wyoming weather can be unpredictable. Many of the rides in this book are in the backcountry, where little assistance can be expected if you need help. Go prepared.

The smartest approach to clothing is to wear layers. Many special fabrics are available that wick moisture away from the skin. Polypropylene or similar material should be worn next to the skin. Stay away from cotton; as you sweat it will absorb water and hold it. When you stop and the temperatures are cool, wet fabric next to the skin can create a dangerous chilling effect.

When going to the high country it is important to remember there can be a drop in temperature of up to 10 degrees F for every 1,000-foot gain in elevation. Typically, if it is 90 degrees F on the prairie at 5,000 feet, temperatures will be in the 60s and 70s at 8,000 to 10,000 feet and even lower at higher elevations or if the wind is blowing.

Carry an extra long-sleeved shirt and a rain jacket even in the middle of August. Some cyclists prefer to carry leg and arm warmers, which are sleeve-like pieces of clothing that you can slide on and off with changes in temperature. Full-fingered gloves, a hat or balaclava that fits under a helmet, and an extra pair of socks are also good additions for spring, early summer, and fall riding.

EXPLORING THE BACKCOUNTRY

There are some "rules of the backcountry" that dictate both courtesy and responsibility.

Fences: There is a cardinal rule in Wyoming concerning gates: when you pass through a gate leave it the way you found it. In other words, if the gate was closed, reclose it. If it was open, keep it open.

Some barbed wire fences can be especially tricky to open and close. The best technique is to put your shoulder against the gate, reach through the fence for the post, and pull it in, using your entire body if necessary. Most gates have a metal staple attached and the gate wire needs to go under this staple to prevent cattle from being able to lift the wire when they rub against the gate.

If you come across a locked gate when you are sure you are on a public access road, be sure to report it to the land manager. It is possible that access is being illegally restricted. In the process of researching this book I occasionally encountered situations where I was sure I was following a public access right-of-way, but still came up to a locked gate and had to abort my route.

Water: It is wise to be prepared to refill water bottles from available natural water sources. Though you may think you are carrying enough water at the start of a ride, it is not unusual to run out. Leaning over and drinking from a cool, clear mountain stream may sound romantic and look good in the movies, but it is not a safe move. Even clear, clean water at high elevations can carry nasty organisms that wreak havoc with the human intestinal tract.

There are a number of commercially produced water filters on the market and the selection of a specific brand and model is a personal preference. As the cost of a filter increases, usually its ability to filter also increases. Less expensive models may not filter out Giardia, so check the product description carefully.

The other option for water purification, aside from boiling water, is to use iodine tablets. Most tablets today are accompanied by a second tablet that will remove the iodine, and thus the iodine taste, from the water once it is purified. I have used the iodine method for years. It is hard to beat the weight and cost. However, if you are getting water with a high sediment content the iodine does nothing to filter out the particles.

Mosquitoes and other annoying pests: Mosquito Lake or Mosquito Creek are frequent monikers in the high country. Although I haven't encountered a Black Fly Lake, No-See-'Em Pond, or Horsefly Creek, these names would be equally descriptive of many places in Wyoming, both in the high country and on the prairie. Mosquitoes and other flying pests are especially numerous in the high country during July and early August. Take along some bug repellent.

Biking in bear country: When I was biking the Great Divide Mountain Bike Route, I camped several nights in bear country in northwest Wyoming. I even found semi-fresh bear sign near one of my campsites. I slept fitfully, grabbing my can of pepper spray at the slightest sound.

A couple of precautions should be taken when in bear country. While cycling, keep alert to bear signs and change your direction if necessary. Making some noise when you bike in areas with dense brush can help alert a bear to your presence. Noise gives the bear notice that you are present; often, violent responses from bears are a result of the bear being surprised. Making noise can prevent this type of response.

If you camp in bear country, do not have food stored or prepared near your tent. In Yellowstone and Grand Teton National Parks large metal bear-proof boxes are provided in the campsites. Store your gear and all food in these boxes. If there is no bear box, store food well away from your sleeping area and sling it high up in a tree.

Pepper sprays are a popular weapon to deter an advancing bear. Some evidence indicates bears may be attracted to pepper spray, but the experts still recommend using a top-strength pepper spray.

Encountering other wildlife: Wyoming is rich with wildlife. Keep your eyes open; you never know what you might see. From big game species, such as elk, moose, mule deer, and pronghorn, to smaller mammals, including pine martens, marmots, and porcupines, the opportunity for wildlife viewing is excellent. Give all wildlife a wide berth both for safety reasons and to ensure the health of the animal.

TIPS TO KEEP YOURSELF FOUND

Compass: It is important to keep track of the direction you are headed and the direction you want to go. Relying on the position of the sun is fine to some extent, but clouds can obscure it and you may not realize you are changing direction or going the wrong way until it is too late. I carry a compass at all times and even have one attached to my bike.

Maps: The maps in this book, when used in conjunction with the route directions, will, in most instances, be sufficient to get you to the trail and keep you on it. However, the maps cannot begin to provide the detailed information found in U.S. Geological Survey 7.5-minute topographic maps (usually at a scale of 1 to 24,000). These "topo" maps are especially useful for determining terrain. The maps have contour lines that are typically spaced to represent a specific change in elevation. An explanation on the legend of the map will define the contour interval—the change in elevation represented between two contour lines; most often, the distance is 40 feet. When the contour lines are closer together, they indicate that the slope is steeper.

Maps printed by land management agencies, such as the Bureau of Land Management (BLM) and the U.S. Forest Service are in a scale of 1 to 100,000. These maps are especially useful in getting the big picture of an area, but they may not always show contour lines.

Helpful hints: Having spent considerable time in the backcountry, there have been times when I was temporarily "misplaced." If this happens to you, don't panic. To help determine your location, here are a few tips:

1. Fences tend to be on section lines. This is not always true, but, in general, fences tend to go along section lines (a section is a 1-mile square designation on a map) or, at least, on half or quarter section lines.

2. All oil and gas pump sites have signs giving their legal description. If you misplace yourself in oil and gas developed areas, it is handy to verify your location by looking at the legal description sign posted at every drill site. Of course, this only helps if you have a map that includes township, range, and section delineations.

3. Look back from time to time. As you ride along, and especially if you are going cross-country, occasionally look back in the direction you have come. Things can look different from the other direction and it can be helpful, if you have to retrace your route, to pinpoint landmarks from a different perspective.

4. Many trails on public lands have blaze marks. These marks, a dot-dash placed one above the other, are especially useful if snow obscures some of the trail. Most blazes are about 7 to 9 feet up on trees and the first mark, or dot, is circular with a diameter of about 4 inches. The second mark, or dash, is right below and is an oblong cut in the tree about 8 to 10 inches long and 4 inches wide. Some dot-dashes are highlighted with bright orange or red paint.

Many backroad trails are marked with a "dot-dash" blaze mark. Some are painted with bright red or orange paint, but most have no color.

5. Trails are often marked with rock cairns when they go across treeless terrain. These cairns range in size from a pile of three or four rocks, to elaborate affairs with a couple dozen rocks arranged in a pyramid fashion. These are especially useful when crossing rock fields or grassy meadows, where a trail is easily obscured.

6. If you lose the trail, relocate it using a systematic process. Rather than wandering forward for an extended period, once you lose a trail, stop and systematically try to relocate it. When this happens to me, I set my bike down at the end of the known trail and then scout the area in a fan-like pattern, searching for dot-dashes on the trees or looking for obvious foot trails. Trails can easily be lost when you enter large meadows or sagebrush openings. In heavily grazed areas cattle can create significant trails. These may look like notable, well-established routes one minute and then suddenly dissipate into nothing or deadend at a waterhole or salt lick. The same can be true of game trails. If you are not familiar with route finding, proceed cautiously. Infrequently used trails can be difficult to locate.

All of the trails in this book were well marked and easy to follow at the time of the initial mapping. But conditions can change with time. Carry a map and compass at all times and don't wander aimlessly if you lose a trail; relax and search in a systematic manner.

RULES OF THE TRAIL

The majority of routes in this book are on multi-use roads and trails. To avoid conflicts with other users, some rules of the trail need to be followed. Do your part to maintain trail access by observing the following rules of the trail formulated by the International Mountain Bicycling Association (IMBA). IMBA's mission is to promote environmentally sound and socially responsible mountain biking.

1. Ride on open trails only. Respect trail and road closures, avoid possible trespass on private land, and obtain permits and authorization as may be required. Federal and state wilderness areas are closed to cycling. The way you ride will influence trail management decisions and policies.

2. Leave no trace. Be sensitive to the dirt beneath you. Even on open (legal) trails, you should not ride under conditions where you will leave evidence of your passing, such as on certain soils after a rain. Recognize different types of soil and trail construction; practice low-impact cycling. This also means staying on existing trails and not creating any new ones. Be sure to pack out at least as much as you pack in.

3. Control your bicycle! Inattention for even a second can cause problems. Obey all bicycle speed regulations and recommendations.

4. Always yield the trail. Make known your approach well in advance. A friendly greeting is considerate and works well; don't startle others. Show your respect when passing by slowing to a walking pace or even stopping. Anticipate other trail users around corners or in blind spots.

5. Never spook animals. An unannounced approach, a sudden movement, or a loud noise startles all animals. This can be dangerous for you, others, and the animals. Give animals extra room and time to adjust to you. When passing horses use special care and follow directions from the horseback riders (ask them if you're uncertain). Running cattle and disturbing wildlife is a serious offense. Leave gates as you find them or as marked.

6. Plan ahead. Know your equipment, your ability, and the area in which you are riding, and prepare accordingly. Be self-sufficient at all times, keep your equipment in good repair, and carry necessary supplies for changes in weather or other conditions. A well-executed trip is a satisfaction to you and not a burden or offense to others. Always wear a helmet.

GETTING READY TO RIDE

You've selected your route and are getting set to head out. To ensure a safe and fun outing, you should carry the following items, either in a small pack on the bike or in a day/fanny pack. This list is not meant to be all-inclusive, but rather includes minimum health and safety items. Longer rides or overnighters will require additional equipment and supplies.

There are several bicycle tools on the market that combine a number of different tools into a small, handy gadget. This equipment list includes individual tools, but these combination gadgets can be substituted.

This book
Additional maps
Compass
Tire levers
Bike pump
Patch kit

Spare tube
Allen wrenches (3, 4, 5, and 6 mm)
6-inch crescent wrench
Small flat-blade screwdriver
Chain rivet tool
Spoke wrench
Baling wire
Duct tape
First-aid kit (sunscreen, aspirin, various bandages and gauze, moleskin, etc.)
Water purification tablets or filter
Extra long-sleeved shirt
Wind jacket
Leggings
Food
Water
More water

How to Use This Guide

Mountain Biking Wyoming provides descriptions and directions for a wide range of rides, from difficult crankers to family cruises. When you select rides in this book, it is easy to match up your technical and fitness levels with an appropriate ride. Most of the rides are either loops or out-and-back routes, although there are also a few a shuttle rides that involve drop-off and pick-up points.

Each ride has been described in one direction. Reversing the route may completely alter the difficulty and make the route seem completely different.

Rides follow a combination of road and trail surfaces. Portions of some rides follow gravel and even paved roads, allowing cyclists to enjoy the scenery and not worry so much about the technical aspects of mountain biking. Others follow doubletrack roads. This is a general descriptor for roads that have two parallel paths, typically for four-wheel drive vehicle use. The condition of doubletracks varies widely, from rough and rocky to smooth and flat.

The increased use of all-terrain vehicles, or ATVs, has added a new type of road. These are narrower than typical doubletrack, with a wide singletrack, and are generally excellent for mountain biking. Other routes follow singletrack paths that are also used by hikers and horseback riders.

The rides in this book are described using the headings and definitions listed below.

Trail name and number: Each ride is given a name and number. Names are based on topographic or other features in the area, official names assigned by land managers, or local custom. Numbers are provided to allow easy reference when one ride can easily be linked with another.

Location: This description provides the general location based on nearby towns or landmarks.

Distance: The overall length of a trail is described in miles. Also, the trail is usually described either as a loop, one-way, or out-and-back route.

Time: A rough estimate of the time needed to complete the ride is provided. This includes actual riding time and does not include rest stops. Strong, skilled cyclists may be able to complete the ride in less time than listed, while others may take considerably longer. Also, trail conditions, weather changes, and mechanical problems can greatly influence the duration of a ride.

Elevation gain: Unless stated otherwise, the figure provided is the total gain of elevation along the trail. For trails where the elevation variation is not extreme, the rides are simply described as flat, rolling, or possessing short steep climbs or descents.

Tread: This describes the type of road or trail, including paved road, gravel road, dirt road, doubletrack, ATV-width singletrack, and singletrack. Often the distinction between the tread types is not always obvious. For example, a doubletrack road, closed to motorized travel, may gradually become a singletrack. Also, gravel roads and dirt roads can be difficult to differentiate.

Season: This is the best time of year to pedal the route, taking into account variations in precipitation from year to year and trail conditions.

Aerobic level: This describes the physical effort required to complete the ride in general terms: easy, moderate, or strenuous. An explanation of this rating system is included later in this chapter.

Technical difficulty: This describes the level of bike handling skills needed to complete the ride. A thorough description of the rating scale is described later in this chapter.

Hazards: Potential dangers or other hazards are listed. These include traffic, weather, trail obstacles and conditions, risky stream crossings, difficult route finding, and other potential perils. It is important to keep in mind that trail conditions can change with time. New fences can be constructed and additional routes may have been added since these routes were originally researched.

Land status: The land ownership and the federal agency managing the land will be listed. All of the rides in this book are on public lands, except for occasional public-access roads where the federal managing agency has secured right-of-way access across private land. When a route crosses private land it will be noted and special care must be taken to remain on the access road until it enters public land.

Maps: U.S. Geological Survey (USGS) topographic maps that cover a ride will be listed along with any special use maps that are available.

Access: A description is provided of how to get to the trailhead or starting point of the ride.

Highlights: This section details the qualities that make the ride unique. You'll find specifics on things you'll see along the way and a general description of natural surroundings.

The ride: A detailed description is provided, listing key points such as landmarks, notable climbs and descents, stream crossings, obstacles, hazards, major turns, and junctions. All distances are measured to the tenth of a mile with a cycle-odometer. Terrain, riding technique, and even tire pressure can affect odometer readings; treat all mileages as estimates.

Elevation and ride description graph: Each ride is illustrated with a graph that includes elevation changes, tread types, and technical ratings. The elevation profile illustrates changes in altitude. This can help in selecting a ride that meets your needs and it helps prepare you for what terrain changes are coming as the ride progresses.

The ratings: I have had friends confide in me their anxiety about an upcoming ride with another friend. "Is this a hard trail?" they ask. Their anxiety arises from concern that what their friend considers an easy ride, will, in reality, be a leg-burning, arm-jarring experience. All they really want is a pleasant and smooth ride through the woods.

Such anxiety is not without merit. One person's easy ride can be a heart-pounding experience for the novice rider. How can you know in advance what the trail is really like? Don't listen to your friends. Read this book instead.

Each ride has two ratings: a technical rating and an aerobic rating. The technical rating provides an indication of the bike skills needed to successfully negotiate a trail. The aerobic scale indicates what your heart rate will be as you pedal the ride. The following sections define the various ratings.

TECHNICAL DIFFICULTY RATINGS

Gnarly. That is the 1990s term that describes a rough and rocky singletrack trail. Gnarly means you won't take your eyes off the trail even for a minute and you had better have your hands ready on the brakes in case you need a quick bailout. The other end of the scale is a smooth paved road where you can watch the scenery and not think twice about where your wheels are headed.

The technical ratings in this book go from a low of 1—the smooth, paved road, to 5—the gnarly hair-raiser. The ratings are based on an objective approach based on such things as the width of the trail and the frequency of obstacles such as rocks and ruts. The addition of a plus (+) symbol helps cover gray areas between levels of difficulty. A rating of 3 + is slightly more technically difficult than a rating of 3. A description for each of the five ratings is provided below.

Level 1: Smooth tread. It is most likely a paved road or has smooth, even gravel. There are no obstacles or ruts. This requires only basic bike riding skills.

Level 2: Mostly smooth tread. This is most likely an improved road, though occasional obstacles, such as ruts and rocks, are present. It may also be a doubletrack or an ATV trail in good condition.

Level 3: Irregular tread with some rough sections. This includes rougher doubletrack where ruts, rock, loose gravel, or sand create obstacles. It also includes singletrack and ATV trails with occasional rocky areas where the less-experienced rider may need to get off the bike and hike around unsafe areas.

Level 4: This is similar to Level 3, except the obstacles are much more frequent. The rocky sections combine with steep terrain and the rider must focus on the road ahead: no daydreaming! Bike-hiking becomes more frequent for the less-experienced rider.

Level 5: This is a continuously broken, rocky, and root-infested trail. Most often it is singletrack trail, but it can also be a doubletrack road. There are frequent and sudden changes in gradient, with some very steep areas going over rocky terrain. The obstacles are nearly continuous. Only the most experienced—or totally insane—cyclist will stay on the bike in these conditions. Bike-hiking, even carrying the bike, is the typical mode of transport on these sections.

AEROBIC LEVELS

The effort involved in pedaling a bicycle varies considerably among individuals as fitness levels vary. Terrain, elevation changes, and duration of a ride can greatly influence the aerobic level of a ride. As the heart rate and breathing rate increase and sweat breaks out, the aerobic level goes up. The physical exertion ratings, from easy to strenuous, are defined below.

Easy: The heart rate is well below maximum and, although the breathing rate may be slightly elevated, it is well within levels that can be maintained over a sustained period. Typically, the ride is going downhill. The easy level may also include rides through rolling terrain with short but gradual climbs. You will get a light workout at this level and a little sweat may break out on your brow.

Moderate: This level will provide a moderate to good workout depending on the duration of the ride. There are some hills and although the climbs are fairly short, they may be fairly steep. The heart rate is still within the aerobic training zone, or 70 to 85 percent below the maximum.

Strenuous: This level may require occasional rest periods. At this level the heart rate can approach maximum. On some of these rides the climbs still level out enough to provide some easing of the heart rate. Other rides can be very strenuous, or "killer," with terrain mostly uphill and quite steep. To continue riding at the very strenuous level requires a high level of aerobic fitness, power, and endurance. Mere mortals will need to walk.

Medicine Bow National Forest Area Rides
Southeast Wyoming

The Medicine Bow National Forest is spread out over three different mountain ranges in southeastern Wyoming. National Forest lands total over 1 million acres. Elevations range from 5,500 to 12,013 feet, creating a diversity of climates from semi-arid lowlands to cold and humid high country.

The Snowy Range Mountains are 30 miles west of Laramie, rising to excellent mountain biking with many old logging roads; these are often closed to motorized travel but open to biking and pedestrian travel. The Savage Run and Platte River wilderness areas are the only areas off-limits to mountain bikes.

Pole Mountain is immediately east of Laramie and provides easy access for residents of both that town and the city of Cheyenne. Consequently, the area is fairly heavily used, at least by Wyoming standards. Activity is focused on areas in Veedauwoo and Happy Jack, but gravel and doubletrack roads provide great places to explore throughout the forest.

The Sierra Madre Mountains rise from the prairie further west of the Snowy Range. The lack of a major population center near this mountain range ensures fewer people in the backcountry, making this an excellent destination for those wanting a more private and isolated biking excursion. Only one route is described in this book, but the U.S. Forest Service map of the area reveals many additional options. Huston Park and the Encampment River, two small wilderness areas, are the only areas closed to mountain bikes.

Libby Flats

Location:	The Snowy Range Mountains, north of Rob Roy Reservoir.
Distance:	32.2 miles, out and back.
Time:	Six to seven hours.
Elevation gain:	1,654 feet.
Tread:	The first 2 miles of the out-and-back ride are on rough doubletrack until the route follows gravel roads for nearly 8 miles. The next 5 miles are on good doubletrack, but then the trail deteriorates into rough doubletrack for nearly 6 miles.
Season:	This route reaches over 10,700 feet and is not snow-free until July. It is best to avoid the route until the snow has melted and the road has dried somewhat to prevent damage to the road. During October, take care to wear a hunter orange vest because the Snowy Range is a popular elk and deer hunting area.
Aerobic level:	Moderate.
Technical difficulty:	Roads are mostly good doubletrack or good gravel with a rating of 2. Segments of rough doubletrack have a rating of 3 due to ruts, potholes, and boulders.
Hazards:	The doubletracks have ruts, potholes, and boulders. The gravel road has some washboarded areas and pockets of thick gravel. Watch for traffic on the gravel road.
Land status:	U.S. Forest Service, Medicine Bow National Forest.
Maps:	USGS Albany, Keystone, Medicine Bow Peak, Centennial.
Access:	From Laramie, take U.S. Highway 130, toward the Snowy Range Mountains. At approximately 22 miles, turn on Wyoming 11, toward Albany. After Albany, continue on Forest Road 500. As the road crosses Douglas Creek, on the northern edge of the reservoir, turn north onto good forest road to Cinnabar Park.

HIGHLIGHTS

This ride begins near Rob Roy Reservoir and climbs toward Medicine Bow Peak. It starts in lodgepole pine forests and climbs from subalpine into alpine habitat. As the route rises over 10,000 feet, open parks become

Libby Flats

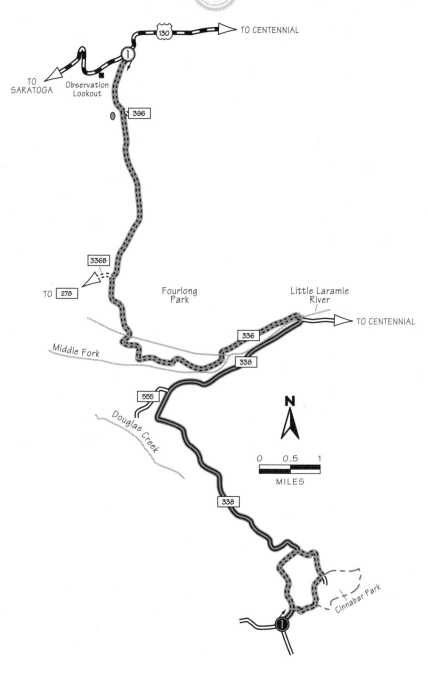

TO CENTENNIAL

130

TO
SARATOGA

Observation
Lookout

396

336B

TO 278

Fourlong
Park

Little Laramie
River

336

TO CENTENNIAL

Middle Fork

338

555

Douglas Creek

N

0   0.5   1

MILES

338

Cinnabar Park

Medicine Bow Peak rises to over 12,000 feet above Libby Flats at the turnaround point for the Libby Flats ride.

more frequent, eventually coming to the largest park, Libby Flats. The stunted trees in this area are strong evidence of the fierce winds that scour the high country in the winter. Branches pointing northwest are much shorter than those pointing southeast; each tree acts as a wind-vane, pointing away from the predominant wind direction.

This mountain range is called the Snowy Range because of the sugary-white quartzite rock that reflects sunlight and looks like snow, even in late summer. From Libby Flats the white glint of Medicine Bow Peak gives this illusion.

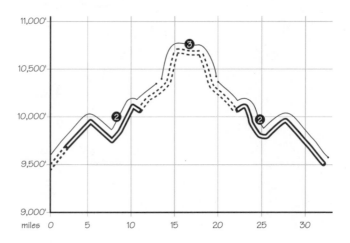

This route is often done as a shuttle, beginning near the Libby Flats Observation Point off US130 and ending either at Rob Roy Reservoir or at Albany. The out-and-back route described here eliminates the hassle of arranging vehicles. The uphill climb is a good workout but the route is not particularly steep.

THE RIDE

0.0 Start at turn from FR 500 onto FR 308 to Cinnabar Park.

0.2 Turn left onto doubletrack road. There are a number of areas to camp along the creek.

0.8 Turn right on old logging road (FR 338J).

1.2 Come to intersection with good dirt road (FR 338).

5.4 FR 555 goes left to Douglas Creek. Stay on FR 338.

8.0 Road forks. Go left onto FR 336 to Libby Flats.

10.2 Road becomes rougher doubletrack.

11.0 At Nelson Park.

11.2 Route turns right, going north. Cross creek.

11.3 Pass by an old cabin.

12.7 Road forks. Stay right. Left goes to South French Creek.

14.1 Cross the creek.

14.9 At highest point across Libby Flats.

16.0 Come to US130. Turn around here.

20.7 Pass by cabin again.

24.0 Return to FR 338. Turn right. Left goes to Centennial.

30.8 Come to intersection with FR 338J. Continue straight to and through Cinnabar Park.

32.2 Back at parking area.

Sheep Mountain Out-and-Back

Location:	On the eastern edge of the Snowy Range Mountains, approximately 30 miles west of Laramie.
Distance:	22 miles, out and back.
Time:	Five to six hours.
Elevation gain:	2,100 feet.
Tread:	The first 0.9 mile is on rough singletrack, then the trail has a short bit of doubletrack before returning to singletrack until mile 2.9. Then it is on wide track or doubletrack as it goes across the crest of Sheep Mountain.
Season:	The trail is open in spring, summer, and fall. It is a popular hiking trail in spring and a popular hunting area in October. The Forbes Game and Fish Access and Trail 386 West are closed from December 31 through June 30 to protect elk winter range and spring calving sites.
Aerobic level:	Moderate.
Technical difficulty:	The trail begins on steep and rocky singletrack with a technical rating of 4 for the first mile. It then goes to doubletrack with a technical rating of 3.
Hazards:	The singletrack segments are steep and rocky. The trail is smooth for a few miles on the top and then becomes rougher and rockier.
Land status:	U.S. Forest Service, Medicine Bow National Forest.
Maps:	USGS Lake Owen, Rex Lake.
Access:	From Laramie, follow U.S. Highway 130 toward the Snowy Range Mountains. After approximately 24 miles, turn south on Wyoming 11 toward Albany. After 6.5 miles, turn left on Fox Creek Road (Forest Road 311). One access point is 5.6 miles farther, at the Forbes Game and Fish Trailhead, Trail 386 West. For the route described here, continue another 1.5 miles farther south to a marked trailhead with a small parking area. Sheep Mountain is surrounded by private property and public access is limited to public access points.

Sheep Mountain Out-and-Back

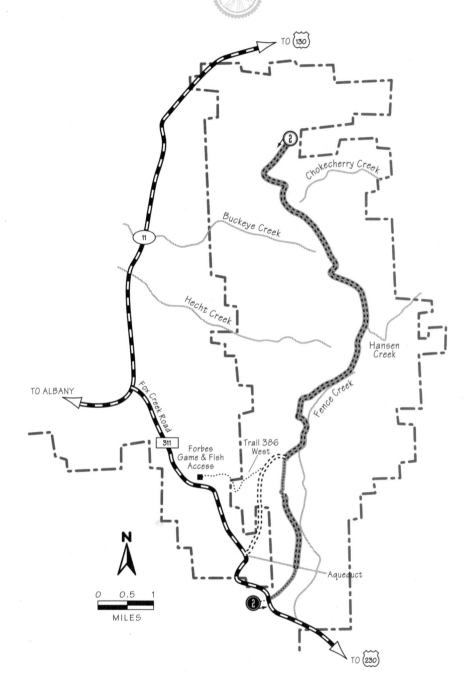

TO (130)

Chokecherry Creek

Buckeye Creek

11

Hecht Creek

Hansen Creek

Fence Creek

TO ALBANY

Fox Creek Road

311

Forbes Game & Fish Access

Trail 386 West

N

0   0.5   1

MILES

Aqueduct

TO (230)

Sheep Mountain rises abruptly from the Laramie Plains on the east side of the Snowy Range Mountains. This mountain has a unique history. In 1924 the mountain was designated a National Wildlife Refuge to be managed by the U.S. Forest Service. Today, approximately 150 head of elk inhabit the mountain year-round and they are joined by four times that number during the winter.

No motorized travel is allowed on Sheep Mountain, making it an ideal mountain biking route. The trails are popular in spring and early summer because they are snow-free earlier than much of the Snowy Range Mountains. By late summer the trails are nearly deserted until hunters invade the area in October.

At its highest point (9,558 feet), the mountain rises above Lake Hattie, providing a majestic panoramic view of the Laramie Basin. The view is well worth the struggle up the mountain, which is fairly steep and rocky. Once on top, the biking is easy and fun as it widens and follows an old doubletrack road. Bring the mosquito repellent if you plan on relaxing for a picnic.

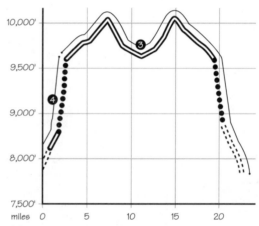

THE RIDE

0.0 Start at singletrack trail at trailhead marker. Trail goes up immediately.

0.9 Trail forks. Aqueduct with doubletrack intersects Forest Trail 386. Continue straight. Trail becomes a rolling doubletrack.

3.1 Come to intersection. Stay right. FT 386 West goes left, leading to the Forbes Game and Fish Access Point. If you take this trail, be sure to stay right when the trail forks approximately 0.3 mile later. Left follows good doubletrack but deadends at a locked gate at the U.S. Forest Boundary.

3.9 Beaver ponds on right.

5.5 Cross small creek.

5.8 Cross another small creek.

11.0 Turnaround point. Return via same route.

22.0 Back at parking trailhead.

Variation: Use the Forbes Game and Fish Access Trailhead. This trail is steeper but shorter than the southern access point. It intersects with a doubletrack road approximately 0.3 mile before the intersection with FT 386. If returning by this route, take care to turn onto FT 386 West. Do not continue down doubletrack. It goes another mile and then deadends at the U.S. Forest Boundary.

North Fork Trail

Location:	Snowy Range Mountains, approximately 36 miles west of Laramie and 6 miles west of Centennial.
Distance:	9.6 miles out and back.
Time:	Two to three hours.
Elevation gain:	1,215 feet.
Tread:	The ride is all on singletrack.
Season:	This ride can be ridden beginning in late spring, once the snow has melted. It is a good trail into mid-fall.
Aerobic level:	Moderate.
Technical difficulty:	Due to rocky areas, this route has a technical rating of 3, with steep areas having a rating of 4.
Hazards:	The trail has segments of rocky terrain and areas with a steep drop-off on one side of the trail. It can be muddy in areas of wet meadows and care should be taken to minimize potential erosion in these areas. Be alert and yield to pedestrians; this is a popular hiking trail.
Land status:	U.S. Forest Service, Medicine Bow National Forest.
Maps:	USGS Centennial.
Access:	Follow U.S. Highway 130 west from Laramie to Centennial. Six miles west of Centennial, turn north on the Sand Lake Road (Forest Road 101). Continue 2.2 miles to the pull-off parking area for the trailhead. The trail can also be accessed at the north end of the North Fork Campground.

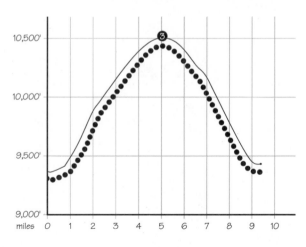

North Fork Trail

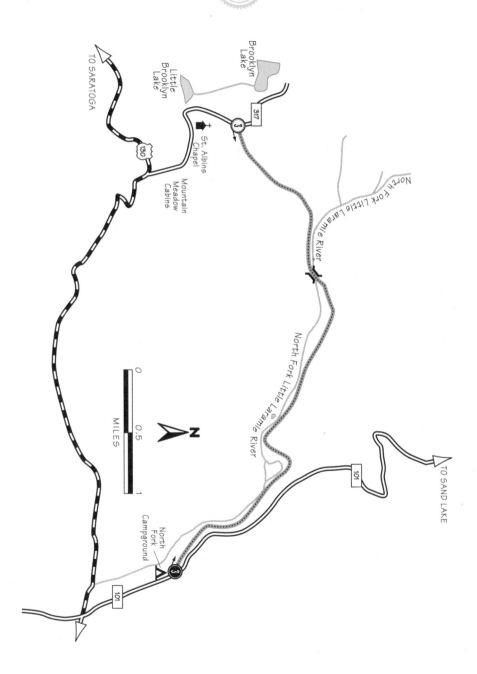

Brown's Peak can be seen rising above a clearing in the Snowy Range Mountains along the North Fork of the Little Laramie River.

Highlights

This trail parallels the North Fork of the Little Laramie River and is a scenic ride on enjoyable yet challenging singletrack trail. The uphill climb is relatively easy. Those wishing to avoid the uphill trek can make this a shuttle ride beginning on the Brooklyn Lake Road and ending at the trailhead on Sand Lake Road.

The trail has been adopted by Big Brothers and Big Sisters of Southeast Wyoming and is well-maintained and well-marked thanks to the volunteer assistance of members from that organization. Foot bridges have been constructed at all river and creek crossings. It is also a popular hiking route and is heavily used by anglers fishing for brook and cutthroat trout in the river.

The Ride

0.0 Take trail exiting on the west side of the parking area. It immediately takes a steep downhill.

0.1 Trail forks. Continue right. Left goes to the North Fork Campground.

0.7 Go through gate.

0.9 Cross the creek on a wooden bridge.

1.6 Cross the creek again, over a wooden bridge.

2.3 Go through gate.

2.6 Rock-hop across little creek.

3.2 Cross the creek on a wooden footbridge.

3.4 Look west for an excellent view of Brown's Peak.

4.6 Trail forks. Stay straight. Left goes to the Mountain Meadow Cabins.

4.8 Come out onto Brooklyn Lake Road (FR 317). This is the turnaround point. Return on same route.

9.5 Back at trailhead.

Quealy Lake Loop

Location:	The Snowy Range Mountains, west of Medicine Bow Peak.
Distance:	17.9-mile loop.
Time:	Five to seven hours.
Elevation gain:	1,840 feet.
Tread:	The first 8 miles follow doubletrack that can be quite rough at times. These roads are used nearly exclusively by ATVs rather than full-sized vehicles. Consequently, much of the doubletrack is gradually reverting to a narrower ATV-sized road. The route joins gravel roads for 1.5 miles, then returns to rough doubletrack and continues until the final mile, which is on slightly better doubletrack.
Season:	This route reaches over 10,700 feet and is not snow-free until July. It is best to avoid the route until the snow has melted and the road has dried somewhat to prevent damage to the road. During October, take care to wear a hunter orange vest because the Snowy Range is a popular elk and deer hunting area.
Aerobic level:	Strenuous.
Technical difficulty:	The first 8 miles have rough and rocky segments with an overall rating of 4. The 1.5 miles of gravel road has a technical rating of 2. The trail becomes rough again, with a technical rating of 4 to 5 up to Quealy Lake. After the lake it has a technical rating of 3 for the remainder of the ride.
Hazards:	The doubletracks have ruts, potholes, and boulders and can be quite rough at times. The gravel road has some washboarded areas and pockets of thick gravel. Watch for traffic on the gravel road.
Land status:	U.S. Forest Service, Medicine Bow National Forest.
Maps:	USGS Medicine Bow Peak, Phantom Lake, Turpin Meadows, Sand Lake.
Access:	From Laramie, take U.S. Highway 130, over the Snowy Range Mountains. Go past Lake Marie and 1.4 miles past the exit to Silver Lake Campground. Turn right (north) onto Forest Road 103. After 1 mile, come to intersection with FR 200. This is the beginning of the ride. Park here or at any of the numerous dispersed camping sites along the road.

Quealy Lake Loop

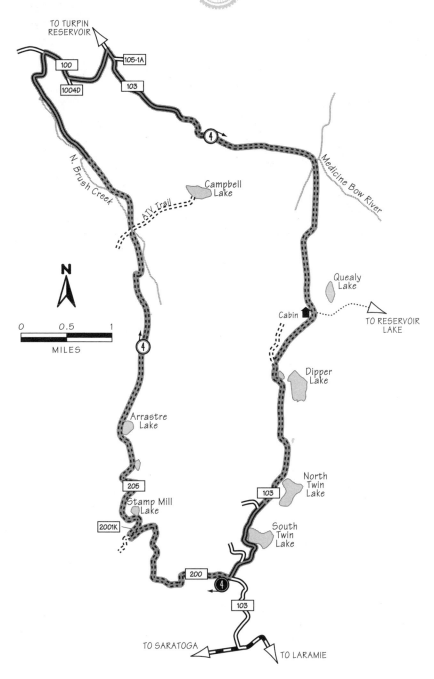

TO TURPIN
RESERVOIR

100
1004D
105-1A
103

4

N. Brush Creek

ATV Trail

Campbell
Lake

Medicine Bow River

N

0   0.5   1
MILES

4

Quealy
Lake

Cabin

TO RESERVOIR
LAKE

Dipper
Lake

Arrastre
Lake

205

Stamp Mill
Lake

2001K

North
Twin
Lake

103

South
Twin
Lake

200

4

103

TO SARATOGA

TO LARAMIE

The alpine Quealy Lake is the high point for this ride before following along the base of Medicine Bow Peak.

HIGHLIGHTS

This 18-mile loop goes through both subalpine and alpine habitats. As it approaches timberline at 10,400 feet, the pine forests give way to open, wet meadows. It is a rough ride with rocky trails and is recommended for more experienced cyclists.

The area is becoming increasingly popular with fishermen, who access the area on ATVs and trailbikes. Foot travelers and mountain bikers are much less common and the ATVers are likely to look at cyclists with some surprise and curiosity. An occasional four-wheel drive vehicle can be seen at Quealy Lake. As you bike the road, you'll wonder why anyone would choose to drive such a rough road.

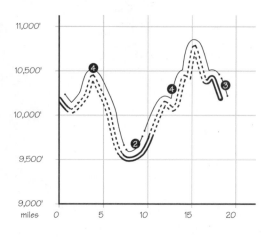

Medicine Bow Peak, to the southeast, overlooks the route as it rises to an elevation of 12,013 feet. Due to the high elevation, be prepared for cool weather regardless of the time of year. Storms can appear unexpectedly and snow has been known to fall during every month of the year. Winter snow drifts can make the going both slow and wet up to mid-July; consequently, this route is best in August and early September.

THE RIDE

0.0 Start down FR 200 at its intersection with FR 103. It starts by going downhill.

1.3 End downhill segment. Crossing private land here on forest road right-of-way. Stay on the road through this area.

1.7 Road forks with a doubletrack road. Stay left. Right goes down to creek. Immediately after, road forks again. Go right on FR 2001K.

1.8 Road joins FR 205. Stay straight on FR 205. Just past intersection is Stamp Mill Lake and a doubletrack road forks to the right just past the lake. This leads to the lake. Stay straight.

2.8 Pass by a larger pond.

3.1 Come to Arrastre Lake. Begin a tough uphill.

3.3 Road forks. Stay right. Left is FR 1D.

4.2 Cross a wet meadow and begin downhill.

5.8 Come to a North Brush Creek crossing. Note the continuing ATV trail on other side. This goes to Campbell Lake and is a nice ride with some good fishing at the lake. To continue this Quealy Lake route, do not cross the main creek. Pick your way along the bank about 50 feet, crossing a small tributary. Join the ATV trail that continues on this west side of the creek.

6.3 Cross creek.

6.4 Cross creek again.

6.9 Cross small creek. Immediately after, the road becomes improved gravel.

8.3 Road joins the main gravel road, FR 100. Turn right. Watch for traffic.

9.3 Turn right onto FR 103 and go over cattleguard.

9.5 Road forks. Go right on FR 103 and up the hill. Left is FR 105-1A.

10.4 Road gets much rougher.

10.6 Pass by "Road Closed" sign on doubletrack to right. Immediately after, cross the creek and go up a very rocky stretch of road. It's safest to bike hike here.

10.9 Cross "Snow Course" signs. Road closed to left. Cross creek and then go uphill on rocky and steep segment.

11.9 Go downhill.

12.2 Come into big open meadow.

12.3 Cross creek.

12.5 Start up rocky hill.

13.0 Trail levels out.

14.0 Come to old cabin above Quealy Lake. The route takes a sharp right here but take the time to wander down to the lake and enjoy the high alpine setting. Down by the lake, Forest Trail 102 forks off to the east and heads toward Reservoir Lake and Gap Lakes.

14.5 Steep creek crossing.

15.3 Come to saddle next to a little pond. The route is mostly all downhill from here.

15.5 Road forks. Stay straight. FR 103-1C goes to Dipper Lake to the left.

16.4 Down and up stream crossing.

16.9 Road forks. Stay straight. FR 103-1B goes left.

17.0 Road joins Forest Road 103 and road improves.

17.2 Pass by Twin Lakes.

17.3 Forest Road 1A goes to the left. Stay straight.

17.5 Road forks. Forest Road 103 deadends right. Go left.

17.9 Back at starting point.

Little Laramie Trails

Location: Eastern slope of the Snowy Range Mountains.

Distance: 3.6 miles for loop described. There are 9.5 miles of trail available.

Time: One to two hours plus additional variations.

Elevation gain: 325 feet.

Tread: These trails are all singletrack, although they are wide in some segments where they follow old logging roads.

Season: These trails are at a lower elevation than most other Snowy Range Mountain trails and, consequently, are snow-free a few weeks earlier in the spring. Typically, they are rideable by mid-June and on through the fall until the snow depths convert the trails to ski use.

Aerobic level: Moderate.

Technical difficulty: These trails have rough and rocky areas with an overall rating of 3.

Hazards: Watch for rocks, ruts, and logs on the trails. They are well marked but tend to be cleared for cross-country skiing rather than mountain biking.

Land status: U.S. Forest Service, Medicine Bow National Forest.

Maps: USGS Centennial. Route ski maps are available at the trailhead.

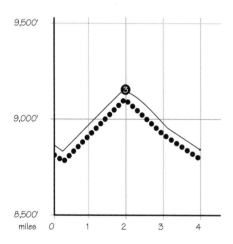

Little Laramie Trails

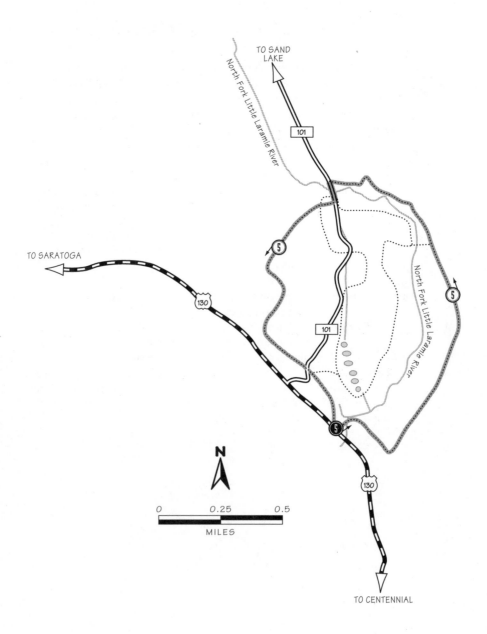

A cyclist enjoys a rest stop while crossing a bridge on the Little Laramie Loop as it crosses a small creek.

Access: From Centennial, follow U.S. Highway 130 up the mountain. Just after the highway passes over the North Fork Little Laramie River, turn right into the Little Laramie Trailhead. Park in parking area.

HIGHLIGHTS

These trails were originally logging roads that were closed to motorized travel and converted to cross-country ski trails. They make good mountain biking trails, although the loop described here is not very long. Still, the route is fairly steep as it leaves the trailhead, providing a good aerobic workout for those looking for a short, early morning or afternoon ride. The downhill portion is not overly technical and is fun for the less-experienced rider. Two additional loops make up the trail complex and can be added to lengthen the distance. Altogether, there are 9.5 miles of trail in this complex, with another 7 miles of trail across US130 at the Corner Mountain trails. Although the trailheads and parking areas are well-developed and the trails are well-marked with blue diamonds, these trails do not attract much traffic outside the ski season.

THE RIDE

0.0 Go to entrance of parking area, past outhouse and onto trail as it passes near the highway.

0.2 Cross creek on good wooden bridge. The trail will go uphill and curve around toward the north.

1.5 Trail forks. Continue straight.

1.8 Trail joins doubletrack.

1.9 Trail comes out onto main gravel road. Turn left and go over creek. Immediately after the bridge, take marked trail going to the right. Trail goes up a short distance and then is a fun downhill.

3.1 Cross gravel road and return to trail on other side. Trail forks immediately. Go right to return to parking area. Left goes up onto Meadow Loop Trail.

3.6 Back at parking area.

Chimney Park

Location:	Snowy Range Mountains, approximately 33 miles west of Laramie and 6 miles west of Woods Landing.
Distance:	4.7-mile loop.
Time:	One to two hours.
Elevation gain:	150 feet.
Tread:	The ride is all on doubletrack roads.
Season:	This ride can be ridden beginning in late spring once the snow has melted. It is a good trail into mid-fall.
Aerobic level:	Easy.
Technical difficulty:	Due to rocky areas this route has a technical rating of 2+.
Hazards:	The trail has segments of steep and rocky terrain. It can be muddy in areas and care should be taken to minimize potential erosion after rain storms or early in the season.
Land status:	U.S. Forest Service, Medicine Bow National Forest.
Maps:	USGS Woods Landing. The Forest Service also has maps of the route as a cross-country ski map.
Access:	Follow U.S. Highway 230 west from Laramie to Woods Landing. Nine miles west of Woods Landing, turn south into parking area at Chimney Park Boy Scout Camp. Park at entrance.

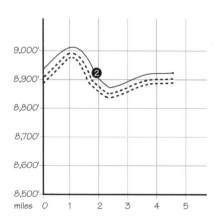

Chimney Park

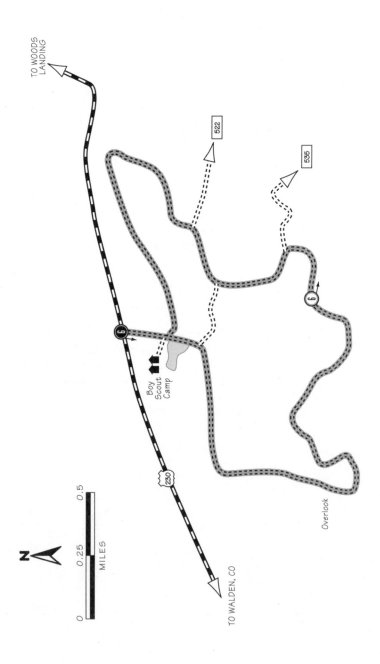

TO WOODS LANDING

522

535

6.0

6

Boy Scout Camp

Overlook

230

TO WALDEN, CO

N

MILES

0   0.25   0.5

HIGHLIGHTS

If you'd like to take a family bike outing, this route is a good choice. It follows forest roads in and out of timbered areas with an overlook at the halfway point providing a panoramic view of both the Wyoming and Colorado mountains.

This area is a Boy Scout camp and when Scouts are using the facility, as a courtesy, be sure to stay on the road when passing the lodge. The buildings are not open to the public but all surrounding permit lands are open for public use. This is a popular ski trail area in the winter and is a pleasant mountain biking trail before the snow flies.

THE RIDE

0.0 From entrance to Scout Camp off US 230, go south on main road.

0.3 Pass by Scout Camp main building. Continue on road past reservoir.

0.4 Road forks. Go right, staying on main road.

0.8 Road forks. Go left.

1.2 Road circles around vantage point.

2.3 Road forks. Go left. Right goes to Forest Road 535.

2.6 Road forks. Go right on FR 522. Left returns to Boy Scout Camp. Go left if you want a shorter loop.

3.0 Road forks. Go left. Straight continues down FR 522.

3.3 Road forks. Go left. Straight goes to FR 533.

3.5 Cross creek and immediately turn sharp left and follow trail next to creek.

4.4 Rejoin main road. Turn right and return to parking area.

4.7 Back at starting point.

Variation: There are a number of old logging roads branching off the loop described here. There are also a number of other routes to explore between US230 and the Colorado-Wyoming border.

Turtle Rock Loop

Location:	15 miles east of Laramie in the Medicine Bow National Forest and Veedauwoo Recreation Area.
Distance:	5.5-mile loop.
Time:	One and one-half to two hours.
Elevation gain:	310 feet.
Tread:	The ride begins on singletrack for 3 miles and then follows rough doubletrack. The final 0.5 mile is on gravel road.
Season:	This ride is good from late spring through the fall.
Aerobic level:	Moderate.
Technical difficulty:	The majority of this ride has a rating of 3+ with segments of 2 and rough, narrow segments with a rating of 4.
Hazards:	The singletrack is a little tricky in places due to rocks and a narrow trail. The rough doubletrack can be rocky, with ruts and potholes. The final gravel road has pockets of loose gravel and can become washboarded.
Land Status:	U.S. Forest Service, Medicine Bow National Forest.
Maps:	USGS Sherman Mountains East, Sherman Mountains West.
Access:	Approximately 15 miles west of Laramie, on Interstate 80, take the Veedauwoo exit. Follow the road 1.1 miles until it forks. Continue on the paved road, going left. A gravel road continues straight. Just after the turn, park in the parking area. Parking farther inside the recreation area requires a daily fee.

HIGHLIGHTS

Veedauwoo (pronounced vee-dah-voo) is Arapaho for "earth-born," which is an appropriate description of this jumbled pile of rocks. The area is popular for its world-class cragging, or crack climbing, as well as its mountain biking and hiking. The Veedauwoo Recreation Area has a campground and several picnic areas; it can get crowded on the weekends and during the summer. Its proximity to Laramie makes it especially popular for an after-work or after-school outing.

Turtle Rock Loop

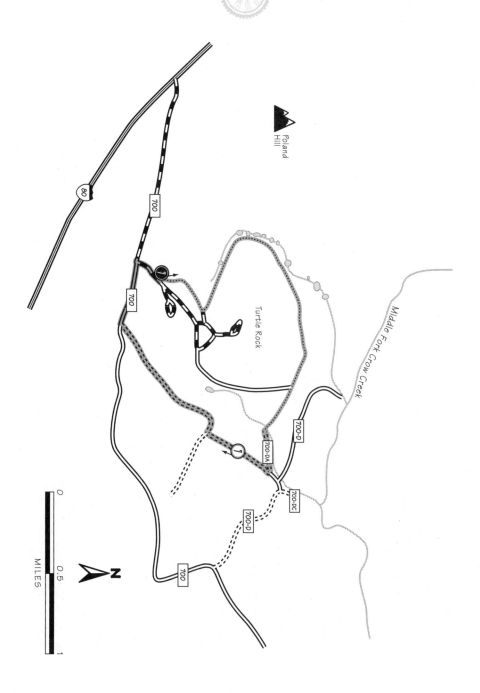

The rock piles that characterize the Veedauwoo area make it a popular climbing area as well as a popular hiking and mountain biking site.

This route is a fun up-and-down roller coaster ride. It begins on singletrack, passing between beaver ponds on one side, and jumbled rock piles and cliffs on the other. The recreation area had a face-lift in 1997 with the construction of paved roads in the most popular climbing and picnic areas, a developed campground, and designated parking and picnic areas. At

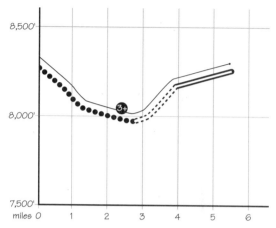

the same time, a number of doubletrack roads were closed to motorized vehicles. Consequently, there are a number of abandoned roads criss-crossing the area, offering mountain bike opportunities. This loop is one of many that could be ridden in this section of the Medicine Bow National Forest.

THE RIDE

0.0 From parking area, go north down paved road.

0.2 Before crossing cattleguard and main road, turn left onto wide singletrack trail marked by sign saying "To Upper Parking Area."

0.3 Trail forks. Stay left. Doubletrack goes right.

0.5 Carry bike over steps (called a stile) going over fence.

0.6 Come onto paved parking lot. Take trail leaving from west side of parking area.

0.7 Go through gate. Reclose.

1.3 Pass by a number of small beaver ponds on lefthand side of trail.

2.8 Trail forks. Go left. For a shorter loop, go right back to upper parking lot.

2.9 Trail becomes rough doubletrack.

3.1 Cross creek. On other side, come to a better dirt road. Go left down road, designated as Forest Road 700-DA.

3.4 Pass by "Road Closed" signs, one on each side of the road. Go right on old doubletrack. Straight goes to intersection with FR 700-DC and, after 0.7 mile, to FR 700 (an alternate route).

3.9 After climbing hill, pass by wooden fence. Just beyond, trail joins a dirt road. Turn right. Left will continue 0.6 mile and deadend.

4.0 Road forks. Stay straight. Immediately after this fork, the main dirt road curves left, while a closed road, connecting to the paved Recreation Area roads, continues straight.

5.1 Pass by FR 700-T, which goes right.

5.4 Come to paved road; turn right to return to parking area.

5.5 Back at parking area.

Happy Jack Ski Trails

Location:	10 miles east of Laramie in the Medicine Bow National Forest and Happy Jack Recreation Area.
Distance:	9.9-mile loop.
Time:	Two to three hours.
Elevation gain:	525 feet.
Tread:	The ride begins on a gravel road as it goes through the campground and then exits onto wide singletrack. The Summit Trail follows an old doubletrack, although use by non-motorized travel is transforming the route from a doubletrack to a wide singletrack.
Season:	This ride is good from late spring through the fall. This area is a non-hunting area, making it safer in the fall than adjacent open hunting areas. To be safe, still wear an orange vest during the hunting season.
Aerobic level:	Moderate.
Technical difficulty:	The majority of this ride has a rating of 3+ with segments of 2 and rough, narrow segments with a rating of 4.
Hazards:	The singletrack is a little tricky in places due to rocky terrain.
Land status:	U.S. Forest Service, Medicine Bow National Forest.
Maps:	Pole Mountain and Sherman Mountains West Quads.
Access:	Approximately 10 miles east of Laramie on Interstate 80, take the Happy Jack exit. Turn left on the Happy Jack Road (Wyoming 210). After 1 mile turn right into the Tie City Parking Area. An alternate access point is the Happy Jack Trailhead, 1 mile farther down the state highway. Also, the trails can be accessed from the northeast corner of the Summit Rest Area. This parking area is a fee area. Season parking passes can be purchased at the Forest Service headquarters in Laramie or a daily fee can be paid at the parking area.

HIGHLIGHTS

In the Medicine Bow National Forest, 10 miles east of Laramie, there is a maze of trails originally designated for wintertime cross-country skiing. After the snow has melted, these trails are quite popular for hiking, trail

Happy Jack Ski Trails

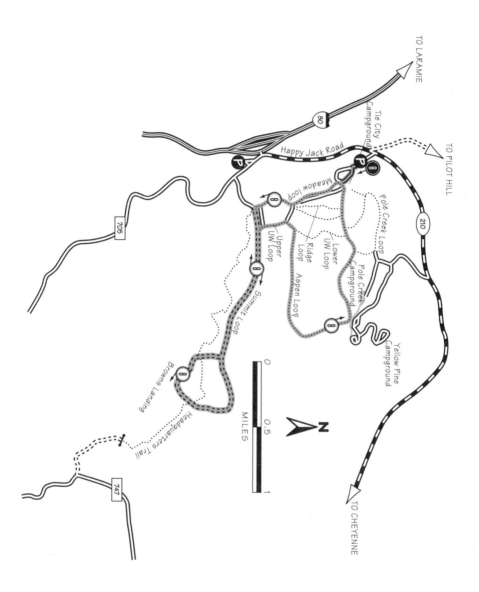

running, and mountain biking as well as horseback riding. The close proximity to Laramie makes these trails especially popular; take care to yield to other users on the trail.

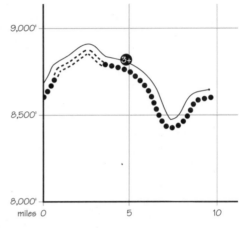

The trail maze includes approximately 27 miles of mostly wide singletrack trails, winding through the forest. The trials are well-marked with blue diamonds. Initially, however, the maze of trails can be confusing. All trails, except the Headquarters Trail, form a loop and all return to any of the three trailheads.

The loop described here passes through the Tie City Campground before taking the trail across a wet sagebrush meadow and heading up the mountain. It follows the Meadow Loop, Upper UW Loop, Summit Loop, and Aspen Loop.

THE RIDE

0.0 From the parking area, go south onto the road that circles around the campground.

0.2 On south side of campground, trail exit is marked. Follow Meadow Loop Trail as it crosses the open meadow and up the hill into the timber.

0.4 Trail enters timber just before a bit of an uphill. Go up hill; at top, several trails converge. Stay right and continue on Upper UW Loop.

0.7 Trail joins the Summit Loop. Continue due east. The summit trail is an old road and follows the fence line.

1.8 Come to "T" intersection. Go right. This is the beginning of the "loop" segment of the Summit Loop Trail.

2.8 Come back around to "T" intersection. Go right and return to Upper UW Loop.

3.9 Return to intersection with Upper UW Loop. Go right. Trail curves left and down a hill.

4.1 Come to convergence of several trails. Stay right and go on Aspen Loop. This loop is rougher. Continue around on loop. When other trail forks off, stay on main Aspen Trail.

9.3 Come to convergence of several trails. Continue straight to return to Tie City Campground.

9.7 Go back through campground.

9.9 Back at starting point.

Variation: There are numerous alternatives for the Tie City and Happy Jack trails. Also, Headquarters National Recreational Trail is a 4.5-mile trail that parallels much of the Summit Loop.

Sierra Madres Continental Divide Loop

Location:	The Sierra Madre Mountains, south of Rawlins.
Distance:	24.4-mile loop.
Time:	Five to six hours.
Elevation gain:	2,200 feet.
Tread:	The first 7 miles follow good gravel roads, then the route follows an old jeep trail that is only open to ATVs, motorcycles, and non-motorized travel; consequently the trail is gradually being reduced in size from doubletrack width to ATV width. The trail follows rough doubletrack to mile 15 where it improves to a narrow gravel road. The road widens and is good gravel for the remainder of the ride.
Season:	This route reaches over 10,000 feet and is not snow-free until July. It is best to avoid the route until the snow has melted and the road has dried somewhat to prevent damage to the road. During October, take care to wear a hunter orange vest because the area is a popular elk and deer hunting area.
Aerobic level:	Moderate to strenuous.
Technical difficulty:	The route starts at a rating of 2 for 7 miles, then goes to a rating of 3, with some steep and rocky areas with a rating of 4. The final 9 miles have a rating of 2.
Hazards:	Watch for traffic on the gravel roads as well as rutted areas and patches of dense gravel. The doubletracks have ruts, potholes, and boulders.
Land status:	U.S. Forest Service, Medicine Bow National Forest.
Maps:	USGS Sharp Hill, Bridger Peak, Singer Peak.
Access:	From Rawlins, go south on Wyoming 71 and take the Jack Creek Road (County Road 500); continue to Jack Creek Campground.
	From Saratoga, take the Jack Creek Road (CR 500) west. After approximately 35 miles, the road passes by the Jack Creek Campground. Park here or, for another option, go 2.2 miles to the intersection with Forest Road 830.

Sierra Madres Continental
Divide Loop

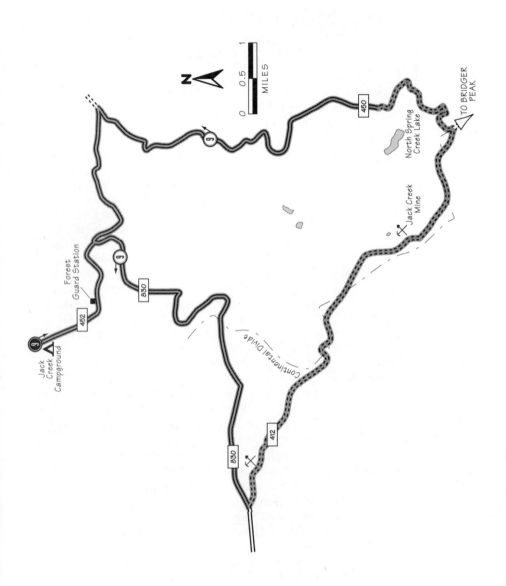

The trail that climbs toward the Continental Divide in the Sierra Madre Mountains has a few steep crankers before meeting the divide.

HIGHLIGHTS

The Wyoming segment of the Sierra Madre Mountains provides great biking, hiking, fishing, and camping without the crowds. There is an interesting mining history on the mountain. Remnants of the old tramway, used to transport ore from the mountain to the town of Encampment, can still be found on the top of Bridger Peak.

The Continental Divide runs down the length of the Sierra Madres and this ride follows a portion of the National Continental Divide Trail. This route has a

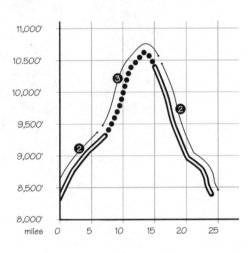

tough climb to the Continental Divide but then rolls along the summit before following a steep and rocky road back down. Camping is available in the Jack Creek Campground or at many dispersed sites throughout the range.

THE RIDE

0.0 From campground, follow gravel FR 452.

2.2 At intersection with FR 830, turn right. Route will loop around to this intersection. This is an optional parking site if you don't want to use the campground.

2.5 Cross Jack Creek and start uphill.

4.1 Deep Jack Trailhead, FR 462 goes left (south). Continue straight.

7.0 Turn left onto FR 412, the Continental Divide National Scenic Trail. This trail is open to ATVs and motorcycles in addition to bicycles, horseback riders, and hikers. Start up rocky road.

12.2 Pass above Jack Creek Mine on fairly flat terrain.

13.1 Come to intersection with FR 450. Turn left onto rocky doubletrack and start down.

15.0 Road improves.

20.7 Come to intersection with FR 452, which is a wider gravel road.

21.3 Cross North Spring Creek.

22.2 Return to intersection with FR 830. Return to campground.

24.4 Back at campground.

Variation: For a shuttle ride, at the intersection with FR 450, go right to Bridger Peak and continue on road to WY 70 leading to Encampment.

Central Wyoming Trails

The Central Wyoming trails are not associated with any individual mountain range or National Forest. There are a series of smaller mountains arranged mostly in a west to east direction beginning north of Rawlins with Green Mountain and ending south of Douglas with Laramie Peak. The routes described in this section are on or near these series of mountains.

Green Mountain, north of Rawlins and southeast of Lander, creates a green and timbered oasis as it rises above the sagebrush prairie. In succession, east of Green Mountain and extending to the edge of the Shirley Basin, are the Ferris Mountains, Seminole Mountains, and Shirley Mountains. Each of these mountains has a checkerboard of public and private land ownership, but many have county roads that provide public access across the private lands. Also, the prairie between and surrounding these mountains is predominantly public land, administered by the Bureau of Land Management. The mountains offer hundreds of miles of doubletrack roads to explore.

Casper Mountain, Muddy Mountain, and Laramie Peak skirt the northern and eastern rim of Shirley Basin. There is an assortment of land ownership on these mountains, including private, state, county, and federal. There are excellent opportunities to explore these areas by bike but carry maps showing land ownership to prevent accidental trespass on private lands.

Shirley Basin is a vast, open area. Travelers driving Wyoming 487 through the Basin often comment there is nothing, absolutely nothing, out there. For those relishing open space this is a paradise. There are miles and miles of open prairie and very little evidence of human use. For the adventurer looking for open space and no people, this is a great place to explore.

Big Bear Canyon

Location:	The Laramie Range, southeast of Douglas.
Distance:	14.4 miles, out and back.
Time:	Two to three hours.
Elevation gain:	1,800 feet.
Tread:	This route follows a gravel road for the first 0.5 mile and then goes onto an ATV trail as it goes up Big Bear Canyon. At the summit, it follows a doubletrack road to Devil's Pass.
Season:	This route is good from spring until late fall.
Aerobic level:	Moderate.
Technical difficulty:	This ride has a technical rating of 2+, with some rocky and rutted areas.
Hazards:	There are some rocky and rutted areas as the route goes up Big Bear Canyon and on toward Devil's Pass.
Land status:	U.S. Forest Service, Medicine Bow National Forest.
Maps:	USGS School Section Mountain, Saddleback Mountain, Toltec, Windy Peak.
Access:	From Douglas, go west on County Road 91 past the KOA Campground. A few miles farther, turn south on the Cold Springs Road and follow this road until it meets the Old Fort Fetterman Road (CR 61). Follow CR 61 approximately 10 miles to the intersection with the LaBonte Canyon Road (Forest Road 658). Continue up the canyon to Curtis Gulch Campground. Park in the campground or in any of the dispersed camping sites along the creek.

HIGHLIGHTS

This is a fun ride and is well-suited for a family outing. The ride up scenic Big Bear Canyon is challenging for the novice rider but is not overly steep. Because this is an out-and-back route, riders can turn around and head back down the canyon whenever they choose. The map indicates a possible 16-mile loop from the top of Big Bear Canyon by turning west on FR 610. Unfortunately, locked gates block this route when it passes across 1 mile of private land. This interspersing of public and private land is common in the Laramie Peak area, making mountain biking a bit difficult. If you plan to explore, be sure to carry a BLM or Forest Service map that clearly delineates private and public lands.

Big Bear Canyon

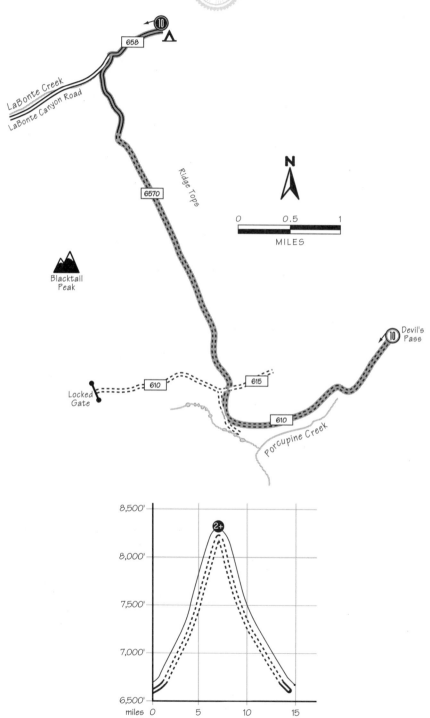

LaBonte Creek

LaBonte Canyon Road

658

10

Ridge Tops

6570

Blacktail Peak

N

0   0.5   1

MILES

10 Devil's Pass

610

615

Locked Gate

610

Porcupine Creek

8,500'

2+

8,000'

7,500'

7,000'

6,500'

miles 0   5   10   15

Camping is available in the Curtis Gulch Campground or in a number of dispersed camping areas along LaBonte Creek. This is a popular camping and fishing area and the Big Bear Canyon trail is popular as an ATV and hiking trail.

THE RIDE

0.0 From campground, go back down LaBonte Canyon Road (FR 658).

0.8 Turn left onto FR 6570. Cross creek.

4.8 Cross cattleguard

5.1 Come to top of canyon. Trail forks. Stay on main route right.

5.2 Road forks. Go left to Devil's Pass.

7.2 At Devil's Pass and turnaround point. Return via same route with fun downhill.

14.4 Back at campground.

Casper Mountain Trails

Location:	This trail is located immediately south of Casper on Casper Mountain.
Distance:	3.3-mile loop (many alternatives available).
Time:	Forty-five minutes to one and one-half hours.
Elevation gain:	250 feet.
Tread:	This ride is a nearly all doubletrack except for a couple of excursions into the woods on singletrack.
Season:	These trails are open following the ski season in late spring and are open until ski season starts again in the winter.
Aerobic level:	Easy to moderate.
Technical difficulty:	The doubletrack is rated a 2+ due to some rocky areas. The singletrack sidetrips are rated with a 3+. These segments are short and can be maneuvered by beginners by going slow.
Hazards:	On the doubletrack watch for rocky and rutted areas. On the singletrack watch for rocks, logs, and other debris. The trail becomes quite narrow in these segments. This trail system is popular; watch for other trail users. Dogs are prohibited on the trails.
Land status:	Natrona County.
Maps:	USGS Crimson Dawn. The best map for this area is printed by Natrona County and shows the cross-country ski trails. Copies are available either through the county or at local bicycle shops.
Access:	From Casper, follow the main Casper Mountain Road (State Road 251) up the mountain. At the fork to Hogadon Ski Area, go left toward Bear Trap Meadow. Just before Bear Trap Meadow, turn left into parking area. Additional parking is available a little farther down the road, on the righthand side of the road.

HIGHLIGHTS

Casper Mountain was once a popular camping and hiking area, some distance from the city of Casper. Today it is nearly a part of the city because subdivisions have expanded to fill the foothills leading up to the mountain and even on top of the mountain. It is still a popular camping and hiking

Casper Mountain Trails

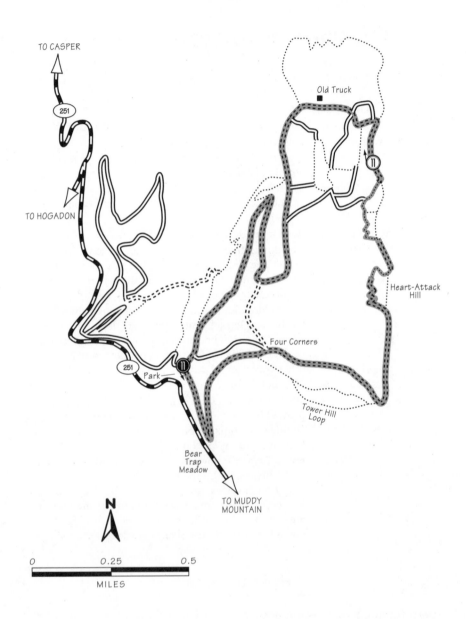

TO CASPER

251

TO HOGADON

Old Truck

11

Heart-Attack
Hill

Four Corners

251

Park

11

Tower Hill
Loop

Bear
Trap
Meadow

TO MUDDY
MOUNTAIN

N

0   0.25   0.5

MILES

The trails at Casper Mountain are popular family rides with their easy access from the city of Casper and peaceful paths throughout the pines.

area but, because of the development of residential housing areas, much of the public use area is within public trail development areas.

One of the most popular areas is the Casper Mountain County Park. During the winter this area is a very popular cross-country ski area complete with a lighted trail for nighttime skiing. During the late spring, summer, and fall, these trails offer excellent hiking and mountain biking.

This maze of loops includes 15 miles of non-motorized singletrack and doubletrack trails. A few narrow and winding singletracks have been added that aren't shown on the ski maps. These are specially designed for the biking season, adding some zigs and some zags and increasing the challenge for advanced and novice cyclists.

The route described here is a good family ride. Additional loops on adjoining trails can increase the challenge.

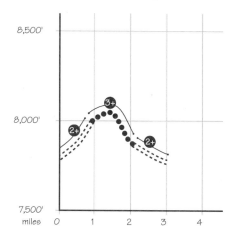

0.0 From parking area, start on trail leaving the southeast corner of the parking lot and leading past an outhouse. Go around gate.

0.1 Bike past outhouse.

0.3 Trail makes a sharp left turn.

0.6 At Four Corners where trails converge. Continue straight, going up the hill.

0.8 Cross Elkhorn Creek.

1.0 Trail comes out on top of hill. Turn sharp left.

1.2 At top of Heart-Attack Hill. You can continue straight down the hill but, for singletrack, turn left into the trees and follow winding trail.

1.4 Return to doubletrack.

1.6 Turn left onto singletrack again and follow trail through the woods.

1.7 Trail forks. Continue straight. Left is another alternative.

1.9 Return to main trail. Continue straight.

2.1 Trail forks. Go left and up hill.

2.3 Pass by abandoned truck on the right. After truck, trail curves left.

2.6 Trail forks with many alternative routes. Turn right. Straight returns to Four Corners (former milepost 0.6).

2.7 Take left hairpin turn at intersection.

3.2 Join another trail. Continue straight.

3.3 Back at parking area and starting point.

Variation: There are 15 miles of trail in this maze, offering many opportunities to explore. All trails are loops that eventually return to the main parking area.

Muddy Mountain Trails

Location:	This trail is located immediately south of Casper, past Casper Mountain, on Muddy Mountain.
Distance:	6.4-mile loop (with many shorter and longer alternatives available).
Time:	One to two hours (add loops to extend the time).
Elevation gain:	250 feet.
Tread:	The first 0.3 mile follows a gravel road and then turns onto a singletrack. After approximately 2 miles, the trail becomes doubletrack, but the trail is becoming more of a singletrack because doubletrack motorized vehicles no longer use the road.
Season:	The Muddy Mountain Road is closed from the end of October until Memorial Day, although it may be open later or earlier based on seasonal weather conditions. The trail can be muddy after wet weather and early in the season. Take care when crossing muddy areas to avoid damage to the trail.
Aerobic level:	Moderate.
Technical difficulty:	The narrow and winding singletrack trails have a technical rating of 3 due to some obstacles. The doubletrack trails also have a technical rating of 3, although there are short stretches with a rating of 2 and 4.

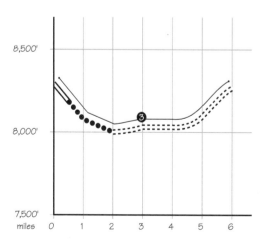

Muddy Mountain Trails

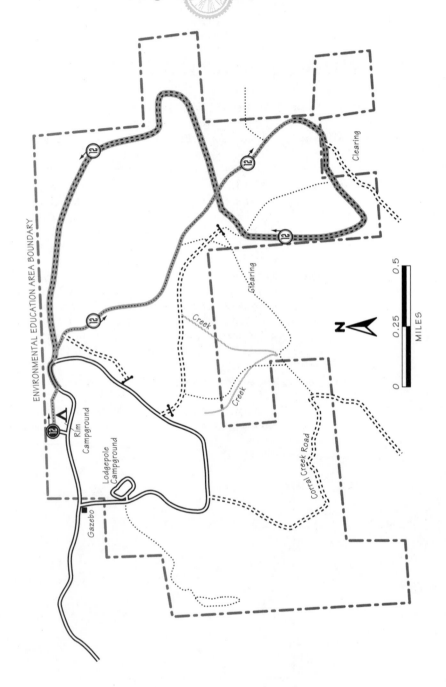

Hazards:	On the singletrack, the trail is quite narrow, seemingly no wider than the width of the handlebars. There are rocky areas as well as logs and debris across areas of both the doubletrack and singletrack.
Land status:	Bureau of Land Management and State of Wyoming.
Maps:	USGS Crimson Dawn, Otter Creek. Hopefully the BLM will prepare maps of the Environmental Education Area with the different trails. Check the gazebo area to see if maps are available.
Access:	From Casper follow the main Casper Mountain Road (State Road 251) up the mountain and onto Circle Drive (Natrona County Road 505) past Bear Trap Meadow. Continue past Casper Mountain. When Circle Drive turns west, toward Wyoming 487, continue straight on Muddy Mountain Road. Follow the road to the entrance to the Muddy Mountain Environmental Education Area; take left fork toward the Rim Campground. Turn in toward campground and park in parking area just before the sign at the entrance to the campground.

HIGHLIGHTS

The Muddy Mountain Environmental Education Area, covering 1,260 acres, was developed over a 20-year period. The area includes a natural area and an interpretive area with an assortment of trails, including multiple-use trails, non-motorized trails, and a nature trail that is accessible to people with disabilities. There are two developed campgrounds and a gazebo with interpretive signs.

These singletrack and doubletrack trails are a kick. The Bureau of Land Management, with the help of some volunteer assistance from local cyclists, has developed a maze of trails that are both entertaining and challenging for a wide array of abilities. Individual loops may be too short for those wanting a longer ride, but there are multiple loop options making it possible to explore the area for hours without repeating any trail. The interconnecting maze of trails can be confusing, but all trails eventually loop around back to the primary Loop Road.

THE RIDE

0.0 From parking area, follow road through campground and back onto graveled Loop Road.

0.3 Turn left at trailhead onto trail and through gate onto doubletrack trail. Just after gate, a singletrack forks to right. Take the singletrack.

0.5 Faint trail forks right. Stay on main trail. As the trail winds through the timber, alternate routes branch off and offer some fun exploration. For this route, though, stay on the main trail.

1.2 Trail forks. Go left.

1.6 Cross the main doubletrack. Continue on singletrack on other side of road.

1.9 Cross a gully and begin uphill.

2.2 Come to a clearing. Trail may be less distinct through the grassy meadow. Continue straight to intercept doubletrack road. Turn right. Take the time to walk to the end of the ridge; it overlooks a beautiful valley.

2.5 Trail forks right, going up the hill toward the timber. This is not a very obvious trail due to the grassy conditions. The doubletrack becomes obvious once it enters the timber.

3.2 Come into clearcut area.

3.8 Come onto doubletrack. Turn right down road and through gate. Follow old logging road as it goes through regrowth areas.

6.1 Back at gate. Go through to main Loop Road and return to campground.

6.4 Back at parking area.

Variation: Rather than list alternative routes, I suggest you check the map and explore the area. Additional routes will be constructed by the BLM in the future and faint singletrack trails developed by local cyclists are already present, providing miles of entertaining riding.

Green Mountain

Location:	On the northern edge of the Great Divide Basin, approximately 10 miles southeast of Jeffrey City.
Distance:	16.2 miles, out and back.
Time:	Three to four hours.
Elevation gain:	1,500 feet.
Tread:	This route is all on developed road but it is very rough in areas. Exploratory routes on the top of the mountain are all doubletrack roads.
Season:	This area opens up earlier than other mountain sites and is bikeable by mid-May, but portions of the road may be closed to motorized travel between November 15 and July 1. It can be pedaled on through the fall, though this is a popular hunting area and can become much more crowded in the fall.
Aerobic level:	Moderate.
Technical difficulty:	The road is rough and rocky in places, for a rating of 3, though most of the route has a rating of 2. The optional logging roads typically have a rating of 3.
Hazards:	The trail is rough and rocky in places. This is the main travel road on the mountain, so watch for traffic, both trucks and ATVs.
Land status:	Bureau of Land Management.
Maps:	Sagebrush Park.
Access:	From Jeffrey City head east on Wyoming 287 toward Muddy Gap. After 6 miles turn south on the well-marked BLM Road 2411. After 6.3 miles the road forks. Go left for three miles to the Cottonwood Campground. Park at entrance to campground or take a camping site.

HIGHLIGHTS

Green Mountain is a pleasant surprise, a forested island on the edge of the desert habitat of the Great Divide Basin. It is snow-free earlier than the higher mountain ranges and is not crowded outside of the hunting season. There are two campgrounds near the base of the mountain and the ride here gives alternative routes from each campground. Once on top of the mountain, take the time to explore the many old logging roads on the

Green Mountain

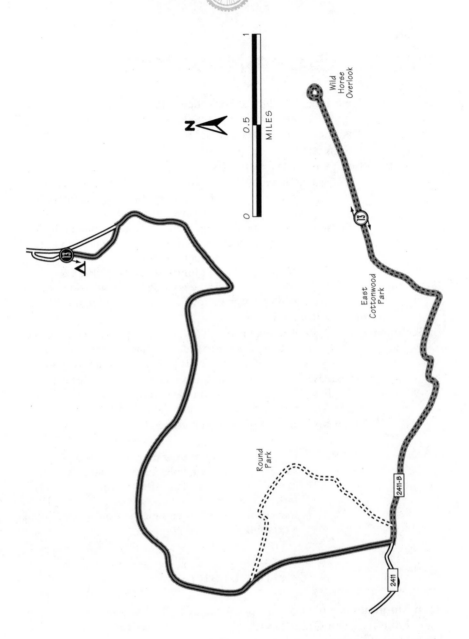

Wild Horse Overlook

East Cottonwood Park

Round Park

2411-B

2411

MILES

N

relatively flat, broad summit. At the time of this writing one portion of the road above the Cottonwood Campground is closed to motorized travel where the road has washed out. Carrying your bike down and up the steep gully is an easy way to negotiate this damaged area.

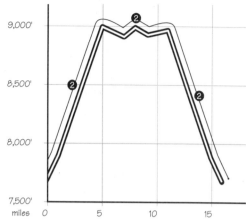

From the summit of Green Mountain, at the Wild Horse Overlook, there is a panoramic view of the vast Great Divide Basin. The Continental Divide splits in two, encircling the basin. Water falling into the basin flows to neither ocean but sits in one of the few playa lakes or evaporates under the heat of the sun.

Elk and mule deer are abundant on the mountain as are other woodland residents such as the gray squirrel, pine marten, junco, and chickadee. The back, or south side, of the mountain shows evidence of uranium mining, although the mine is currently inactive.

THE RIDE

0.0 Beginning at the campground, go uphill through the campground until reaching the main gravel road. Turn right on the road. Begin tough crank up the mountain.

1.5 Come to area where road has washed out (this may get repaired before too long, in which case it may be just a simple creek crossing). Negotiate area by walking bike down and back up the gully.

4.9 At intersection. Go left on BLM Road 2411-B. On right is BLM Road 2411, which continues around on summit of Green Mountain before dropping back down past the Green Mountain Park Campground.

7.1 Road forks right. Stay straight. Road to right goes down the mountain.

8.1 At Wild Horse Overlook. Return on same route but take the time to explore the broad mountain summit on the old logging roads.

16.2 Back at campground.

Variation: Begin the route from the intersection of Wyoming 287 and BLM Road 2411. This adds 19.2 miles (round trip) to the route. Another alternative is to begin and end your ride at the Green Mountain Park Campground.

Bates Hole Loop

Location:	Southwest of Casper on the north end of the Shirley Basin.
Distance:	15.6-mile loop.
Time:	Three and one-half to four and one-half hours.
Elevation gain:	1,650 feet.
Tread:	The first 4.4 miles follow a gravel road and then turn onto doubletrack for 6.8 miles before returning on a gravel road.
Season:	This route can be ridden early in the season beginning in spring and through the fall. Watch for cold winds that can make for lower wind chill temperatures.
Aerobic level:	Moderate.
Technical difficulty:	The gravel road is a technical rating of 1, while the doubletrack, with some rocky areas, has a technical level of 3.
Hazards:	On the gravel road watch for rutted areas and deeper gravel. There may be some traffic on the road, but it is not a heavily traveled route. On the doubletrack watch for rutted and rocky areas.
Land status:	Bureau of Land Management and State of Wyoming.
Maps:	USGS Twin Buttes, Sheep Creek, Mud Springs, Horse Peak.
Access:	From Casper, follow Wyoming Highway 220 west approximately 18 miles. Turn south onto WY 487. Continue approximately 20 miles and turn east on the Bates Creek Stock Trail (County Road 403). Park on CR 403 by the large sign near the intersection with WY 487.

Bates Hole Loop

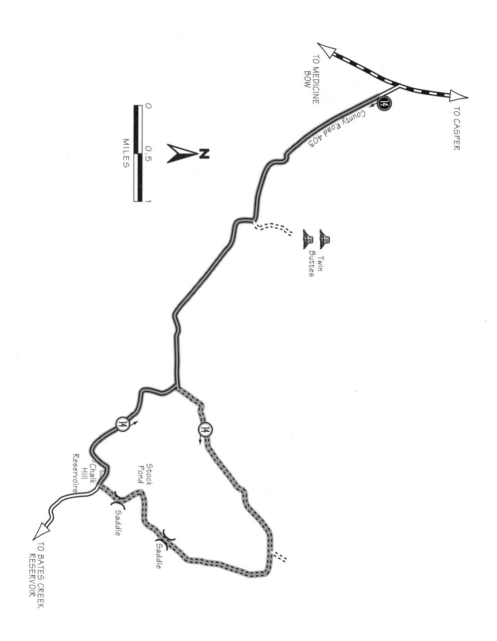

The Bates Hole Loop provides scenic views across the vast valley of the northern end of Shirley Basin.

HIGHLIGHTS

Between the Laramie Range, south of Casper and Douglas, and the Freezout and Shirley Mountains north of Medicine Bow, lies the Shirley Basin. This big basin contains large deposits of uranium. Mining activity in the 1970s and 1980s created the town of Shirley Basin, which was closed in the 1990s when the low price of uranium caused a drastic decline in mining activity. Since then, the Shirley Basin has returned to its former open expanse of sagebrush, buttes, and miles upon miles of open space.

The northern end of the basin has white sandstone formations, creating rolling and hilly terrain between the scattered buttes. This route explores a small part of the northern basin as it passes near Twin Buttes and looks over the Bates Creek drainage. The route described is one of many possibilities within the Shirley Basin.

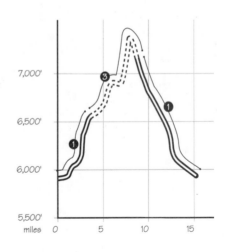

0.0 Start up gravel CR 403.

2.2 Road forks. Stay on right (south) fork. Left leads to Twin Buttes.

2.5 Pass by stock pond on right.

2.8 Come to top of hill.

2.9 Doubletrack goes right. Stay on main road.

3.4 At bottom of hill.

3.8 At top of hill.

4.4 Come to fork in road. Go left (north) on doubletrack. Go through gate just off the main road.

4.5 Go through gate.

4.6 Faint doubletrack goes left. Stay on main doubletrack.

4.9 Begin uphill.

5.3 At ridge top. Beautiful view into the Bates Creek drainage.

5.7 Trail forks. Go right. An old windmill is off the trail to the right about 200 yards.

6.3 Go through gate.

6.6 Trail forks. Stay right.

7.3 Go through gate.

8.1 Come to saddle on ridge.

8.7 Pass by a stock pond. Trail curves to left around pond.

8.9 At saddle.

9.0 Go through gate.

9.2 Back on county road. Turn right.

11.2 Back at fork (milepost 4.4 earlier). Continue down county road to starting point.

15.6 Back at starting point.

Black Hills Area Rides
Northeast Wyoming

The name Black Hills comes from the Lakota Sioux words "Paha Sapa," or "hills that are black." Seen from a distance, these hills rising from the surrounding grassland prairie do appear to be black. Once you are in the hills, though, they offer a combination of green forests and colorful vegetation that is unique in Wyoming.

The Bear Lodge Mountains are a segment of the Black Hills National Forest, located between Sundance and Hulett, Wyoming. Elevations range from just under 5,000 feet to 6,650 feet at the summit of Bear Lodge Mountain. These mountains are considerably lower than those in other U.S. National Forests in Wyoming, where the elevations rise above 11,000 feet. This lower elevation provides snow-free bicycling earlier in the spring than in other forested areas.

The vegetation and wildlife in the Black Hills are unique in Wyoming. The forests include not only pine and aspen trees, but also birch and dense scrub oak. White-tailed deer are especially abundant and are visible during the early mornings and evenings. Elk, wild turkeys, great horned owls, and ospreys also make their home in these hills.

Mountain bikers are made to feel very welcome in the Bear Lodge Mountains, with over 60 miles of non-motorized trails. These include old logging roads, doubletrack roads, and singletrack trails. The routes are shared with hikers and horseback riders, but use is not especially heavy.

The Bear Lodge Mountains trail system includes the Carson Draw Trails out of the Reuter Campground, the extensive Sundance Trails southeast of the Fire Lookout on Warren Peaks, and trails near Cook Lake.

Cliff Swallow Trail

Location:	14 miles north of Sundance in the Black Hills.
Distance:	3.7-mile loop.
Time:	One and one-half hours.
Elevation gain:	310 feet.
Tread:	3.5 miles are on singletrack and 0.2 mile is on gravel road.
Season:	Due to the lower elevation of the Black Hills, this trail will be snow-free earlier than most other mountain trails. The trail can be biked from spring through fall.
Aerobic level:	Moderate.
Technical difficulty:	The overall rating is 3, with segments of 2 and 4.
Hazards:	There are some rocky areas on the trail. Thick vegetation can obscure the trail and make it difficult to anticipate what is coming. Watch for exposed log waterbars that cross the trail to divert runoff.
Land status:	U.S. Forest Service, Black Hills National Forest.
Maps:	USGS Black Hills. The U.S. Forest Service has a map of the Cliff Swallow and Cook Lake trails. Check the map box at the entrance to the campground for a copy.
Access:	From Sundance follow the signs for Cook Lake, following Forest Roads 838, 843, and 842. FR 838 is paved for the first few miles before becoming a winding gravel road. There are two campgrounds and a picnic area at Cook Lake Recreational Area. Daytime trail users must park in the day use parking lot. Trail users wanting to park overnight must pay for a campsite and park in the campground. The trailhead begins in Campground Loop B, although it can also be accessed from the day use parking lot.

HIGHLIGHTS

This is a delightful ride, although it ends much too soon. A second time around the loop would solve that problem. It gets its name from the cliff swallows that make their nests in the limestone cliffs above Beaver Creek. It is both moderately technical and moderately aerobic, making it a good

Cliff Swallow Trail

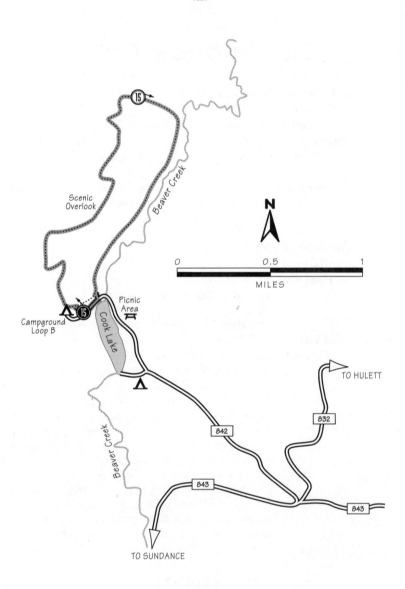

Scenic
Overlook

Beaver Creek

Campground
Loop B

Cook Lake

Picnic
Area

N

0   0.5   1

MILES

842

832

TO HULETT

Beaver Creek

843

843

TO SUNDANCE

The Cliff Swallow Trail follows Beaver Creek before dropping down to Cook Lake.

challenge for all abilities, although novice riders may choose to bike hike some of the more difficult sections.

The ride begins by climbing above Cook Lake following a scenic overlook of the lake and the Beaver Creek drainage. Eventually, the trail drops down to the creek and parallels it until it meets the dam at Cook Lake. The trail allows only non-motorized travel and is well-marked as it winds its way through the pine, birch, and oak forest. Plan for a post-ride swim in Cook Lake.

This is fun habitat to explore. Keep your eyes open for white-tailed deer and wild turkeys, although these skittish wildlife species are difficult to spot in the dense vegetation. Water ouzels can be seen running underwater in Beaver Creek as they feed on aquatic insects. Great blue herons, mallards, and other waterfowl can be found in the marsh areas next to Beaver Creek.

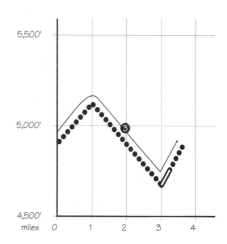

THE RIDE

0.0 Begin ride at the trailhead located in Campground Loop B. Go through gate at start of trail and begin uphill climb.

0.4 Trail levels off.

0.6 Great overlook view of Cook Lake and Beaver Creek.

1.5 Begin fun downhill.

2.0 Another trail forks to the left and connects to an old logging road. Stay on main trail. Shortly after this, another trail forks right. Stay left.

2.2 Go through gate.

3.3 Go over wooden bridge.

3.4 Go through gate and past information board. Climb the wooden stairs and join main gravel road, turning right. Bike past the day use area.

3.6 Just before the day use parking area, take wooden steps and return to singletrack. This trail connects to Campground Loop B. Another option would be to stay on the gravel road from the day use area to Campground Loop B.

3.7 Back at start of trail.

Carson Draw-Reuter Springs Loop

Location:	3 miles north of Sundance, on Forest Road 838 in the Black Hills National Forest.
Distance:	6.3-mile loop with numerous options to extend the ride.
Time:	One and one-half hours.
Elevation gain:	925 feet.
Tread:	The trail is on old logging roads, which were once good doubletracks but are now less distinct and often have only a single distinct track. In some areas the track is grass-covered.
Season:	Due to the lower elevation of the Black Hills, this trail will be snow-free earlier than most other mountain trails. The trail can be biked from spring through fall.
Aerobic level:	Moderate.
Technical difficulty:	The majority of the route is a technical 3 due to sandy areas and indistinct trail. There are some areas rated 2 on good doubletrack.
Hazards:	The trail is quite sandy in spots, making it difficult to get traction.
Land status:	U.S. Forest Service, Black Hills National Forest.
Maps:	Sundance West. The U.S. Forest Service has an excellent map of the area. Check the map box at the area campgrounds for a copy.
Access:	Take U.S. Highway 14 north out of Sundance. After 1 mile turn right on Forest Road 838. After two miles the road enters the Black Hills National Forest and the Reuter Campground is on the left. One access point is within the campground. A second access point is on a gravel road that goes left 0.4 mile past the campground. If you use the second access point, the ride begins at mile-marker 0.6.

Carson Draw-Reuter
Springs Loop

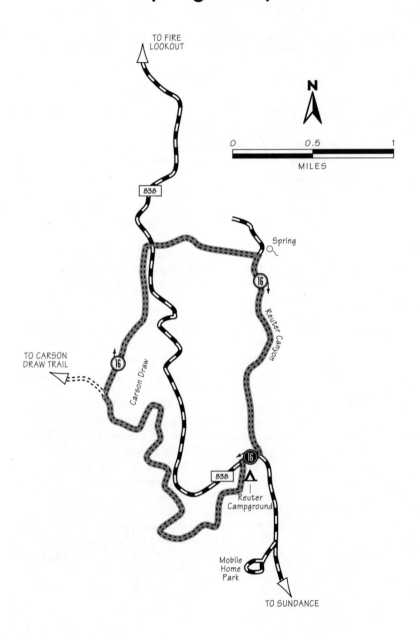

TO FIRE
LOOKOUT

N

0   0.5   1
MILES

838

Spring

16

Reuter Canyon

TO CARSON
DRAW TRAIL

16

Carson Draw

16

838

Reuter
Campground

Mobile
Home
Park

TO SUNDANCE

HIGHLIGHTS

This trail has easy access from the town of Sundance, being only 3 miles north of town. It is more popular in the winter as a cross-country ski trail, but attracts mountain bikers who are looking for a less-traveled route. It primarily follows old logging roads that are closed to motorized travel. The trail has enough of an uphill climb to provide an aerobic challenge, yet, with a lower technical rating, it allows for plenty of viewing and searching for wildlife while pedaling the wide trail.

The second half of the loop crosses the paved FR 838, and comes down Reuter Canyon to end near Reuter Campground.

THE RIDE

0.0 Start at trailhead in Reuter Campground. Begin climb on doubletrack road.

0.6 Trail comes to intersection. Another doubletrack goes left; stay right up to better graveled road and turn left.

0.65 Go under "Road Closed" gate. Trail is on old logging road.

0.8 The road forks. Go right.

0.9 Pass by stock tank on the right.

1.9 Trail forks. Go right, up hill, past a wooden ski hut. Left continues on Carson Draw Trail.

3.2 Cross paved FR 838. Rejoin trail on opposite side of the road where the trail becomes the Carson Cut-Across.

3.9 Trail joins the main Reuter Springs Trail. Go right, into canyon and down hill.

6.1 Come out onto paved FR 838. Turn left and return to starting point.

6.3 Back at starting point.

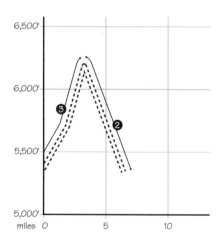

Sundance Trails

Location:	The Sundance Trails can be accessed 4 miles north of Sundance from Forest Road 838. Another access point is located 3.5 miles north of Sundance from the Government Valley Road.
Distance:	Total distance for the ride is 9 miles. This loop includes all or part of five Sundance Trails, including the Sand Pit Trail, the South Fork Trail, the Tent Canyon Ridge Trail, the North Fork Tent Trail, and the Ogden Ridge Trail.
Time:	Three to four hours.
Elevation gain:	1,545 feet.
Tread:	The loop starts out on good doubletrack road for 1.4 miles and then drops onto a singletrack constructed specifically for mountain biking. After nearly 4.5 miles, it joins an old doubletrack for approximately 2 miles before following a singletrack trail again for 1.2 miles. The final 1.2 miles are on good doubletrack road.
Season:	Due to the lower elevation of the Black Hills, this trail will be snow-free earlier than most other mountain trails. The trail can be biked from spring through fall.
Aerobic level:	Moderate.
Technical difficulty:	The doubletrack and old logging roads are levels 2 + and 3 due to rocky and sandy areas. The narrow singletrack along the South Fork Trail rates a technical 4 due to rocky segments, logs, and other obstacles on the trail.
Hazards:	There are rocky and sandy sections on the Sand Pit Trail. As the route follows the South Fork Trail, the singletrack is narrow with numerous rocks, logs, and other obstacles. The Tent Canyon Trail starts out rocky on the lower segments but smoothes out at the higher elevations. The North Fork Tent Trail has low branches and other obstacles in the trail. The Ogden Ridge Trail has few hazards.
Land status:	U.S. Forest Service, Black Hills National Forest.
Maps:	USGS Sundance West, Sundance East. The U.S. Forest Service has an excellent map of the area. Check the map box at the area campgrounds for a copy.

Sundance Trails

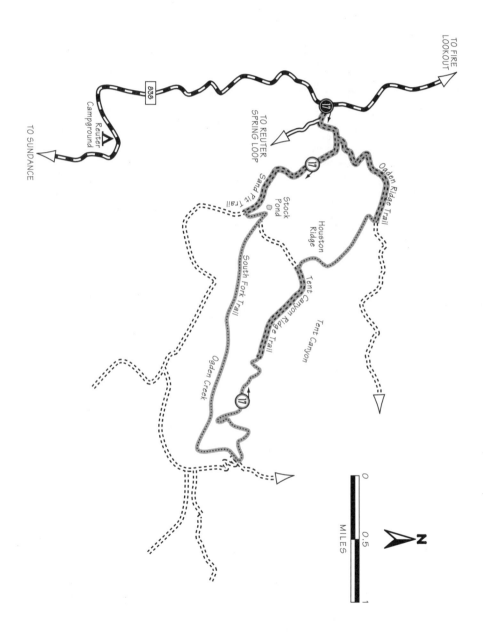

The Sundance Trails offer a panoramic view of the valley below.

Access: Take U.S. Highway 14 north out of Sundance. After 1 mile, turn right on Forest Road 838. After 2 miles the road enters the Black Hills National Forest and the Reuter Campground is on the left. Continue up the paved road approximately 3 miles, turning right onto gravel FR 884. Park adjacent to the road.

There are two alternate access points for the Sundance Trails. You can park in the Reuter Campgrounds and take the Reuter Springs Trail that goes left right before the campground. The Reuter Springs Trail goes 2.9 miles and connects to the starting point of this ride. A third access point is from the Sundance Trails Campground, located 3 miles north of Sundance and US14 adjacent to Government Valley Road.

HIGHLIGHTS

The Sundance Trails in the Bear Lodge Mountains are great to explore. The trail system includes 50.3 miles of gravel, doubletrack, and singletrack routes. Many of the trails are old logging roads that have been closed to motorized travel. There are many different options on where to ride; one loop option is described in detail here but other trails are shown on the map.

Several of the Sundance Trails have been named for some of the first families who homesteaded the Bear Lodge Mountains in the late 1800s and early 1900s. Originally, some of the trails were the routes to reliable water, while others provided the only access to some parts of the mountains and were a key part of the rich mining history in the area.

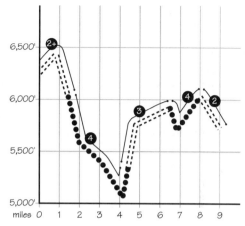

This Tent Canyon Ridge Loop ride includes challenging singletrack as it drops 1,000 feet along Ogden Creek. The ascent takes a more circuitous route and is less steep. If you prefer to do the uphill segment first and don't mind adding a few miles to the route, start at the Sundance Trailhead and follow the Sundance Trail until it connects to the Tent Canyon Trail.

Keep your eyes peeled (when you aren't focused on the segments of singletrack) for wildlife as you go through pine, birch, and oak forests

THE RIDE

0.0 Start out at the intersection with the Reuter Springs Trail and FR 838. (Reuter Springs Trail goes to the right (south), ending at the Reuter Campground.) For this ride, go straight on good doubletrack road.

0.4 Continue right on Sand Pit Trail. Ogden Ridge Trail goes left.

1.4 Cross cattleguard and immediately after, turn left onto the Tent Canyon Ridge Trail and follow singletrack down into drainage. An alternate and easier route is to continue on the Sand Pit Trail. This road is open to motorized traffic for another 1.6 miles, then it continues for another 1.7 miles before intercepting with the Tent Canyon Trail.

1.6 Go past a stock pond. Immediately after the pond, trail forks. Take the right fork to the South Fork Trail. This is a singletrack trail that runs parallel to Ogden Creek. It cross the small creek a number of times as it continues down the drainage.

4.1 Come to trail intersection. Go left up the Tent Canyon Ridge Trail. Right continues to Sundance Trailhead.

4.7 Trail becomes wider as it follows an old logging road but is still primarily a singletrack. Be sure to look back into the beautiful Government Valley.

4.9 Come to a newer road (this area was under construction when I rode it for this book).

6.5 Trail forks. Take the right fork onto singletrack. (To go straight is an easier route. It continues up the old logging road and, after 0.9 mile, it rejoins the Sand Pit Trail at the cattleguard, from milepost 1.4.) The singletrack is heavily used by cattle but is an obvious trail as it heads steeply down to Tent Canyon Creek.

6.8 Cross a little creek.

7.0 Go past a stock tank.

7.3 Trail comes out onto a newly constructed logging road. Follow this road for a short distance.

7.4 Singletrack trail can be found immediately south of the logging road. Take the singletrack.

7.6 Trail comes out onto logging road. Go through gate.

7.8 Road joins the Ogden Ridge Trail, an old logging road. Go left.

8.5 Go under "Road Closed" sign on gate.

8.6 Come to intersection with Sand Pit Trail. Go right.

9.0 Back at the start.

Bighorn Mountain Area Rides

Wyoming's Bighorn Mountains stretch down from the Montana border, reaching into central Wyoming. This range of mountains offers spectacular diversity from the heights of Cloud Peak in the Cloud Peak Wilderness Area to the cliffs and buttes of the Paintrock Canyon in the Bighorn Basin.

Trails leading into the wilderness area, especially near the Hunter Corrals above Buffalo and near Battle Park above Tensleep, are heavily used by horsepackers. These trails can be rough when crossing wet areas where horse hooves have churned the trail. The horseback riders and backpackers seem to accept the less-numerous mountain bikers easily, although bikers must turn around before reaching the wilderness boundary. Trails that do not lead to the wilderness are less traveled and offer especially enjoyable mountain biking.

The lower-elevation southern Bighorns, west of the Hole-in-the-Wall and within an hour's drive of the city of Casper, offer spectacular scenery for early-season riding. Butch Cassidy and Flat Nose George "Kid" Curry operated out of the Hole-in-the-Wall, stealing and hiding livestock. They would head to the Hole-in-the-Wall to escape capture and hide from posses of lawmen. The "hole" is actually a gap in a 50-mile wall of red hills paralleling the Bighorn Mountains. Buffalo Creek flows between them and cuts a rugged and picturesque canyon, making a perfect hideout for outlaws and thieves.

At the other extreme is the ride to Grace Lake, on the border of the wilderness area, as it ascends over 10,000 feet; it is only open in the middle of the summer.

The Bighorns offer miles and miles of doubletrack and singletrack rides at a wide range of elevations, making it easy to gradually ascend the mountains as the spring snowmelt occurs. The singletrack ski trails near Willow Park and leading to East Tensleep Lake are among the most enjoyable in the state. Take fishing gear along and combine pedaling with casting for brook, rainbow, cutthroat, and golden trout. Grayling are even found in a few isolated areas.

Wildlife is especially numerous in the Bighorns, including both elk and mule deer. The moose population has experienced a gradual increase and these animals can be found along willow-lined creeks. Give these gangly creatures a wide berth, especially if you disturb a cow with a calf. These homely mothers can be especially protective of their young. Also, keep your eyes open for bighorn sheep, which have been introduced near both the Hole-in-the-Wall and Shell Canyon.

Hunter Loop

Location:	This ride is in the southeastern Bighorn Mountains, 28 miles west of Buffalo.
Distance:	10.8-mile loop.
Time:	Three and one-half to four and one-half hours.
Elevation gain:	1,525 feet.
Tread:	This ride begins with a nice doubletrack that deteriorates quickly into a very rocky doubletrack; it is singletrack from mile 4.1 to 4.9.
Season:	This ride begins at 7,900 feet and tops out at 9,125 feet. The best season to ride this trail is in summer, once the trail has dried from snowmelt, and into early fall. Hunting activity is fairly heavy in the fall; wear bright orange and be especially cautious.
Aerobic level:	Strenuous.
Technical difficulty:	The doubletrack up to Triangle Park is quite rough and rocky with a rating of 3+ with some rougher segments of 4 and some easier segments with a rating of 2+. The downhill ride has a rating of 3+ except for the down-and-up segment leading to and from South Rock Creek, which has a rating of 4+.
Hazards:	This trail is very rocky in some stretches. Proceed with caution! Watch for horseback riders on the trail.
Land status:	U.S. Forest Service, Bighorn National Forest.
Maps:	USGS Hunter Mesa, Lake Angeline. The Cloud Peak Wilderness map and the Bighorn National Forest map, both put out by the U.S. Forest Service, are good maps for this route.
Access:	Take U.S. Highway 16 out of Buffalo and go up the highway approximately 28 miles. On the righthand side of the road is the turnoff to the Hunter Corrals, North Fork Picnic Ground, and Hunter Forest Service Work Station. Take this good gravel road, following the signs to the Hunter Corrals. After 2.4 miles turn left into the Hunter Trailhead. Park here. There are several overnight camping sites within the trailhead. Other options for more rustic camping can be found by going through the trailhead area and taking Forest Road 394. Dispersed camping is available adjacent to the road within the first mile of this rough doubletrack road.

Hunter Loop

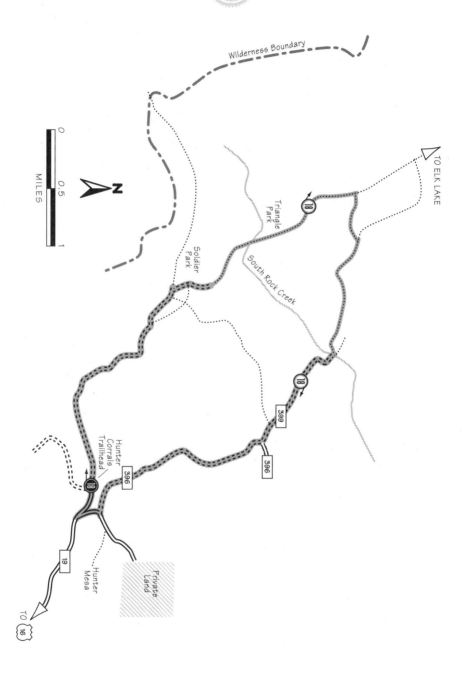

The Hunter Loop trails of the Bighorn National Forest are popular with riders as they make their way to Cloud Peak Wilderness Area.

Highlights

This is a rough ride due to the rocky condition of the road and trail. The route begins at the trailhead and climbs steadily, going from approximately 7,900 feet at the trailhead to 9,125 feet. After the first mile the route goes through an old forest fire burn with the skeletal remains of large lodgepole pine trees on the hillsides. The forest rebirth is evident in the dense young pines covering the forest floor.

The Hunter Trailhead is a popular entrance to Cloud Peak Wilderness Area for horseback riders. Consequently, the trails can be fairly rough from all the horse hooves. Be cautious when approaching or being approached by horseback riders. A horse's reaction to a moving cyclist can be unpredictable.

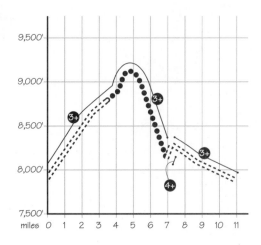

THE RIDE

0.0 The trail leaves west through the back gate of the trailhead corrals and campsite/ parking area.

0.1 Cross bridge. Continue on up the hill.

1.2 Timber opens up to a large clearing. Some horse trailers may be parked here and there is dispersed camping. The view across the valley to the peaks is awesome. After the clearing the trail becomes quite rocky and gets steeper.

1.3 Pass by a small pond. Hunter Creek can be seen at the far side of the pond.

1.5 Cross bridge over Hunter Creek.

2.3 Pass by two graves. Terrain flattens out beginning here.

2.6 Road forks. Go to the right. Left goes up to Cloud Peak Wilderness Area. The big opening is Soldier Park. Follow FR 365 along the edge of the Park.

2.7 At the edge of the clearing the trail narrows and becomes rough and rocky as it enters the forest. A faint doubletrack forks to left just before entering the timber. Stay on main road into the woods. The trail continues up hill, steep at times. The rocky trail may require more bike hiking than actual bike riding.

3.5 Trail opens up into a meadow called Triangle Park. Trail marker indicates no motorized travel allowed past this point. At the meadow, a trail branches off to the right, following adjacent to the creek. Stay left and go into meadow and cross the creek. After the creek crossing, the trail is flat but the horse travel has made the trail quite rough, especially in the boggy areas.

4.1 All singletrack after leaving Triangle Park.

4.5 Trail begins to level out and is easier to ride.

4.6 Trail forks. Take the right fork, which goes to French Creek Swamps. Left fork leads to Elk Lake in the wilderness area.

4.9 Trail forks again. Go right to South Rock Creek, Hunter Corrals, and Paradise Ranch. Left fork goes to Elk Park.

7.0 Cross South Rock Creek. Wet crossing with no footbridge. On the other side the trail goes up a steep hill.

7.3 End of tough uphill push out of creek drainage. Trail comes into an opening with a trail going off to the left with a marker indicating the trail is only for non-motorized travel. Don't take that trail; stay to the right as the main road goes in through the trees.

8.0 Road forks. Take left fork. Right fork goes to Soldier Park.

8.2 Road forks. Stay right on trail to Hunter Corrals. Left goes to Paradise Ranch and Keno Creek.

9.8 Cross creek. Crude footbridge is present.

10.1 Go through gate.

10.2 Go through another gate.

10.4 Go right on main gravel road.

10.6 Turn into trailhead.

10.8 Back at trailhead parking area.

Variation: There are several options with this route. One option is to continue another 0.5 mile at milepost 4.7 to another fork. This adds about another mile to the original loop. Elk Lake is in the Cloud Peak Wilderness and is not an optional destination for mountain bikers. Other trails create a bit of a maze near Soldier Park and offer exploration options.

Red Wall Loop

Location:	Southern Bighorn Mountains.
Distance:	41.3-mile loop.
Time:	Six and one-half to seven and one-half hours.
Elevation gain:	2,440 feet.
Tread:	This route is all on gravel road, but it is deeply rutted, rough, and rocky in areas.
Season:	This route is open from the spring through the fall. Its lower elevation provides early riding opportunities while the higher country is still impassable.
Aerobic level:	Strenuous.
Technical difficulty:	The route is quite rough and rocky in places for a technical rating on the entire route of 3.
Hazards:	The road has areas that are deeply rutted, rough, and rocky. Some vehicle traffic is present but, due to the rough road, speeds are minimal.
Land status:	Bureau of Land Management and public-access right-of-way across private land.
Maps:	Cherry Creek Hill, Grave Spring, First Water Draw, Roughlock Hill, Three Buttes, and Deadman Butte Quads. The majority of the ride is on the BLM 1:100,000 scale Lysite map, with small portions on Nowater Creek and Midwest maps.
Access:	Exit from U.S. Highway 20-26 at Waltman, turning north on County Road 104. At Armento, continue north on CR 105, the Buffalo Creek Road. After 12 miles the road forks, first to CR 108 and, shortly after, a major fork with CR 109 going left and CR 105 going right. Park here and begin ride going up CR 109.

HIGHLIGHTS

The Red Wall country offers spectacular scenery with a long series of red bluffs paralleling the southern Bighorn Mountains. The Hole-in-the-Wall is the most famous trail in this area, climbing the Buffalo Creek drainage of the upper Middle Fork of the Powder River. It is a famous route that was used by outlaws to escape from the Powder River Basin into the narrow valleys and canyons of the Bighorns. The breathtaking beauty of the Red

Red Wall Loop and
Easy Red Wall Out-and-Back

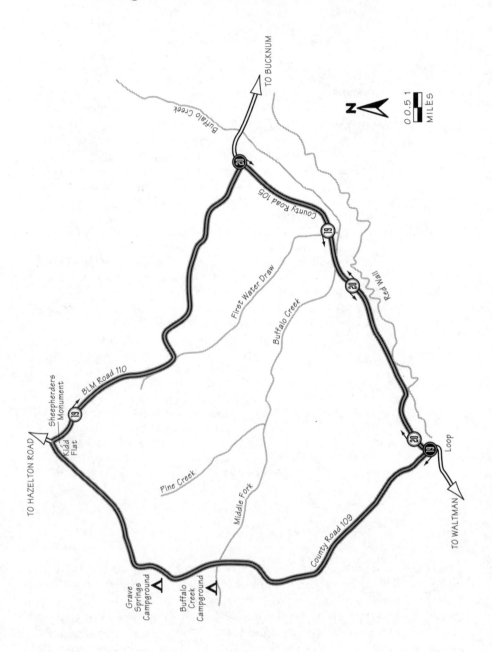

TO BUCKNUM

Buffalo Creek

N

0 0.5 1
MILES

20

County Road 105

19

First Water Draw

20

Red Wall

Buffalo Creek

BLM Road 110

Sheepherders Monument

19

Kidd Flat

TO HAZELTON ROAD

Pine Creek

Middle Fork

20

19

Loop

TO WALTMAN

County Road 109

Grave Springs Campground

Buffalo Creek Campground

Wall, and the history of the outlaws, Indians, cattlemen, and trappers who lived there, combine to give the Red Wall country a fascinating character.

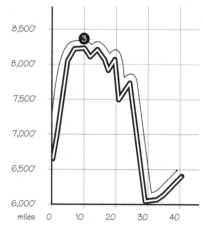

This route is part of the BLM-designated national backcountry byway that begins on CR 104 at Waltman and ends 15 miles northwest of Casper on CR 125 at Bucknum. The route is graded and drained but areas are rough and rocky and require higher clearance vehicles. It is well-suited to mountain biking, despite the fact that this loop has a challenging uphill climb. There are two BLM campgrounds along the western half of the loop and there are also areas of dispersed camping.

Currently, there is no public-access route to the Hole-in-the-Wall on the Middle Fork of the Powder River. The BLM is hoping to negotiate a trail in the future that will connect with this Red Wall Loop.

THE RIDE

0.0 Begin by heading northwest up the hill on CR 109.
0.3 Cross a creek.
0.9 Cross a creek.
5.5 Doubletrack goes left. Stay on main road.
7.6 Cross a creek.
9.8 Cross a creek.
11.3 Entrance to Buffalo Creek Campground is to the left.
11.8 Cross a creek.
11.9 Entrance to Grave Springs Campground is to the left.
12.3 Cross a creek.
13.3 Road curves to the right.
17.0 Enter Washakie County and cross Kidd Flat.
18.3 At Sheepherders Monument. Turn sharp right onto Thirty-three Mile Road (BLM Road 110).
19.3 Start up hill.
20.3 At top of hill called Eagle Creek Hill.
21.5 Pass First Water Draw Reservoir.
24.6 Doubletrack goes left. Continue straight going up the hill.
24.8 At top of hill.
30.6 Turn right at fork onto the Buffalo Creek Road (CR 105).
31.7 Pass old homestead.
41.3 Come to intersection with CR 109 where the ride started.

20

Easy Red Wall Out-and-Back

See Map
on Page 90

Location: Southern Bighorn Mountains.

Distance: 21 miles, out and back.

Time: Three to four hours.

Elevation gain: 490 feet.

Tread: This route is all on gravel road, but it can be muddy with ruts and rough areas.

Season: This route is open from the spring through the fall. Its lower elevation provides early riding opportunities.

Aerobic level: Easy.

Technical difficulty: The route is all on roads with a rating of 2.

Hazards: The road has areas that are muddy, rutted, and rocky.

Land status: Bureau of Land Management and public-access right-of-way across private land.

Maps: Cherry Creek Hill, First Water Draw, and Roughlock Hill Quads. The majority of the ride is on the BLM 1:100,000 scale Lysite map, with small portions on the Midwest map.

Access: Exit from U.S. Highway 20-26 at Bucknum Road (County Road 125), 15 miles west of Casper. Approximately 4 miles north of Bucknum the road joins the Thirty-three Mile Road (CR 110). Continue for approximately 30 miles to the intersection with the Buffalo Creek Road (CR 105). Park at intersection.

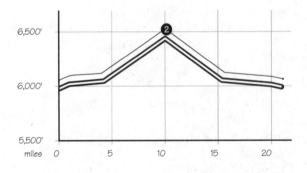

HIGHLIGHTS

This ride is one portion of the Red Wall Loop route and offers a shorter and much easier alternative. It is a relatively flat ride, going along the base of the beautiful Red Wall. The route is described as it begins on the east end and heads west, but it can begin at the same point as the Red Wall Loop route and go east.

THE RIDE

0.0 Start out on the Buffalo Creek Road (CR 105), heading west.

1.1 Pass by an old homestead.

10.5 Come to intersection with CR 109. This is the turnaround point. Return on same route.

21.0 Back at beginning of ride.

Willow Park Ski Trails

Location:	Southwestern Bighorn Mountains.
Distance:	5.1-mile loop.
Time:	One to two hours.
Elevation gain:	250 feet.
Tread:	This ride is all on singletrack.
Season:	This area can be ridden once the snow melts in the spring and before it starts drifting in the fall. Take care at wet patches and mud holes to minimize potential erosion.
Aerobic level:	Moderate.
Technical difficulty:	This trail has an overall technical rating of 3, although there are steep and rocky segments with a rating of 4 and easy segments with a rating of 2.
Hazards:	There are some rocks and logs on the trail and the maintenance level varies throughout the ski trail maze. Horseback riding tours are offered in the area; yield to horseback riders.
Land status:	U.S. Forest Service, Bighorn National Forest.
Maps:	USGS Meadowlark Lake. A free map of the ski trails is available through the Forest Service.
Access:	From U.S. Highway 16, between Buffalo and Tensleep, take the turnoff to Willow Park Picnic Area. Go to the picnic area and park in the area provided. Trail begins on west side of parking area at end of buck-rail fence.

HIGHLIGHTS

If you are looking for either a few hours or a full day of biking, these trails offer a fun and easily accessible maze of singletrack. The trails are not overly technical and offer enjoyable riding for less-experienced riders while still challenging advanced cyclists. The trails can be accessed from three areas: 0.5 mile north of Tyrell Ranger Station off West Tensleep Road (Forest Road 27), the Willow Park Picnic Area, or Sitting Bull Campground.

These cross-country ski trails wind through pine forests and sagebrush meadows and past lily pad-covered ponds. Most of the trails have been adapted for use outside the snow season, with cleared singletrack riding and hiking paths. A few have no clear ground path, though, and are a little

Willow Park Ski Trails

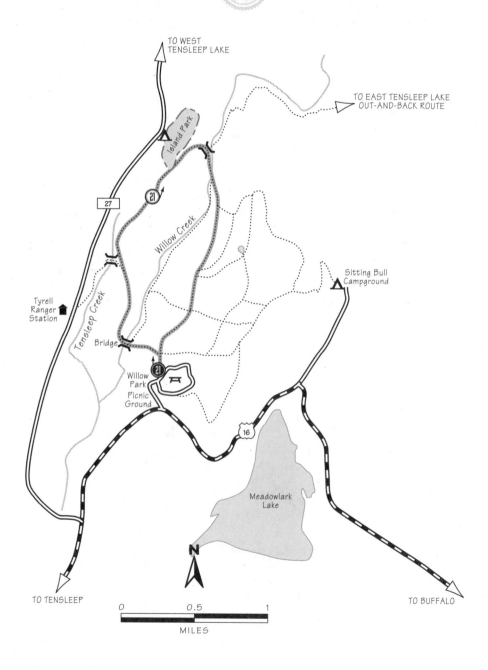

TO WEST
TENSLEEP LAKE

TO EAST TENSLEEP LAKE
OUT-AND-BACK ROUTE

Island Park

27

21

Willow Creek

Tyrell
Ranger
Station

Tensleep Creek

Sitting Bull
Campground

Bridge

21

Willow
Park
Picnic
Ground

16

Meadowlark
Lake

N

TO TENSLEEP

TO BUFFALO

0   0.5   1

MILES

more challenging to bikes due to debris still present on the ground. The trails are well-marked with blue diamonds and, even if you get turned around, they always loop around and return to the Willow Park Picnic Area.

Only one loop is described here but the maze of trails and adjacent routes to Island Park and up to East Tensleep Lake offers a wide array of distances as well as a range of technical and aerobic levels.

THE RIDE

0.0 Begin ride on the west side of buck-rail fence.

0.9 Cross creek on old wooden bridge.

1.2 Trail re-enters timber.

1.4 Come to fork. Continue straight. Left crosses West Tensleep Creek.

1.6 Trail forks. Stay straight. Right returns to ski trails.

2.3 Come to Island Park. Campground is on the west side of the clearing. Follow trail as it skirts around the edge of the clearing and then into the timber.

2.8 Just before trail crosses the creek, it forks. Go right. Left is the East Tensleep Lake Out-and-Back Loop.

2.9 Cross creek. Trail forks. Go left. The other trail goes right and follows Willow Creek. Begin fun downhill. From here, trail returns to Willow Park Picnic Area. Numerous alternative routes branch and cross the trail. Continue straight at each fork and continue down the hill.

5.1 Back at picnic area.

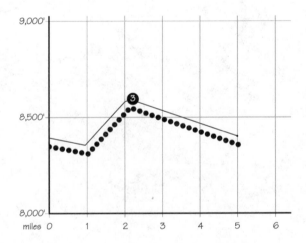

East Tensleep Lake Loop

Location:	Southwestern Bighorn Mountains.
Distance:	8.1-mile loop.
Time:	Three to four hours.
Elevation gain:	1,100 feet.
Tread:	The ride starts out on dirt road and then goes to rough doubletrack. The return loop is on singletrack with the final 2 miles on doubletrack road.
Season:	This ride begins at nearly 9,000 feet and tops out at 9,700 feet. The best season to ride this trail is in summer once the trail has dried from snowmelt and early fall. Hunting activity is fairly heavy in the fall; wear bright orange and be especially cautious.
Aerobic level:	Moderate.
Technical difficulty:	The trail begins on easy doubletrack with a rating of 2 but gets steeper and rockier after 1.5 miles, going to a rating of 3. The narrow singletrack on the downhill has a rating of 4 due to rocks and logs on the trail. The final 2 miles are on doubletrack with ratings of 3 and 2.
Hazards:	The trail going toward the lake is a rough doubletrack going through areas with boulder fields. The creek crossing below East Tensleep Lake is wet; there is no bridge. The singletrack trail on the way down has some rocky areas but is a good trail.
Land status:	U.S. Forest Service, Bighorn National Forest.
Maps:	USGS Meadowlark Lake.
Access:	From U.S. Highway 16, between Buffalo and Tensleep, take the turnoff north to Sitting Bull Campground. Drive 0.5 mile toward the campground and park in the small parking area just before the entrance to the campground.

HIGHLIGHTS

This trail begins and ends next to the Sitting Bull Campground. It goes through a big open meadow before entering the timber and climbing up toward East Tensleep Lake. ATV riders use the trail to the lake but it is quite rough in some segments. At the lake the route passes by a few dispersed camping

East Tensleep Lake Loop

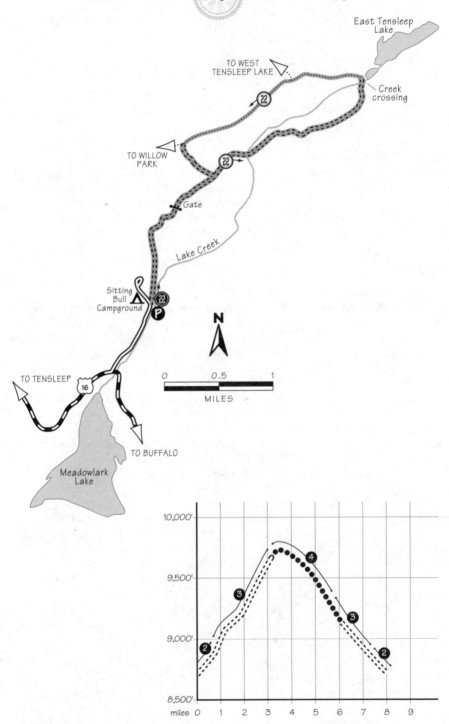

East Tensleep Lake

TO WEST
TENSLEEP LAKE

Creek
crossing

22

TO WILLOW
PARK

22

Gate

Lake Creek

Sitting
Bull
Campground

22

P

N

TO TENSLEEP

16

TO BUFFALO

Meadowlark
Lake

| 0 | 0.5 | 1 |

MILES

10,000'

9,500'

9,000'

8,500'

miles 0   1   2   3   4   5   6   7   8   9

Both East Tensleep Lake Loop and the Out-and-Back routes pass by East Tensleep Lake, on the edge of the Cloud Peak Wilderness Area.

sites before coming to a wet meadow where the road deadends. East Tensleep Lake is a short hike up the creek edge and is worth the trek, especially for the fisherman interested in catching some brook trout.

At the wet meadow the route crosses the creek and meadow to join the singletrack on the other side. For the next 1.2 miles the trail winds through the timber on a fun but challenging downhill ride until meeting an old logging road and then a doubletrack to return to Sitting Bull Campground.

THE RIDE

0.0 Begin ride from the small parking area. Go north toward Sitting Bull Campground. Just before the campground turn right onto the dirt road. Stay on main dirt road as it crosses a large open meadow.

1.0 Come to end of the dirt road; go around the "Road Closed" gate.

1.5 Trail forks. Take right fork that is designated for ATV use. This is an old road, rocky in parts. It rises steadily.

1.9 Cross the creek. There is a crude log bridge near the point where the trail crosses, or you can wade across the creek.

3.3 Another road comes in from the right; keep straight. There may be some bike hiking on the steeper segments, especially where the trail crosses some boulder fields.

3.4 Come to campsite area. Take road to the left, going past campsites.

3.5 The road deadends at the creek.

Take the time to follow the creek up the hill to East Tensleep Lake. To get to the lake, it is easiest to park the bike in the trees and hike the 500 yards up to the lake. You will come to a smaller lake first; continue up the hill past this little lake to reach East Tensleep Lake. Bring your fishing rod for some good fishing at the lake.

To continue loop, cross the creek. This is a wet crossing; wade across the creek and through the wet meadow. A trail marker is on the other side of the meadow. The trail forks at the marker. Right goes to Highline Trail and West Tensleep Lake. Go left on a fun singletrack trail. This trail is well-marked with dot-dash tree blaze marks.

4.9 Trail enters a clearing and is less distinct. Follow the rock cairns through the meadow.

6.1 Fun downhill singletrack. Trail comes out on an old logging road. Turn left. Right goes up the hill on easy road and deadends in about a mile.

6.6 Trail forks. This is the same point as mile marker 1.5.

7.1 Go around "Road Closed" gate. Follow dirt road back across meadow.

8.1 Back at parking area.

East Tensleep Lake
Out-and-Back

Location:	Southwestern Bighorn Mountains.
Distance:	12.6 miles, out and back.
Time:	Three and one-half to four and one-half hours.
Elevation gain:	1,400 feet.
Tread:	This ride is all on singletrack.
Season:	The ride begins at nearly 8,300 feet and tops out at 9,700 feet. The best season to ride this trail is in summer, once the trail has dried from snowmelt, and into early fall. Hunting activity is fairly heavy in the fall; wear bright orange and be especially cautious.
Aerobic level:	Moderate.
Technical difficulty:	This trail has an overall rating of 3, but there are some steep and rocky segments with a rating of 4.
Hazards:	There are some rocks and logs on the trail, but it is fairly well-maintained. It gets a little difficult to follow when crossing open meadows. Look for rock cairns and tree blaze marks.
Land status:	U.S. Forest Service, Bighorn National Forest.
Maps:	USGS Meadowlark Lake.
Access:	From U.S. Highway 16, between Buffalo and Tensleep, take the turnoff to Tyrell Ranger Station, Forest Road 27. Go a half-mile past the ranger station; turn right onto the doubletrack road leading to the trailhead parking area.

HIGHLIGHTS

This trail meanders its way through timbered forest, crossing Willow Creek and passing through Island Park. It is an excellent ride for cyclists of intermediate ability looking to improve their bike-handling skills. There are brief steep and rocky segments that may require some bike hiking for the less experienced cyclist.

East Tensleep Lake
Out-and-Back

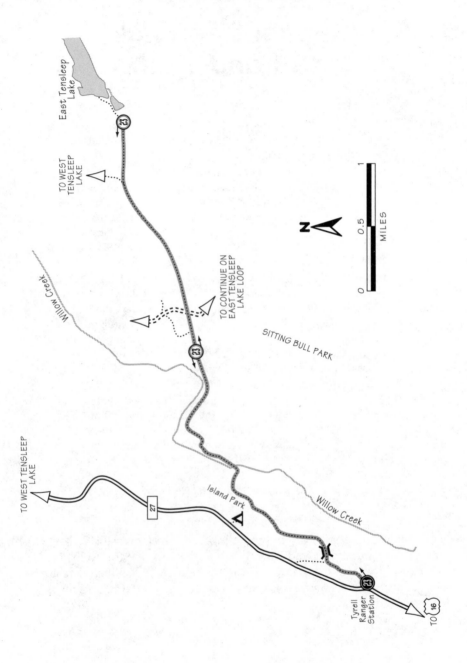

East Tensleep Lake

TO WEST TENSLEEP LAKE

Willow Creek

TO CONTINUE ON EAST TENSLEEP LAKE LOOP

SITTING BULL PARK

TO WEST TENSLEEP LAKE

27

Island Park

Willow Creek

Tyrell Ranger Station

TO 16

N

0   0.5   1

MILES

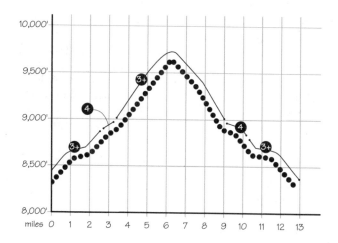

As the trail climbs toward the Cloud Peak Wilderness Area, it breaks into a large open meadow, allowing for a panoramic view of the wilderness peaks. Stark cliffs surround East Tensleep Lake on two sides, creating a striking alpine view. Bring a fishing rod and spend some time angling for brook trout in the lake and creek.

THE RIDE

0.0 Begin ride from the small parking area. Go north past the gate on the old logging road.

0.3 Trail forks. Straight goes to Forest Road 27. Go right over rocky stream crossing and then cross good wooden bridge going over West Tensleep Creek.

0.4 Trail forks. Go left.

0.6 Trail forks. Stay left.

1.3 Trail enters Island Park. The campground is along the western border of the park. Stay on trail as it borders eastern edge of clearing.

1.8 Cross creek on a good wooden bridge. After bridge, trail forks. Stay left.

2.2 Begin steep uphill with switchbacks.

2.7 The trail becomes less steep.

2.9 Cross small creek.

3.2 Come to open meadow with a great view of the high peaks. Trail becomes less distinct as it enters meadow. Stay near the eastern edge of the meadow. Approximately halfway across the meadow, the trail re-enters the timber. If you miss the trail as it enters the timber, just go to the northern end of the meadow where a doubletrack road crosses the creek.

3.5 Come to old road sign. Go left to continue on singletrack trail.

3.7 Trail crosses old logging road. Trail continues on opposite side of the road but it is not obvious. Look for dot-dash blaze marks on trees. If you turn left on the old logging road, it continues up the hill for a pleasant 1.5 miles, then it dead-ends at an old clearcut. The old logging road, turning right, connects with the East Tensleep Lake Loop ride.

4.8 Trail becomes less distinct as it crosses a meadow. Follow rock cairns.

6.3 Come to trail marker. Trail continues to the northwest on the Highline Trail to West Tensleep Lake. East Tensleep Lake is up the hill. To get to the lake, it is easiest to park the bike in the trees and hike the 500 yards up to the lake. You will come to a smaller lake first; continue up the hill past this little lake to reach East Tensleep Lake. Bring your fishing rod for some good fishing at the lake. Return along same singletrack trail. It is a very fun ride down!

12.6 Back at trailhead.

Bald Ridge Shuttle

Location:	Southwestern Bighorn Mountains.
Distance:	11.7 miles, one way.
Time:	Three to four hours.
Elevation gain:	3,200 feet.
Tread:	The ride is on a rough ATV trail for the first 9 miles and then it follows doubletrack.
Season:	This high-elevation ride (10,200 feet) should be snow-free in mid- or late-June and remain open until snow returns in the fall.
Aerobic level:	Moderate.
Technical difficulty:	This trail starts out as a challenging ride on a rough ATV trail with a technical rating of 4. It becomes an easier 3 when it follows an ATV trail. The final doubletrack road has a rating of 2, with some rocky areas.
Hazards:	The trail has some very rocky and rutted areas. It is at high elevation so be prepared for cooler temperatures.
Land status:	U.S. Forest Service, Bighorn National Forest.
Maps:	USGS Lake Solitude, Lake Helen, Brokenback Narrows, Meadowlark. An excellent map is the Cloud Peak Wilderness map, available through the Forest Service.
Access:	From U.S. Highway 16, between Buffalo and Tensleep, take the turnoff to Tyrell Ranger Station, Forest Road 27. After passing Boulder Park Campground turn left on FR 24. Continue 1.7 miles to the turnoff at FR 411. Park the pick-up vehicle here. To begin the ride, continue on FR 24 for another 13 miles to the Lily Lake Trailhead (1.3 miles before the road ends at the Battle Park Trailhead).

HIGHLIGHTS

The route begins near Battle Park and follows an ATV trail to Lily Lake. This is a steep uphill climb, even for an ATV, but this is the toughest part of the ride. Lily Lake is known for its grayling fishing and would be worth an out-and-back biking/fishing trip of its own. From Lily Lake the trail continues

Bald Ridge Shuttle

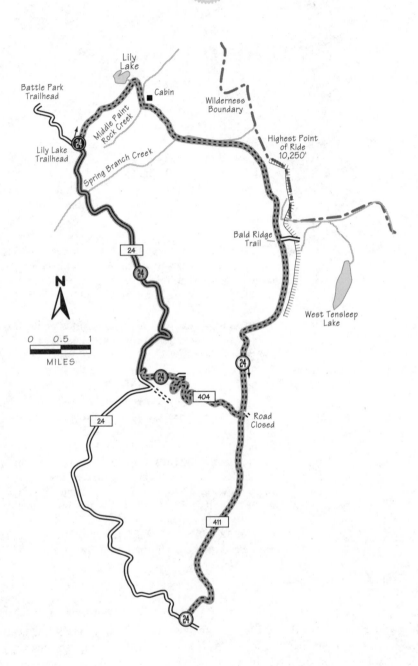

Lily Lake

Battle Park Trailhead

Cabin

Wilderness Boundary

Middle Paint Rock Creek

24

Lily Lake Trailhead

Spring Branch Creek

Highest Point of Ride 10,250'

Bald Ridge Trail

West Tensleep Lake

24

24

N

0   0.5   1
MILES

24

404

Road Closed

24

411

24

A glance back along the Bald Ridge route is worth a pause to enjoy the view of the high country peaks in the Cloud Peak Wilderness Area.

southeast to its highest point on the north end of Bald Ridge above West Tensleep Lake. After the summit the remaining ride is virtually all downhill with an enjoyable ride through open grasslands and lodgepole pine forest.

Two alternative loops are also possible. Both begin and end at the same starting point, by going up the main FR 24. One loop exits on an old logging road and climbs toward Warner Draw and joins the shuttle route. The other loop follows FR 24 all the way to the Lily Lake Trailhead.

THE RIDE

0.0 Start at Lily Lake Trailhead. Take the trail (Forest Trail 66) leaving on the north side of the parking area. Begin steep uphill.

0.8 Come to top of steep climb.

1.0 Cross creek. Begin another uphill climb.

1.5 Trail gets easier.

1.8 Trail forks. Continue right. Left goes to Lily Lake.

2.0 Trail forks. Go right on FR 402, an ATV road. Left goes to wilderness area.

2.2 Pass by cabin on the left. Trail will go left (east) across meadow and start uphill climb.

2.3 Cross creek.

3.2 Cross creek. Trail gets steeper.

4.4 At highest point of ride.

5.6 Cross small creek.

5.9 Trail to West Tensleep Lake goes left. Continue straight.

7.0 Enter timber.

7.6 Cross little creek.

8.9 Come to intersection with FR 404. Left goes to "Road Closed" area. Right goes back to main gravel FR 24. Continue straight down Warner Draw.

9.9 Cross cattleguard.

11.3 Cross cattleguard.

11.7 Come to intersection with FR 24 and end of shuttle ride.

Variation: For a 23.6-mile loop, park vehicle at intersection of FR 24 and FR 411. Ride 11.9 miles on FR 24 to the Lily Lake Trailhead, then begin the ride as described.

For a 13-mile loop, park vehicle at intersection of FR 24 and FR 411. Ride 5.2 miles on FR 24 to turnoff on FR 404. Follow FR 404 for 3.9 miles until it meets FR 411. Continue on FR 411 as described.

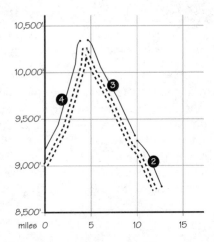

Bellyache Flats

Location: Southwestern Bighorn Mountains.

Distance: 8-mile loop.

Time: One and one-half to two and one-half hours.

Elevation gain: 700 feet.

Tread: The ride begins on good gravel road for the first 4.2 miles and then turns onto doubletrack for the remainder of the ride.

Season: The doubletrack road (Forest Road 360) is closed to motorized travel from September 20 through June 15. It can be quite muddy prior to mid-June and is best during the summer and early fall.

Aerobic level: Moderate.

Technical difficulty: This trail is all a technical rating of 2, although there are a few rocky segments with a rating of 3.

Hazards: The trail has some very rocky and rutted areas.

Land status: U.S. Forest Service, Bighorn National Forest.

Maps: USGS Lake Solitude.

Access: From U.S. Highway 16, between Buffalo and Tensleep, take the turnoff to Tyrell Ranger Station, Forest Road 27. After passing Boulder Park Campground turn left on FR 24. Continue on this road for 10.3 miles. Immediately after a cattleguard FR 360 goes left. Park your vehicle here.

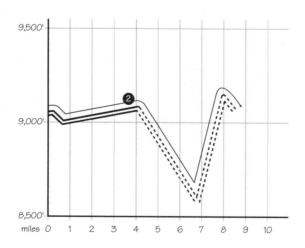

Bellyache Flats

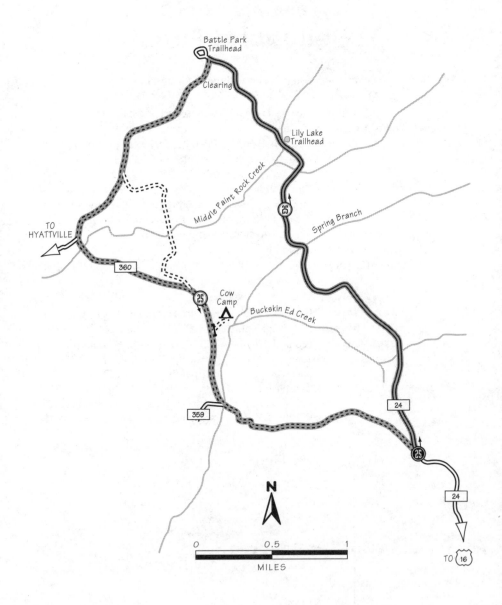

Battle Park
Trailhead

Clearing

Lily Lake
Trailhead

Middle Paint Rock Creek

Spring Branch

25

TO
HYATTVILLE

360

25

Cow
Camp

Buckskin Ed Creek

24

359

25

24

N

0   0.5   1
MILES

TO 16

HIGHLIGHTS

This easy route is great for cruising and sightseeing as it alternates from open grass meadow, to sagebrush prairie, to forested habitat. Half of the route follows gravel road (FR 24) and then it goes on doubletrack that rolls across open meadows, providing a panoramic view of the Paintrock country and the Bighorn Basin. There is dispersed camping along FR 24, but there are no developed campgrounds.

THE RIDE

0.0   Go north (uphill) on FR 24.

1.9   A logging road goes left. Stay on main road.

2.8   Cross cattleguard.

3.0   Pass by trailhead parking area to Lily Lake.

3.8   Go over cattleguard.

4.0   Come into big clearing. This is a popular parking and camping area, especially for horseback riders.

4.2   Just before the end of the clearing, turn onto a doubletrack road, FR 360.

4.3   Cross creek. Begin uphill climb.

4.5   At top of hill.

5.3   Trail forks. Go right, staying on FR 360.

5.8   Cross creek.

6.1   Road forks. Stay straight.

6.5   Go through a series of two gates. A Cow Camp goes left.

7.0   Cross creek.

7.4   Road goes left. Stay straight.

7.6   Road goes right. Stay straight.

7.7   Come to saddle.

8.0   Back at intersection with FR 24.

Grace Lake

Location:	Southwestern Bighorn Mountains.
Distance:	Loop: 8.6 miles; out-and-back: 9.5 miles.
Time:	Loop: three to four hours; out-and-back: two and one-half to three and one-half hours.
Elevation gain:	Loop: 1,840 feet; out-and-back: 1,625 feet.
Tread:	The ride is all on singletrack.
Season:	This high-elevation ride should be snow-free in late June or July. Once the snow flies in late summer or early fall, it should be avoided to reduce the chance of damaging the trail.
Aerobic level:	Strenuous.
Technical difficulty:	This singletrack trail starts out as a rock-free easy ride but it quickly changes into a challenging ride for even the advanced mountain cyclist. Steep and rocky terrain, with a technical rating of 4+, requires some bike hiking. As the optional loop passes over a boulder-strewn and steep trail 2 miles from Grace Lake, the technical rating is a 5 and requires bike hauling. There are several easier, open stretches with a technical rating of 3.
Hazards:	The trail has some very rocky and rutted areas. This is a popular horsepacking trail leading to the Cloud Peak Wilderness. Some wet meadow areas are rough due to horse travel.
Land status:	U.S. Forest Service, Bighorn National Forest.
Maps:	USGS Lake Solitude. An excellent map for this route is the Cloud Peak Wilderness map, available through the Forest Service.
Access:	From U.S. Highway 16, between Buffalo and Tensleep, take the turnoff to Tyrell Ranger Station, Forest Road 27. After passing Boulder Park Campground turn left on FR 24. Continue on this road approximately 15 miles to Battle Park. At Battle Park, continue to end of road and trailhead, where parking is available.

Grace Lake

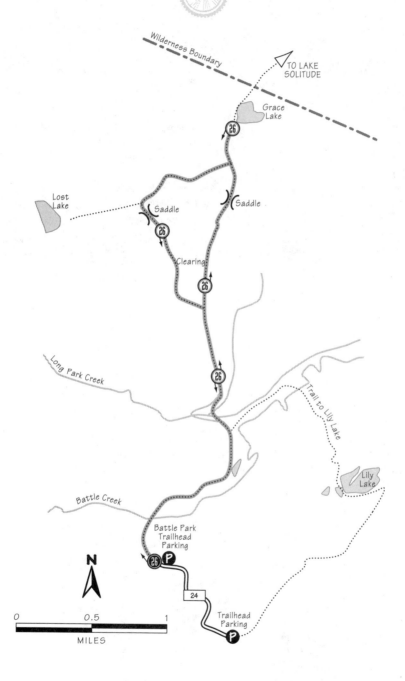

Wilderness Boundary

TO LAKE SOLITUDE

Grace Lake

Lost Lake

Saddle

Saddle

Clearing

Long Park Creek

Trail to Lily Lake

Lily Lake

Battle Creek

Battle Park Trailhead Parking

Trailhead Parking

N

0   0.5   1

MILES

Lilypads float along the surface of Grace Lake, on the edge of the Cloud Peak Wilderness Area.

Highlights

This is a tough route as it passes from subalpine to alpine habitat. It provides gorgeous views of rocky peaks off to the north and east in the Cloud Peak Wilderness. The route described includes a tough loop that climbs a rough and rocky saddle before dropping down to Grace Lake. It involves climbing up and down a boulder field and requires some bike carrying. For those wanting a less challenging route, avoid the loop and stay on the main out-and-back route. It is still quite challenging but not as difficult as the loop.

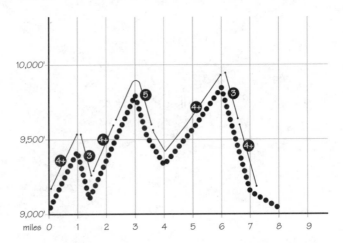

THE RIDE

0.0 Start at Battle Park Trailhead. Take Battle Park Trail 164, which exits just before the circular parking area.

0.2 Forest Trail 173 forks to the left. Stay right on FT 164. After the fork the trail crosses Battle Creek. Trail becomes rough due to heavy horse traffic.

0.8 Go through gate.

1.1 Start fun downhill as you enter big sagebrush and wetland meadow.

1.4 Cross creek.

1.6 Main trail crosses creek again. Note wooden posts going northeast across clearing. Follow these posts for the tough loop to Grace Lake. For easier route, do not turn, but continue straight up hill. For the out-and-back route, continue on main trail for 3.1 miles to Grace Lake. This route is still quite strenuous but requires only bike hiking rather than bike carrying.

2.6 (Via tough loop). Pass by small ponds. Trail is deeply rutted in places due to horse travel.

2.8 Begin very rocky uphill. Some bike carrying may be necessary.

3.1 At saddle. Trail goes down through rough boulder field.

3.3 At bottom of boulder field. Continue right at bottom of boulder field.

4.1 At Grace Lake. Trail continues around the western edge of lake and the trail continues on toward Lake Solitude. This is the turnaround point.

4.9 Just before trail starts up the boulder field, it forks. Take the right loop (avoiding the boulder field).

5.3 Trail forks. Continue straight.

5.7 At saddle. Unmarked narrow trail forks to right (west), leading to Lost Lake. Continue straight.

7.2 Cross the creek. Back on route that you followed on the way up. Continue back on same route to trailhead.

8.6 Back at trailhead.

Tensleep Canyon

Location:	Southwestern Bighorn Mountains.
Distance:	7.9 miles, one-way shuttle.
Time:	One to two hours.
Elevation gain:	There is no significant elevation gain on this ride. There is an overall 2,280 feet elevation loss.
Tread:	The trail is a gravel road with some areas of old pavement. The final 1.5 miles are on pavement but the road does not have a shoulder area.
Season:	This road can be pedaled as soon as the snow melts in the spring and is open into mid- to late fall.
Aerobic level:	Easy.
Technical difficulty:	This trail is nearly all downhill on gravel roads, with a rating of 2.
Hazards:	There are some gravel patches and areas of rough old asphalt. Watch for vehicle traffic.
Land status:	U.S. Forest Service, Bighorn National Forest, and state highway.
Maps:	USGS Meadowlark Lake, Onion Gulch, Old Maid Gulch.
Access:	From Tensleep, follow U.S. Highway 16 up Tensleep Canyon. At the top of the canyon Forest Road 18 goes to the south. Start the ride at the gate. A second vehicle can be parked at a public parking area next to Tensleep Creek, 0.2 mile from US16, on Wyoming 435, leading to Tensleep Fish Hatchery.

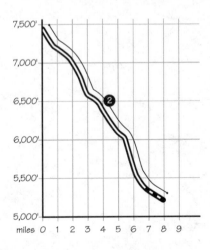

Tensleep Canyon

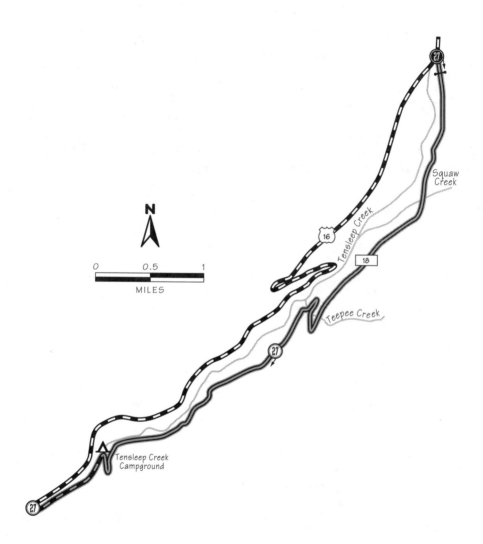

Squaw Creek

Tensleep Creek

16

18

Teepee Creek

27

N

0   0.5   1

MILES

Tensleep Creek
Campground

27

27

HIGHLIGHTS

The highway though Tensleep Canyon was once on the south side of the canyon but in the late 1960s or early 1970s a new highway was constructed on the north side of the canyon. The old highway gradually deteriorated and was eventually resurfaced as a gravel road, although some patches of the old asphalt can still be seen.

When the highway was moved to the north side of Tensleep Canyon, there was concern for the big game, especially mule deer and elk that wintered in the canyon. Elk generally tend to favor the more open slopes found on the north, or south-facing, slopes. These south-facing slopes also get more direct sunlight in the winter and tend to be free of snow earlier in the spring.

This is a delightful ride as it passes through aspen and pine forests. The occasional open sagebrush hillsides allow excellent views of the magnificent canyon. Cliffs rise over 1,000 feet above the trail, and Tensleep Creek can be heard rushing 100 feet below the trail.

THE RIDE

0.0   Ride begins at gate on FR 18, immediately south of US16.
0.1   Go over cattleguard.
1.5   Cross Squaw Creek.
3.1   First switchback.
3.5   Second switchback.
4.8   Pass by split rock.
6.3   Third switchback.
6.5   Road turns off to Tensleep Creek Campground. Stay on main road. Pavement begins.
7.7   Fishing access parking area (a good place to leave a pick-up vehicle).
7.9   WY 435 joins US16. Tensleep is 7.5 miles down the highway.

Variation:
1. This trail can be done as an out-and-back ride for a total of 15.8 miles. The ride up the canyon is relentless as it climbs the canyon, but the grade is steady and not overly steep.
2. Another alternative is to make the route into a loop, going either up or down the canyon via US16. The shoulder on the highway is fairly wide and the traffic moves slowly.

Bench Trail

Location:	Northwest Bighorn Mountains.
Distance:	10.6 miles, one-way shuttle.
Time:	Top racers in the annual bike race complete the course in about an hour. Average mortals complete it in two to three hours.
Elevation gain:	60 feet.
Tread:	The trail is all singletrack.
Season:	The trail begins at 7,600 feet and is snow-free earlier in the spring than trails higher up in the Bighorns. It can be ridden until mid-autumn, depending on seasonal snowfall.
Aerobic level:	Easy.
Technical difficulty:	This is a sometimes narrow, sometimes steep and rocky trail. It has a rating of 3+ for the first 8.5 miles and a rating of 4 for the final 2 miles.
Hazards:	The trail has rocky and steep segments as well as logs and debris. It becomes especially rough in the final 2 miles.
Land status:	U.S. Forest Service, Bighorn National Forest.
Maps:	USGS Shell Falls and Black Mountain.
Access:	On U.S. Highway 14, between Dayton and Shell, approximately 5 miles east of Shell Falls, turn south onto Forest Road 17, the Paintrock Road. Follow this road for 3 miles, past Shell Creek Campground and to Ranger Creek Campground. Take the right road into the west half of the campground. Go left at the first fork and park in parking area near the big picnic ground. Start on the singletrack trail to the right of the "Road Closed" sign and gate. Do not take the old logging road.
	Park a second vehicle or have a pick-up arranged for the Post Creek Picnic Ground, approximately 5 miles west of Shell Falls off US14.

Bench Trail

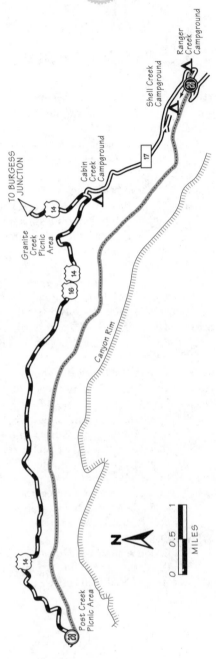

Ranger Creek Campground

Shell Creek Campground

TO BURGESS JUNCTION

Cabin Creek Campground

17

Granite Creek Picnic Area

14

16 14

14

Canyon Rim

Post Creek Picnic Area

28

N

0   0.5   1
MILES

HIGHLIGHTS

Shell Canyon is part of the Bighorn Scenic Byway and features steep rock escarpments in a very scenic canyon. The Bench Trail follows singletrack on a forested bench halfway up the canyon, above US16. The upper end of the trail is fairly easy, but as the trail heads down the canyon it becomes rockier, steeper, and more technical. The trail is well-maintained, with volunteer cyclists assisting to keep the trail safe for mountain biking. A bike race is held on this trail each year, sponsored by Larson's Bicycles in Worland.

THE RIDE

0.0 From "Road Closed" gate, take singletrack trail (Forest Trail 184) to the right of the gate. Follow the trail as it passes by the campground.

0.5 Pass above Shell Creek Campground. The trail continues on a mostly downhill ride all the way down the canyon.

8.5 Trail becomes rougher.

10.6 Come to Post Creek Picnic Ground and end of ride.

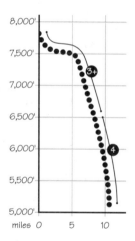

Freeze Out Point

Location:	The ride begins at Freeze Out Point north of Burgess Junction in the northern Bighorn Mountains.
Distance:	9-mile loop.
Time:	Three to four hours.
Elevation gain:	1,120 feet.
Tread:	This trail is on doubletrack except for the final 0.2 mile on gravel road.
Season:	This trail is best in late spring once the snow has melted, and into the fall.
Aerobic level:	Moderate.
Technical difficulty:	The technical rating is 2 except for a few steep and rocky segments, which rate a level 3.
Hazards:	There are steep and rocky segments on the trail.
Land status:	U.S. Forest Service, Bighorn National Forest.
Maps:	USGS Skull Ridge.
Access:	From Dayton, take U.S. Highway 14 up the mountain to Burgess Junction. At Burgess Junction, turn north on Forest Road 15. Continue approximately 4 miles to FR 168. Take this road approximately 8 miles to a parking area loop near Freeze Out Point.

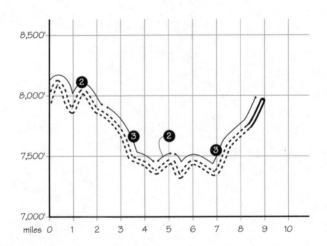

Freeze Out Point

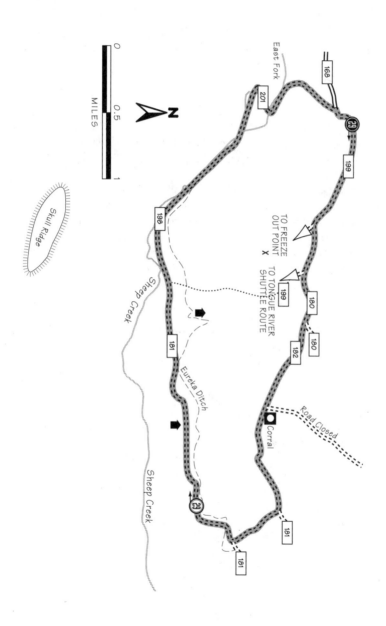

HIGHLIGHTS

Freeze Out Point provides an amazing view of the valley below. As the route follows the doubletrack road northeast, it presents an unobstructed view into Montana and across the Wyoming Powder River Basin. This is an enjoyable ride with some challenging uphill segments followed by fun downhill segments. As the route passes by Sheep Creek, the route for the Tongue River Shuttle crosses the creek and continues down the canyon.

THE RIDE

0.0 Start at the parking area at end of FR 168. Take FR 199 headed east.

0.4 Trail forks; go left through gate. Right goes up the hill to the top of Freeze Out Point.

0.8 Trail forks. Go left on FR 180 down the hill.

1.0 At bottom of hill. Go through the gate and take right fork on FR 182.

1.4 Go through gate; water collector for livestock is off to the left. Great view all the way to Montana.

1.5 At top of the hill with a great view of the valley.

2.0 A doubletrack with "Road Closed" sign forks to left. Stay right on main route.

2.5 Go through gate and take fun downhill.

3.4 Come to end of the road. Go right (onto FR 181).

3.9 Go through gate.

4.1 Road forks. Go left and follow road around to bottom of ridge.

4.6 A cabin is down below the road.

5.2 Go through the gate and take steep downhill.

5.5 Cross the creek.

5.6 A closed road branches to the right. Stay straight on main road.

5.7 Go through gate. There is a nice cabin uphill.

5.9 Come to an intersection. Right (FR 199) goes up the hill to Freeze Out Point. Go left on FR 198, down the hill toward the creek.

6.9 At bottom of hill; trail parallels the creek, then begins steep uphill.

7.0 Trail becomes less steep.

7.5 Cross creek.

8.0 Road forks. Go right onto better road.

8.2 Cross East Fork Sheep Creek.

8.8 Come into main gravel road. Continue right.

9.0 Back at parking area.

Tongue River Shuttle

Location:	The ride begins at Freeze Out Point in the northern Bighorn Mountains.
Distance:	10.5 miles, one way.
Time:	Five to six hours.
Elevation gain:	510 feet.
Tread:	The first 4.1 miles are on doubletrack and the final 6.4 miles are on singletrack.
Season:	This trail is best in the summer when the river and creek levels are lower, but the trail can be ridden once the snow melts and into the fall.
Aerobic level:	Easy.
Technical difficulty:	This route is rated 4 due to rocky and steep segments.
Hazards:	There are steep and rocky segments on the trail.
Land status:	U.S. Forest Service, Bighorn National Forest.
Maps:	USGS Skull Ridge, Dayton South.
Access:	From Dayton, take U.S. Highway 14 up the mountain to Burgess Junction. At Burgess Junction, turn north on Forest Road 15. Continue approximately 4 miles to FR 168. Take FR 168 approximately 8 miles to parking area near Freeze Out Point. The end point is at the Tongue River Trailhead, approximately 4 miles southwest of Dayton.

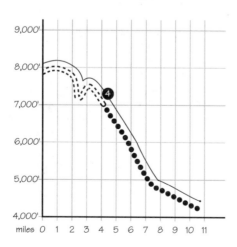

Tongue River Shuttle

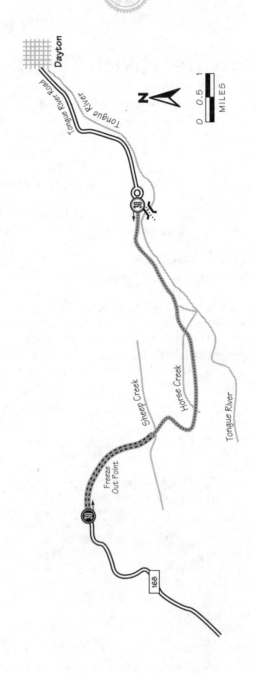

HIGHLIGHTS

This is a popular one-way shuttle ride that follows a good trail and goes through spectacular scenery. An alternative starting point is 13 miles west of Dayton on FR 184. The starting point from Freeze Out Point eliminates the need to cross the Tongue River. The trail crosses Sheep Creek and Horse Creek; only Sheep Creek requires a little wading.

THE RIDE

0.0 Start at the parking area that is at end of FR 168. Take FR 199 headed east.

0.4 Trail forks; go left through gate. Right goes up the hill to the top of Freeze Out Point.

0.8 Trail forks. Go right, down hill toward cabin.

1.2 Go through gate (it may or may not be open).

2.1 Go past cabin on the right.

2.3 Go through gate.

2.5 Cross creek. Wade across then start uphill. Trail begins to get narrower. There are a few switchbacks on the way up the hill.

3.1 At top of ridge. Start down again. Trail becomes less distinct. Head down hill.

3.8 Trail comes in from right. Continue straight.

4.1 Cross Horse Creek. This is an easy crossing but it may be deeper earlier in the season or following heavy precipitation. After the creek crossing, the trail becomes singletrack and goes downhill with some steep and rocky segments.

5.9 Cross Horse Creek again.

7.3 Cross Sheep Creek.

8.1 Cross a little creek.

10.4 Come to wooden bridge where trail forks. The trail across the bridge leads to the Tongue River Caves. Continue straight.

10.5 Come to trailhead.

31

Fool Creek

Location:	Northwest Bighorn Mountains.
Distance:	9.8-mile loop.
Time:	Two to three hours.
Elevation gain:	650 feet.
Tread:	The first 3 miles follow a rough doubletrack before a wet crossing of Fool Creek. Then the route joins a good gravel road for the remaining 7 miles.
Season:	This trail is best in late spring, once the snow has melted, and into the summer and fall.
Aerobic level:	Moderate.
Technical difficulty:	This ride begins on doubletrack with a rating of 2. After 2.5 miles it becomes rough and rocky with a rating of 3+. The route follows gravel roads for the final 6.9 miles with a rating of 2.
Hazards:	The trail has rocky and steep segments on the doubletrack. The first crossing of Fool Creek is a wet crossing without a bridge. The gravel road can be washboarded and may have pockets of dense gravel.
Land status:	U.S. Forest Service, Bighorn National Forest.
Maps:	USGS Burgess Junction.
Access:	From U.S. Highway 14A, between Dayton and Lovell, turn north on Forest Road 15 immediately west of Burgess Junction. Continue north past the North Tongue Campground and picnic area. Approximately 2.5 miles past the Picnic Area, FR 167 forks to right. Park vehicle near intersection.

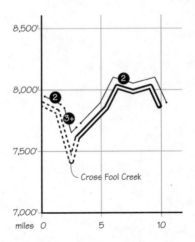

Fool Creek

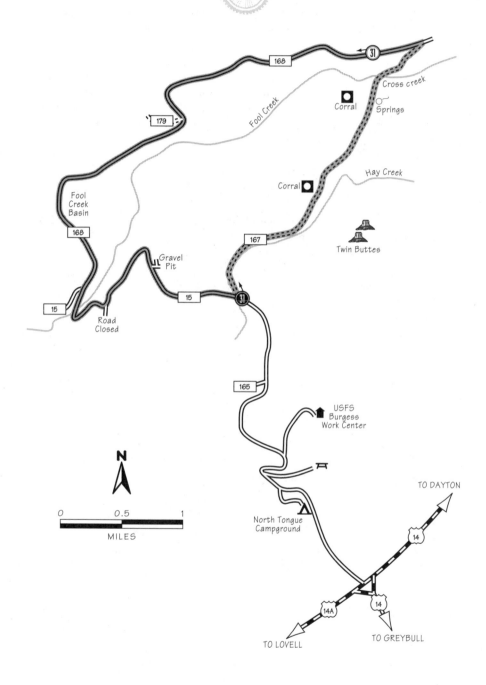

Fool Creek

168

31

Cross creek

Corral

Springs

179

Hay Creek

Corral

Fool
Creek
Basin

168

167

Twin Buttes

Gravel
Pit

15

15

31

Road
Closed

165

USFS
Burgess
Work Center

N

North Tongue
Campground

TO DAYTON

14

0   0.5   1

MILES

14A

14

TO LOVELL

TO GREYBULL

HIGHLIGHTS

This route follows a rough doubletrack road alongside Hay Creek as it flows down to meet Fool Creek. Twin Buttes rises nearly 1,000 feet from the creek bottom to overlook the open grassland drainage bottom. The trail crosses Fool Creek and begins a steep climb to the adjacent ridgeline. The route joins a good gravel road that overlooks Fool Creek and then drops down to Fool Creek Basin, a peaceful-looking wet meadow opening that attracts anglers. The route crosses Fool Creek again but on a good road crossing and then climbs out of the drainage again before returning to Hay Creek and the starting point of the ride.

THE RIDE

0.0 Begin ride at intersection between FR 15 and FR 167. Head north on FR 167.

0.2 Cross creek over earthen bridge.

1.4 Trail becomes rockier. Pass by a little pond to the left.

1.7 Go over cattleguard.

2.4 Cross the creek. On other side, begin steep uphill.

2.7 At top of steep section.

2.9 Come to good gravel road. Go left.

4.2 Cross cattleguard.

5.1 Doubletrack goes right. Stay on main road.

5.5 FR 179 goes right. Stay on main road.

7.6 Go over cattleguard and to intersection with FR 15. Go left.

7.9 Cross Fool Creek and go up hill.

9.0 Dirt road goes left. Stay on main road.

9.8 Cross Hay Creek and return to starting point.

Variation: Begin and end in the North Tongue Campground. This adds 2.3 miles one way, 4.6 miles round-trip to the route.

Black Mountain

Location:	Northeastern Bighorn Mountains above Dayton.
Distance:	16.4-mile loop.
Time:	Four to five hours.
Elevation gain:	1,800 feet.
Tread:	This trail begins on rough doubletrack. After 5 miles it goes to singletrack and continues on a footpath for 3 miles until it joins old logging roads. The final 3 miles are on a good gravel road.
Season:	This trail can be wet and muddy where it crosses creeks and seeps. It is best in the summer and early fall, but can be ridden once the snow melts in late spring.
Aerobic level:	Strenuous.
Technical difficulty:	The ride begins with a fun but rocky doubletrack with a rating of 3. The steep drop to Wolf and Quartz Creeks has a technical rating of 4 and requires some bike hiking. The climb out of the drainage has a technical rating of 3 until it reaches logging and gravel roads with a rating of 2.
Hazards:	There are steep and rocky segments on the trail along with a number of creek and seep crossings. The downhill singletrack that drops down to Wolf Creek is especially rocky and steep. Once on Forest Road 16, watch for vehicle traffic.
Land status:	U.S. Forest Service, Bighorn National Forest.
Maps:	USGS Walker Mountain, Dayton South, Skull Ridge, Woodrock.
Access:	From Dayton, take U.S. Highway 14 up the mountain to the Black Mountain Road, FR 16. The ride begins 2.6 miles down the road at the intersection with FR 186. There are parking and dispersed camping areas along the road and at the intersection.

HIGHLIGHTS

This ride begins in the timber and passes by a number of wet meadows, seeps, and creeks. Elk are attracted to these wet areas in the spring and summer and the bull elk may even use the shallow mud holes as wallows

Black Mountain

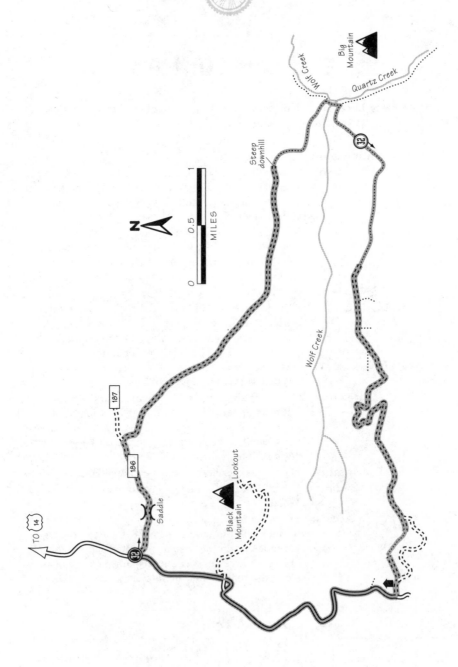

MILES

N

0   0.5   1

Wolf Creek

Quartz Creek

Big Mountain

32

Steep downhill

Wolf Creek

187

186

Saddle

32

TO 14

Black Mountain

Lookout

during the rut. The route continues up onto a hillside that was burned during a forest fire about a decade ago.

The first segment of the route is included in the Black Mountain Out-and-Back route. As it drops down to Wolf Creek, the route becomes much more difficult both aerobically and technically. The climb up from Wolf Creek through the burn and old logging area is an aerobic challenge that is rewarded by a fun downhill along a good gravel road for the final 3 miles.

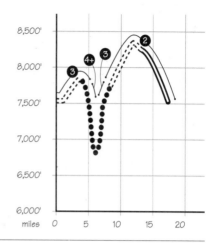

THE RIDE

0.0 Start at intersection of FR 16 and FR 186. Go east down doubletrack. Cross the creek within the first 100 yards and head up the hill.

0.4 At top of hill; begin fun downhill.

1.2 FR 187 forks left. Stay right. After 50 yards, cross small creek.

1.5 Cross creek/seep area. There are a number of seep and wet bog areas in the next couple of miles.

3.6 "Road Closed" trail goes left. Stay straight on main route.

4.3 Trail becomes rockier and steeper.

4.5 "Road Closed" trail goes left; stay right. Trail becomes easier.

4.8 Enter burn area.

5.0 Begin steep downhill as trail goes to singletrack. Most likely, this will require some bike hiking.

5.9 At bottom of steep hill. The trail comes to a creek crossing and the trail is obvious on other side. You can cross the creek but you will have to cross back over within 50 yards. To stay dry, don't cross the creek but follow bank to the right (south), crossing Wolf Creek. Continue south to a clearing with a corral. Sign calls this "Big Bend Picnic Area."

6.0 In clearing, go behind the corral (to the west) to connect with trail. The trail is obvious just up the hill from the corral.

6.2 Uphill climb becomes a little easier.

7.5 Enter old burn area. Trail continues uphill. The trail can become a little less distinct but continue west through burned clear-cut.

8.0 Come to old logging road.

9.1 Enter the timber. Trail is a good old logging road now.

10.4 Road forks; go right.

11.5 A singletrack goes right while the main road continues straight. Take the singletrack for a fun ride.

12.0 Come to gravel FR 223. There is a small creek crossing just after intersection.

12.5 Cross another creek. There is an old cabin off to the right.

12.6 Come to intersection with FR 16. Turn right.

15.1 Closed logging road goes left.

15.5 Road to lookout goes right (FR 222); stay on main road.

16.4 Back at intersection with FR 186.

Black Mountain Out-and-Back

Location:	Northeastern Bighorn Mountains above Dayton.
Distance:	10 miles, out and back.
Time:	Three to four hours.
Elevation gain:	340 feet.
Tread:	This trail follows doubletrack that can be rough and rocky at times.
Season:	This trail can be wet and muddy where it crosses creeks and seeps. It is best in the summer and early fall, but can be ridden once the snow melts in late spring.
Aerobic level:	Moderate.
Technical difficulty:	The doubletrack can be rough and rocky in areas, giving it a rating of 3.
Hazards:	There are steep and rocky segments on the trail along with a number of creek and seep crossings.
Land status:	U.S. Forest Service, Bighorn National Forest.
Maps:	USGS Walker Mountain, Skull Ridge.
Access:	From Dayton, take U.S. Highway 14 up the mountain to the Black Mountain Road, Forest Road 16. The ride begins 2.6 miles down the road at the intersection with FR 186. There are parking and dispersed camping areas along the road and at the intersection.

HIGHLIGHTS

This is a fun ride with just enough down and up to make it a challenging workout, yet you'll spend most of the time on the seat of your bike rather than pushing it. You'll pass by and through some wet areas that would make great elk wallows in the fall. There is a brief segment through an old burn that has young trees and thick undergrowth, showing that forests can regenerate after fire.

The turnaround point is at a rock outcrop overlooking Wolf and Quartz creeks, with the Powder River Basin off to the horizon. The Black Mountain Loop Trail continues down to the creek.

Black Mountain Out-and-Back

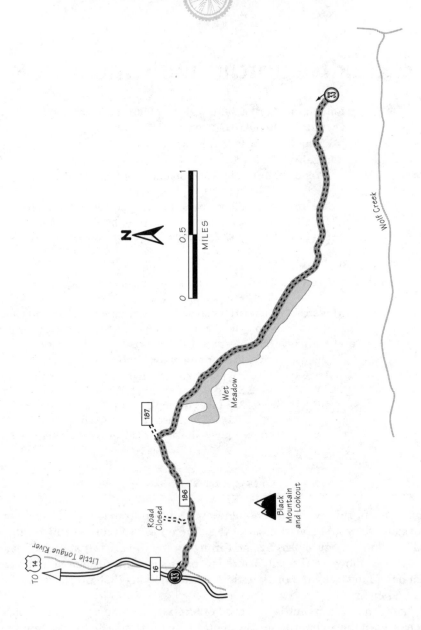

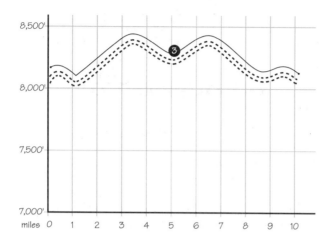

The Ride

0.0   Start at intersection of FR 16 and FR 186. Go east down doubletrack. Cross the creek within the first 100 yards and head up the hill.

0.4   At top of hill; begin fun downhill.

1.2   FR 187 forks left. Stay right. After 50 yards, cross small creek.

1.5   Cross creek/seep area. There are a number of seep and wet bog areas in the next couple of miles.

3.6   "Road Closed" trail goes left. Stay straight on main route.

4.3   Trail becomes rockier and steeper.

4.5   "Road Closed" trail goes left; stay right. Trail becomes easier.

4.8   Enter burn area.

5.0   Come to a small clearing. This is the turnaround point, but take the time to climb the nearby rock outcrop for a grand view of Wolf and Quartz creeks below.

         Return on same route.

10.0 Back at parking area.

Burnt Mountain

Location:	The Northwestern Bighorn Mountains.
Distance:	12-mile loop.
Time:	Three to four hours.
Elevation gain:	1,500 feet.
Tread:	The first 4 miles follow doubletrack and then join gravel forest roads for the remaining 8 miles.
Season:	Ride this route in the late spring through the fall. It is popular during the hunting season and special care should be taken during that season.
Aerobic level:	Moderate.
Technical difficulty:	The first 4 miles follow doubletrack with a rating of 3 due to rough areas and ruts. The final 8 miles follow gravel and dirt roads with a rating of 2.
Hazards:	The old logging road and doubletrack at the start of the ride has rocky and rutted areas. The gravel and dirt roads have pockets of dense gravel, potholes, and ruts. This is a popular fishing area; watch for traffic.
Land status:	U.S. Forest Service, Bighorn National Forest.
Maps:	USGS Bald Mountain.
Access:	Take U.S. Highway Alternative 14 into the Bighorn Mountains from Lovell. From the base of the mountain, drive approximately 36 miles east then turn north on Forest Road 14/11. Turn right on second right, on Burnt Mountain Road. Continue down road to parking area at end of road.

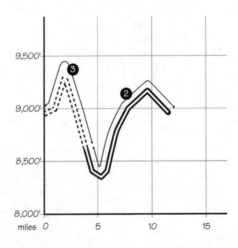

Burnt Mountain

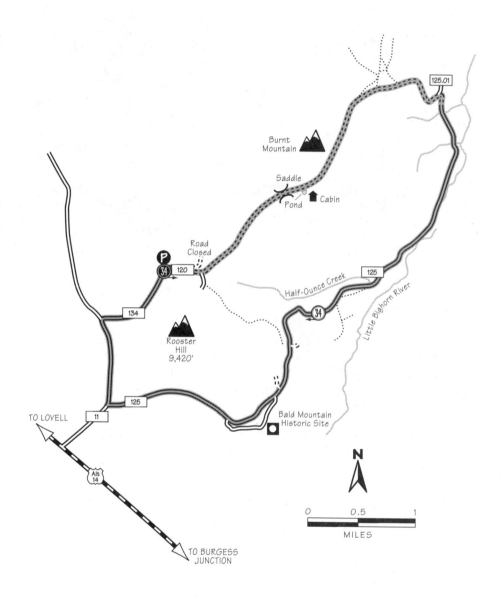

Burnt Mountain burned during a major forest more than two decades ago. Burnt trees still stand while new pines emerge from the forest floor.

HIGHLIGHTS

In 1978 a forest fire, known as the Half-Ounce Burn, spread across 1,320 acres of forest land. Since then, young trees have sprouted across the old timbered areas and the undergrowth grasses are lush and green. Elk frequent the area, especially in the spring and summer, and are attracted to the wet meadow and seep area on the east side of Burnt Mountain.

The route parallels the scenic Little Bighorn River, a popular trout fishing area. It also passes by the old Bald Mountain City, once a booming mining town. Today a few log cabins and other debris are all that remain.

THE RIDE

0.0 Follow doubletrack leaving east side of parking area.

0.7 Main road ends. Go left onto old logging road with "Road Closed" sign. Go up hill and through burn area.

0.9 Go through gate.

2.0 At summit of Burnt Mountain. Go over the ridge and down the east side. Just below is a spring with evidence of an old cabin.

3.1 Pass through gate.

4.3 Road becomes more distinct but still a doubletrack. End of fun downhill.

4.5 Cross creek and start on better road, which is FR 125.

8.0 Pass by Forest Service sign describing the Half-Ounce Burn.

9.0 Pass through the remains of Bald Mountain City.

10.4 Back onto main gravel FR 14/11.

11.3 Turn onto FR 134.

12.0 Back at parking area.

Bighorn Basin Rides

The Bighorn Basin covers approximately 10,000 square miles in the north central part of Wyoming. It is bordered on the west by the Beartooth, Absaroka, and Washakie mountains, to the south by the Owl Creek and Bridger m ountains, and to the east by the Bighorn Mountains. A wide variety of habitats can be found in the basin, including irrigated croplands near the flat center of the basin, arid badlands in the south and extreme north, and forested foothills near the base of the mountains.

The Crow Indians claimed much of the Bighorn Basin as their hunting ground when vast herds of bison, deer, elk, and pronghorn roamed the area. In 1807, mountain man John Colter was the first white man known to have passed through the area.

The two rides presented here explore the badlands in the southern Bighorn Basin. Biking opportunities abound throughout the basin, with hundreds of miles of gravel and doubletrack roads. During the summer months, the Bighorn Basin consistently has the highest daytime temperatures in the state, easily reaching into the low 100s for extended periods. Use caution when biking during the hot, dry periods of July and August.

Honeycomb Buttes–Nowater Trail Overnighter

Location:	The ride begins 6.5 miles west of Tensleep and crosses the southern end of the Bighorn Basin through the Honeycomb Buttes.
Distance:	60.6 miles one way.
Time:	Two days. The total riding time is 11 to 13 hours with a loaded bicycle.
Elevation gain:	3,350 feet.
Tread:	The ride begins on a dirt road with some rough areas, mud holes, and ruts. After 37.4 miles, the road becomes gravel.
Season:	This ride can get quite hot and dry by mid-summer. Spring and fall are the best times to ride it.
Aerobic level:	Moderate.
Technical difficulty:	This ride has a technical rating of 2+.
Hazards:	The first 37 miles have some rocky segments, while the final 23 miles have pockets of dense gravel and ruts. But the road is in good condition as long as it's dry. The road is especially slick after significant rainfall. Watch for potential vehicular traffic beginning at mile 37, on the Nowood Road.
Land status:	All of the route is on BLM roads with right-of-way passage on the few segments of private land. The private land is well-marked and care must be taken to stay on the roads when crossing these areas.
Maps:	USGS Wild Horse Hill, Castle Gardens, Deadline Draw, Sand Point, Lightening Ridge, Cornell Gulch, Cottonwood Pass, Lysite SE. Another option is to use BLM 1:100,000 maps: Worland, Nowater Creek, Lysite.
Access:	From Tensleep, go west on U.S. Highway 16 for 6.5 miles. Turn south onto the Blue Bank Road (BLM Road 1411). The ride begins at this point. If you leave a vehicle at the end destination, there are a couple of options for parking. The best place is near an unnamed reservoir. To get to this site, turn off US20-26 (the Shoshone to Casper highway) at the Moneta exit, going north. After 8.6 miles, go through Lycite past the store and post office. At the north end of

Honeycomb Buttes–Nowater
Trail Overnighter

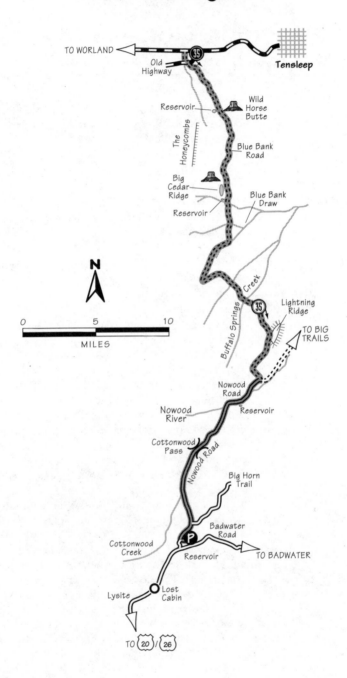

TO WORLAND

Old Highway

Tensleep

Reservoir

Wild Horse Butte

The Honeycombs

Blue Bank Road

Big Cedar Ridge

Reservoir

Blue Bank Draw

N

0   5   10
MILES

Buffalo Springs Creek

Lightning Ridge

TO BIG TRAILS

Nowood Road

Nowood River

Reservoir

Cottonwood Pass

Nowood Road

Big Horn Trail

Badwater Road

Cottonwood Creek

P

Reservoir

TO BADWATER

Lysite

Lost Cabin

TO 20 / 26

The overnighter from Tensleep to Lysite winds through the Honeycomb Buttes in the southern Bighorn Basin.

town, turn right on County Road 17 to Lost Cabin. Continue on this road through Lost Cabin and, after 4.5 miles, turn north onto the Nowood Road (CR 295). Continue 0.7 mile to a reservoir on the east side of the road. Park your vehicle here (it is on BLM land). A dam goes across the reservoir, with potential parking on the other side.

Highlights

This ride rolls through the badlands of the southern Bighorn Basin and along the foothills of the Bighorn Mountains. It passes by color-banded mud cliffs of the Honeycomb Buttes on a roller-coaster ride from ridgetops to drainage bottoms. The buttes and mesas and sporadic creeks and reservoirs break the miles of sagebrush prairie. After a day of pedaling the route drops down to the Nowater River and parallels the river valley until climbing up to Cottonwood Pass.

It is best to plan a two-day ride, carrying overnight gear and plenty of water. The name of the ride provides a good clue about one of the concerns on this ride. Water is scarce. Include a water purification system with your camping gear.

There is little, if any, traffic on the Blue Bank Road. Increased traffic and some residences are present on Wyoming 434, 10 miles to the east.

0.0 Go south on the Blue Bank Road, BLM Road 1411. The BLM sign indicates it is 26 miles to the Nowater Trail.

1.2 Come to old Tensleep highway; turn left.

1.6 Turn right on the Blue Bank Road.

3.4 On top of ridge; start down.

4.3 At bottom of drainage.

4.8 At top of next ridge.

6.2 BLM sign indicates 16 miles to the Nowater Trail. 2-Mile Road goes left with 5 miles to Castle Gardens. Continue on Blue Bank Road.

12.4 Pass by a reservoir. There is no flowing water here but water could be used in an emergency using a filter.

14.9 At reservoir. Immediately after the reservoir, go left at fork and up hill.

16.4 At top of hill.

18.5 At rim, now heading down.

24.5 Come to intersection with the Nowater Trail. Go left (east).

29.9 Cross over Buffalo Spring Creek. Water is available here. If there is no water where the road crosses, hike up to the spring, approximately 0.5 mile up the drainage. After the creek begin a long uphill.

37.3 On ridgetop with a magnificent panoramic view.

37.4 Road improves to gravel. Some easy riding and then road goes on steep downhill.

41.4 Join the Nowood Road. There is potential traffic on this road.

45.9 Cross a small creek.

46.3 Cross over the Nowood River. The flow is such that calling this a river is a bit misleading. It is barely a creek. Begin final uphill to Cottonwood Pass.

52.3 At Cottonwood Pass. Begin downhill.

55.2 Cross a creek.

59.6 Big Horn Trail goes left. Continue straight.

60.6 At reservoir. The route ends but you can continue for 17.6 miles to US20-26, passing through Lost Cabin and Lycite.

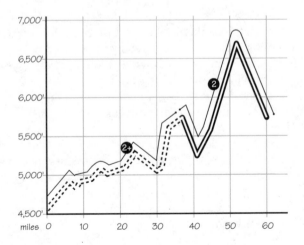

Tensleep to Worland

Location:	Bighorn Basin, north central Wyoming. The ride begins in the community of Tensleep and ends in Worland.
Distance:	26.9 miles, one way.
Time:	Six to seven hours (The time is quite variable, depending on the number of rest breaks, wind direction, and heat/weather conditions.).
Elevation gain:	1,155 feet.
Tread:	The first 0.5 mile and final 3 miles are on pavement. The majority of the trail varies from old pavement with potholes and invading vegetation to gravel and doubletrack.
Season:	Because it is on the prairie and not in the mountains, this ride can be made earlier in the spring and later in the fall. It is best to avoid the ride in the middle of the summer when temperatures in the Bighorn Basin can reach above 100 degrees F.
Aerobic level:	Moderate.
Technical difficulty:	This road is mostly unmaintained and has rough areas with potholes, ruts, and invading vegetation, giving it an overall technical rating of 3.
Hazards:	There are areas with potholes, ruts, and invading vegetation. Traffic is nearly non-existent until the route gets near Worland, where oil and gas development has resulted in construction of improved gravel roads.
Land status:	Bureau of Land Management.
Maps:	USGS Ten Sleep, Wild Horse Hill, Broom Draw, Worland SE, Worland. Most of the ride is on the BLM 1:100,000 Worland map.
Access:	The ride begins on the western edge of Tensleep, on U.S. Highway 16 and ends in Worland.

HIGHLIGHTS

It took mountain man Jim Bridger ten sleeps to get to the western base of the Bighorn Mountains, traveling on foot or horseback from Fort Laramie or Fort Yellowstone. That's how this charming little community got the name Tensleep.

147

Tensleep to Worland

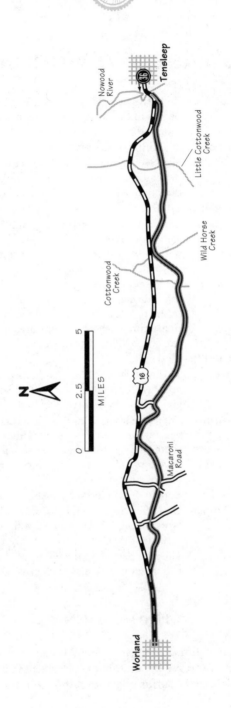

Nowood River

Little Cottonwood Creek

Wild Horse Creek

Cottonwood Creek

Tensleep

16

Macaroni Road

MILES

0 2.5 5

N

Worland

The ride from Tensleep to Worland follows the old highway past buttes and mesas that create a maze through the badlands.

This is a fascinating ride through arid badlands. Watch for raptors, especially northern harriers, ferruginous hawks, golden eagles, and Swainson's hawks. Pronghorn can be seen congregating near water sources.

This ride begins in Tensleep as it leaves the pavement just 0.5 mile west of town and follows the old highway to Worland. The route roller-coasters up and down from drainage to drainage, providing stark panoramas of buttes and mesas as it crosses the southern edge of the Bighorn Basin. As the route nears Worland, oil and gas activity increases and there is the occasional odor coming from sour gas wells. Sour wells emit hydrogen sulfide gas that can be harmful if inhaled in large quantities. Stay away from the well sites and, if you smell sour gas, ride through the area quickly.

THE RIDE

0.0   Begin at the western end of Tensleep, at the city limits, on US16.

0.5   Turn left (south) onto unmarked dirt road. A sign on the right side of the highway says "Lower Nowood Road." Cross cattleguard

0.7   Go on bridge over the Nowood River. There are patches of old pavement still evident on the road.

1.3   Road forks; stay right.

2.0   At top of a hill. Stay straight (road goes to Castle Gardens); road to the left returns to US16.

3.0   Road forks; stay straight. Left goes to Castle Gardens and Blue Bank Road.

4.0 Cross over bridge.

5.6 A doubletrack forks to right. Stay on main road.

5.8 At top of hill. Road changes to a doubletrack.

6.2 Doubletrack goes right. Stay straight on main road.

7.6 Road forks; stay straight on main road. The doubletrack going right returns to US16.

8.0 Cross bridge and start up hill.

8.9 At top of hill.

9.2 Cross cattleguard.

9.6 A gravel road enters from the left.

9.8 Cross bridge. After the bridge a road to the right goes to the Blue Bank Road. Stay straight on main road.

13.1 Road forks; stay straight on main gravel road. Road to the right goes to a well.

15.4 Top of hill. Come to a four-way intersection. Continue straight.

15.8 Road forks; stay straight.

17.1 Turn left onto paved US16.

17.5 Turn left onto gravel road. Immediately cross a cattleguard and then a bridge.

19.3 Cross bridge.

19.5 Cross bridge.

19.8 Stay straight on main road. Road to left is the Marconi Road.

20.3 Top of hill.

21.5 At top of hill, cross a cattleguard and come to a four-way intersection. Continue straight. Road right returns to US16.

22.5 Pass by "The Pits" on the left. This is a popular dirt bike and ATV area.

23.9 Go left onto US16. Historical Marker for "Mammoth Kill Site" is immediately after the turn onto the highway.

26.9 Enter Worland city limits.

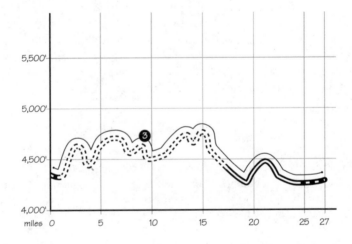

Eastern Wind River Mountains
Lander Area Rides

The eastern side of the Wind River Mountains includes the popular Loop Road, that heads south from Lander and into the Wind River Mountains, going into Sinks Canyon. The "Sinks" of the Popo Agie River (pronounced po-po-sha) are created where the river sinks into an underground cavern and flows underground for about 600 feet to the "rise," where it reappears. Be sure to stop at the rise area and see the humongous trout.

The loop road winds up a narrow gravel road and continues into the mountains, looping past Frye Lake, Fiddler's Lake, and Louis Lake before dropping out of the mountains to South Pass. Mountain biking opportunities abound on trails and doubletrack roads that twist and turn through this rough country.

South Pass was made famous by pioneers traveling the Oregon Trail. South Pass is not a typical mountain pass, but it does cross the Continental Divide. It is a gentle rise reaching only 7,526 feet, creating a crossing point that opened the door to the West as wagon trains crossed the country. This edge of the Great Divide Basin, where the alpine forests meet the high-elevation desert, provides some interesting mountain biking. Few people travel these areas, making the backroads peaceful, if not a bit lonely.

Middle Fork Popo Agie River

Location:	Sinks Canyon Road, 7 miles south of Lander.
Distance:	8.9 miles or 5.8 just to trailhead. Both are out-and-back routes.
Time:	Two to three hours for the full distance. Shorter route from campground to trailhead is 45 minutes.
Elevation gain:	1,000 feet for entire route; 360 feet for shorter route.
Tread:	The first 0.2 mile is on wide singletrack, then the ride follows easy doubletrack for 2.6 miles. At the Middle Fork Trailhead the ride returns to singletrack for the final 1.5 miles to the turnaround point.
Season:	This ride is best once the snow melts in the spring and into summer and fall. Avoid the singletrack trail after heavy rainfall to reduce potential erosion damage to the trail.
Aerobic level:	The first section is easy, but the ride is moderate overall.
Technical difficulty:	The first and final 3 miles have a technical level 2, with good doubletrack road. The Middle Fork Trail has a technical rating of 4 due to rocks and boulders on the trail.
Hazards:	The first and final 3 miles of this ride are on easy doubletrack with few hazards. The singletrack trail leading to the Popo Agie Falls has rocks and boulders. It is also a popular hiking trail and caution must be taken to yield to other trail users.
Land status:	U.S. Forest Service, Shoshone National Forest.
Maps:	USGS Fossil Hill, Cony Mountain.
Access:	Follow Wyoming 131, the Sinks Canyon Road, past Sinks Canyon State Park. Turn left into U.S. Forest Service Sinks Canyon Campground. Park in the open area to the right of the entrance or use a campground if you plan to spend the night.

Highlights

The whitewater rush of the Middle Fork of the Popo Agie (pronounced po-po-sha) River can be heard as this route parallels the river. You'll meet fishermen and women in waders with flyrods as well as dayhikers wandering

Middle Fork Popo Agie River

Frye Lake

Popo Agie Falls

Middle Fork Popo Agie River

37

300

336

Fossil Hill
9,089'

Sinks Canyon Campground

37

131

TO LANDER

N

MILES

0   0.5   1

toward the Popo Agie Falls.

The first 3 miles of this ride, which follow an easy doubletrack, make a good family ride. Beginners may want to turn around once they reach the Middle Fork Trailhead or lock their bikes and continue up the trail on foot. The singletrack foot-trail is rough, rocky, and difficult to ride.

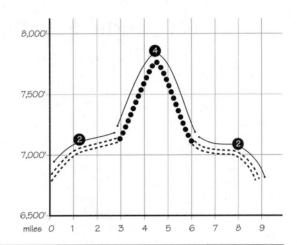

THE RIDE

0.0 Take the path going south from the parking area and go over footbridge. Immediately after the bridge is a large sign where the trail forks. Go right.

0.1 Go over a little wooden bridge and stay right.

0.2 Go past the cross-country skiing warming hut and outhouse. Take the doubletrack that leads to the southwest.

0.4 Another ski trail crosses the doubletrack. Stay on the road.

2.4 Another ski trail crosses the doubletrack. Stay on the road.

2.5 Trail comes next to the Middle Fork of the Popo Agie River.

2.6 Pass by horse corrals.

2.8 Come out onto paved parking lot. Continue across parking lot toward the kiosk at the southwest corner.

2.9 After kiosk, cross the paved road (WY 131) and footbridge to get to the Middle Fork Trail. This is a rough and rocky singletrack that is a popular hiking trail. It is open to bicycles but you may choose to lock your bike at the parking area and continue on foot.

4.5 Come to Popo Agie Falls. This is the turnaround point. Return on the same trail.

6.1 Back at parking lot. Continue back to Sinks Canyon Campground on same doubletrack route.

8.8 Cross footbridge.

8.9 Back at parking area in campground.

Variation: The Middle Fork Trail continues past the falls. An 18-mile loop can be taken by continuing up the trail for approximately 4.5 miles and then crossing Sheep Bridge over the Middle Fork Popo Agie River at an elevation of 8,450 feet. Continue on the trail as it goes past Worthen Meadow Reservoir and to the Sheep Bridge Roaring Fork Trailhead. The trail returns on Forest Road 302 and then to the Louis Lake Road, FR 300.

Indian/Wolf Trails Loop

Location:	Wind River Mountains above Sinks Canyon.
Distance:	17-mile loop.
Time:	Five to six hours.
Elevation gain:	2,400 feet.
Tread:	This trail is primarily on doubletrack roads except for a section of singletrack for 2 miles from milepost 5.3 to 7.3.
Season:	This route is best from summer through fall. In spring and early summer, heavy runoff can make the Sawmill Creek crossing more difficult.
Aerobic level:	Strenuous.
Technical difficulty:	The trail throughout this ride has a rating of 3+ due to rocky and rutted sections.
Hazards:	There are steep, rocky segments that may require bike hiking for safety reasons. The Sawmill Creek crossing is a wet crossing and can be deep during periods of heavy runoff.
Land status:	U.S. Forest Service, Shoshone National Forest.
Maps:	USGS Fossil Hill.
Access:	From Lander, drive up the Sinks Canyon Road (Wyoming 131) past the end of the pavement and continue up the gravel Frye-Louis Lake Road (Forest Road 300). At top of switchbacks, take first doubletrack left, FR 352. Park just past the intersection.

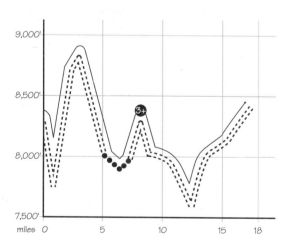

Indian/Wolf Trails Loop

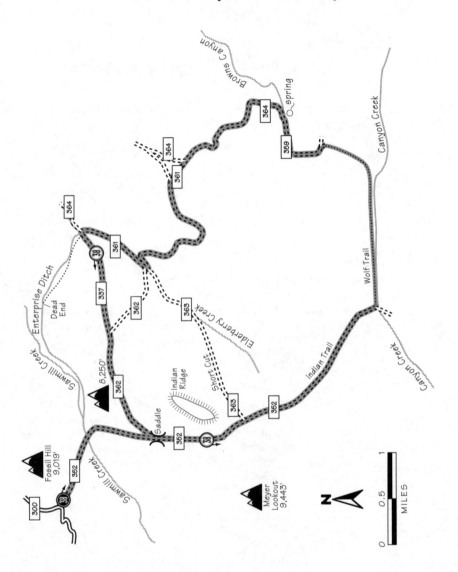

Fossil Hill rises above the winding trail at the beginning of the Indian Wolf Trails Loop.

HIGHLIGHTS

This is a strenuous trail that has several tough climbs and some fast downhill. It passes by steep cliffs, through canyons, and across open hillsides. Much of the trail is through open grassland and sagebrush, but it enters timber habitat often enough to provide shade and wind protection. It crosses several creeks and passes by a man-made ditch. These creeks offer refreshing breaks and supplemental water (use a purification system). An optional shortcut that follows Elderberry Creek can reduce the mileage by about 7 miles.

THE RIDE

0.0 Head east, down doubletrack FR 352.

0.1 Go through gate and reclose.

1.0 At bottom of hill. Follow trail to right that crosses Sawmill Creek.

1.1 Go through gate and up the hill. Stay on main doubletrack as it climbs the hill.

2.0 Trail forks. Continue straight and continue up hill.

3.1 At saddle. Trail forks. Continue straight, going down the hill to Canyon Creek. Left is an alternative shortcut that goes along Elderberry Creek.

5.3 Just before Canyon Creek, the trail forks. Go left and follow the creek on the north side as it follows above Canyon Creek, on Forest Trail 907.

6.2 Trail curves north and continues over ridge.

7.3 Trail joins old logging road (FR 3581A). Go left.

7.6 Come to fork in road. Go right on FR 359.

7.9 Trail forks. Go left on FR 364.

9.7 Trail forks. Go left on FR 361 and follow around hill.

10.7 Cross Crooked Creek.

11.6 Come to creek. To cross, follow road uphill to crossing. After crossing, FR 362 forks left. Stay right on FR 361.

12.6 Come to intersection at Enterprise Ditch. Do not cross the ditch but turn left and go back up hill across sagebrush hillside on FR 337. The doubletrack that parallels the ditch deadends a mile down the road.

13.8 Trail forks. Go right on FR 362.

14.4 Go through gate.

15.0 At summit return to FR 352. Go right and back down to Sawmill Creek.

17.0 Back at starting point.

Variation: At 3.1 miles, turn left on FR 363 along Elderberry Creek to reduce the loop by about 7 miles.

Miner's Delight

Location:	Near South Pass, east of the Wind River Mountains.
Distance:	6.4-mile out-and-back route, with numerous side roads to explore.
Time:	Three to four hours.
Elevation gain:	320 feet.
Tread:	The trail is all on doubletrack roads.
Season:	Although this ride is on the edge of the Great Divide Basin, it is still at fairly high elevation and is not passable until late spring. It can be traveled into the fall, but avoid it after heavy rains.
Aerobic level:	Moderate.
Technical difficulty:	The ride is all on good doubletrack and has an overall technical rating of 2.
Hazards:	The greatest hazard in the area is not on the trail but rather with the many abandoned mine sites in the area. Avoid exploring in the mineshafts and adits (mine shafts are vertical tunnels, mine adits are horizontal).
Land status:	This route begins on National Forest Service land and crosses onto Bureau of Land Management lands. The road numbers and markings appear to be forest road numbers and are listed as such in the ride description.
Maps:	USGS Miner's Delight.
Access:	From Wyoming 28 (between Lander and South Pass) go east on Forest Road 321, which leads to two BLM campgrounds. Immediately after the cattleguard off the state highway, turn north toward a highway department gravel storage pile. Park your vehicle here. Another option is to go to the campground and ride from campground back to the starting point.

HIGHLIGHTS

Miner's Delight was once a thriving mining town created by the Sweetwater gold rush that brought nearby South Pass City and Atlantic City into existence. It sprang up in 1868 with the opening of the Miner's Delight Mine, and its population fluctuated with the success and failure of the mine.

Miner's Delight

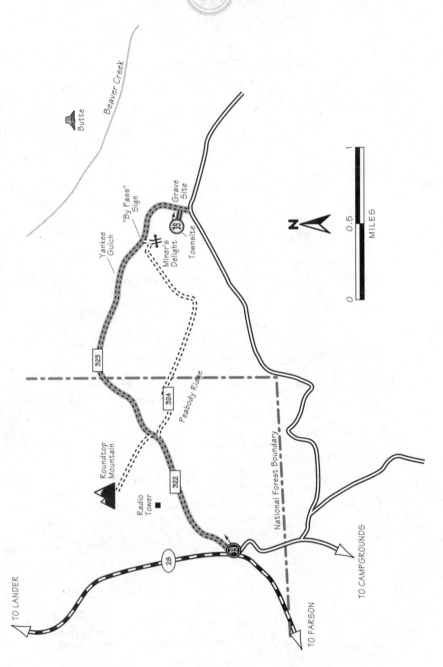

Beaver Creek

Butte

"By Pass" Sign

Yankee Gulch

Grave Site

Miner's Delight

Townsite

39

325

324

Peabody Ridge

322

Roundtop Mountain

Radio Tower

National Forest Boundary

39

28

TO LANDER

TO FARSON

TO CAMPGROUNDS

N

MILES

0   0.5   1

Graves mark the Miner's Delight townsite, a stark reminder of how tough life must have been in the small nineteenth-century mining town.

Today, Miner's Delight is a ghost town with over a dozen wooden buildings and structures. A stroll among the buildings evokes images of the hustle and bustle of horses and buggies, saloon halls, and livery stables.

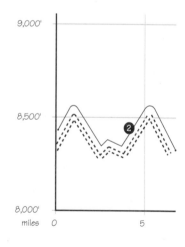

The trail is an out-and-back, or, as an alternative, it can follow a loop through the townsite. It is a scenic ride with panoramic views of the Continental Divide. It rolls past beaver ponds and a number of old mine sites. Many of the old mine shafts remain. An adjacent pile of rocky debris, long ago excavated from the depths of the mine, is all that remains to give warning of a potential mine shaft. Avoid these sites; 100 years of abandonment has made them very unstable.

THE RIDE

0.0 Go north along fenceline, past gravel piles, onto doubletrack road (FR 322).

0.8 Two doubletracks go left. Stay straight on main road.

0.9 Road forks. Stay right. Left goes up hill to radio towers.

1.0	Faint doubletrack goes right. Stay left.
1.2	Reach saddle summit. Now road goes down.
1.6	Doubletrack goes left. Stay right.
2.0	Go past beaver ponds on left.
2.1	Road forks. Stay right and go up the hill.
2.3	At crest of hill, road forks. Stay right. At the bottom of "Yankee Gulch" doubletracks go left and right. Stay straight.
2.6	At ridgetop, road forks. Go left on "Miner's Delight By-Pass Road."
2.7	Road forks. Go right on by-pass road.
3.1	Doubletrack goes left. Stay straight and go over cattleguard. Left goes to main gravel road.
3.2	Come to fenced gravesite. Follow road to right, past "Road Closed" gate and down the hill to townsite.
3.3	At townsite. This is the turnaround point or, as an alternative, walk through townsite and connect with road on other side that joins the by-pass road.
3.5	Back at gravesite. Return by same route.
6.4	Back at start.

Western Wind River Mountains
Pinedale Area Rides

The western slope of the Wind River Mountains extends from the Red Desert all the way north past Pinedale. Much of the forested area is part of the Wind River Wilderness Area, limiting where mountain bikers can pedal. The largest non-wilderness area is above the Green River Valley and extends north to Togwotee Pass (pronounced toag-a-tee) and Dubois. These high-elevation areas have a brief mountain biking season, with old snow remaining in the trees well into late June and even July, and new snow flying as early as late August.

There are other options, however, including trails surrounding Fremont Lake and Half Moon Lake, and rides as far south as the Big Sandy Recreation Area. Many foothill areas are also on public land and offer challenging biking through sagebrush openings that create a mosaic with the timbered forest.

The vast basin, extending west from the base of the Wind River Mountains to the base of the Wyoming Range, is nearly all public land managed by BLM. Although this area is experiencing change with oil and gas development, dirt roads and doubletracks abound and provide plenty of areas to explore when the high country is impassable.

Sweeney Creek Loop

Location:	Above Fremont Lake in the Wind River Mountains.
Distance:	9.2-mile loop.
Time:	Two and one-half to three and one-half hours.
Elevation gain:	1,550 feet.
Tread:	The first and final 3.5 miles of this out-and-back route are on good doubletrack. The remainder is on rough and steep singletrack.
Season:	This route is clear of snow in late spring to early summer and it can be ridden until snowfall in the autumn.
Aerobic level:	Moderate.
Technical difficulty:	The first 3.6 miles has a rating of 2 as it follows doubletrack. After the bog and to the intersection with the Kelly Park Trail, the route has a rating of 4 due to steep, rocky, and narrow sections. The return route on the Kelly Park Trail has a rating of 2.
Hazards:	There is a wet bog area to cross either by wading across where the road crosses or by working through the dense willows near the creek. The singletrack has steep and rocky segments, requiring some bike hiking. The return trip has some ruts and rocky areas.
Land status:	U.S. Forest Service, Bridger National Forest.
Maps:	USGS Fremont Lake South and Fayette Lake. There is a Wind River Wilderness Area map that covers most of the route. The Forest Service has a free map that illustrates the cross-country ski trails.
Access:	From Pinedale follow the Fremont Lake Road, also called the Skyline Drive, up past the exit to Half Moon Lake entrance. After approximately 1 mile, turn right into small parking area at ski trailhead.

HIGHLIGHTS

This trail is a part of the 36-mile ski trail system above Pinedale, just past Fremont Lake. The ski trail maze, marked with blue diamonds, has a number of optional routes for the mountain biker, with most routes becoming steeper and rockier as they rise in elevation and approach the Wind River Wilderness Area.

Sweeney Creek Loop

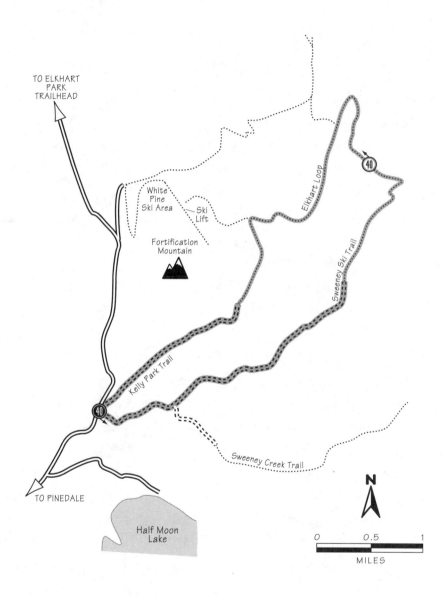

TO ELKHART
PARK
TRAILHEAD

White
Pine
Ski Area

Ski
Lift

Fortification
Mountain

Elkhart Loop

40

Sweeney Ski Trail

Kelly Park Trail

40

Sweeney Creek Trail

TO PINEDALE

Half Moon
Lake

N

0   0.5   1
MILES

The Sweeney Creek Loop twists through thick timber as it rises toward the Wind River Wilderness Area boundary.

The loop presented here starts out on the Sweeney Creek Ski Trail, an easy doubletrack that gradually winds though sagebrush meadows and pine forests as it rises into the high country. The doubletrack ends at a wet meadow and bog area where most motorized travel ends. The trail after the bog becomes steep and rough as it narrows down to a singletrack trail. The Sweeney Creek Trail eventually connects with the Kelly Park Trail where it overlooks one of the ski runs. The loop returns via the Kelly Park Trail, going through a large, wet meadow before it follows a doubletrack back to the parking area.

THE RIDE

0.0 Begin up doubletrack trail going northeast out of the parking area.

0.7 Road forks. Go left (sign indicates it is the Sweeney Creek Ski Trail).

3.6 Trail passes through a bog area. It is easiest just to wade through the water where the road crosses. For a dry crossing, push your bike and wind through the willows between the road and the creek. After the bog area the trail becomes a singletrack as it begins a steeper climb up the mountain.

6.3 Come to "T" intersection at top of downhill ski run. Right goes on up Elkhart Trail. Go left onto Kelly Park Trail and down steep downhill with switchbacks.

6.9 Come to big, open, wet meadow. Trail goes around edge of meadow.

7.4 Re-enter timber on better doubletrack road.

8.0 Trail forks to right. Stay straight on Kelly Park Loop.

8.4 Come to end of doubletrack at little parking area. Continue left on main paved road.

9.2 Back at starting point.

Variation: Check the ski trail route map for alternatives. There are 34 miles of ski trails, although not all are cleared for mountain biking and may have debris on the trail. Follow the blue diamonds that mark the trail.

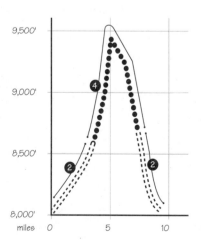

Half Moon Mountain

Location:	15 miles southeast of Pinedale, near Half Moon Lake.
Distance:	4.4-mile loop with longer optional loops.
Time:	One to one and one-half hours.
Elevation gain:	210 feet.
Tread:	This route is all on doubletrack. Some of the roads have been closed to motorized travel and are less distinct.
Season:	The Half Moon Wildlife Area is closed to human travel, be it motorized, mechanized, or foot travel, from November 16 through April 30 to prevent disturbing wintering wildlife. This route is clear of snow in late spring to early summer and it can be ridden until snowfall in the autumn.
Aerobic level:	Easy.
Technical difficulty:	This route is all on doubletrack that has a few rocks and ruts for a technical rating of 2+.
Hazards:	There are a few rough and rutted areas on the route. The trail becomes less distinct when crossing open areas.
Land status:	U.S. Forest Service, Bridger National Forest.
Maps:	USGS Fayette Lake, South Fremont Lake.
Access:	From Pinedale, go east on County Road 23-121 for 9.2 miles until the pavement ends. Go an additional 0.8 mile and turn north on the dirt road, following the signs to Half Moon Wildlife Area. After 2.5 miles, road forks. Right goes to the lake and left goes up the mountain. Follow the road on around to the northwest side of the base of the mountain. For a challenging ride, park your vehicle at the base and ride up the mountain. For a more leisurely ride, drive up the steep road on the north side of the mountain and park at the first intersection on top of the mountain. The ride starts on the main road as it follows the east rim of the mountain.

Half Moon Mountain

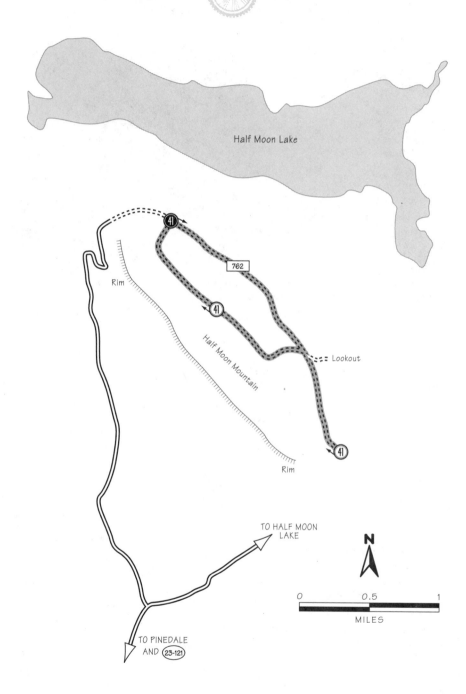

Half Moon Lake

762

Rim

Half Moon Mountain

Lookout

Rim

TO HALF MOON LAKE

N

0   0.5   1

MILES

TO PINEDALE AND 23-121

The view from Half Moon Mountain is breathtaking as it overlooks Half Moon Lake and the peaks of the Wind River Wilderness Area.

HIGHLIGHTS

Half Moon Mountain rises from the prairie and forms a timber-covered island immediately southwest of Half Moon Lake. There is one doubletrack road along the eastern rim of the mountain, overlooking Half Moon Lake. Other old logging roads, closed to motorized traffic, add a few optional loops, but these trails can be a little difficult to decipher when crossing grassy meadows. Areas of the mountain were burned during a forest fire a little over a decade ago. Many of the tree carcasses are still standing, while the undergrowth has regenerated and young trees have emerged.

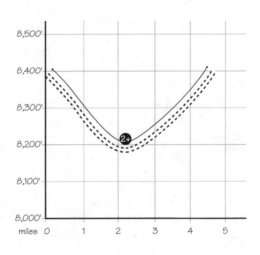

This ride is suitable for a family outing; the terrain is relatively flat and the loop described here is short. Additional loops on the west side of the mountain are also possible.

THE RIDE

0.0 Start by heading southeast at intersection of Forest Road 762 and unnumbered closed road (first intersection at the top of the mountain). Go down main road.

1.8 At southeast corner of mountain. From the edge of the rim, there is an incredible view of Half Moon Lake below and the Wind River Wilderness Area overlooking the valley. Trail begins uphill. Continue down main trail.

2.0 Abandoned doubletrack forks right and up steep slope. Continue straight for a short out-and-back trip to the southeast edge of the mountain.

2.1 Road fades out. Turn around here.

2.4 Pass by the lookout point (described at mile 1.8).

2.5 A faint doubletrack goes left, toward a small rock outcrop. Follow this; as it enters the timber it becomes more distinct. Steeper uphill begins.

3.0 Route flattens out as it enters the old burn.

4.1 Come to "T" intersection with another doubletrack. Go right. Left continues for a 0.5 mile and then fades away.

4.2 Pass near a weather station.

4.3 Doubletrack forks off to the left (southwest). An alternative ride continues on to west rim of mountain.

4.4 Back at starting point.

Variation: There are a number of other routes, but they can be faint and difficult to locate as they cross open meadows or through the burn area. For an easier ride, follow the rim road to mile 1.8, turn around, and return on same road.

Little Sheep Mountain

Location:	Near the Green River Lakes in the Wind River Mountains, approximately 45 miles north of Pinedale.
Distance:	15.8 miles, out and back.
Time:	Four to five hours.
Elevation gain:	1,900 feet.
Tread:	This ride is all on doubletrack road.
Season:	This ride goes up to nearly 10,000 feet and will not be snow-free until late spring or early summer. It is best in the summer, but it can be ridden in the fall until the snow flies.
Aerobic level:	Strenuous.
Technical difficulty:	The primary challenge with this ride is the aerobic challenge. The technical rating is a 2+.
Hazards:	There are rocks and ruts along the road.
Land status:	U.S. Forest Service, Bridger National Forest.
Maps:	USGS Big Sheep Mountain.
Access:	Follow paved County Road 352 as it goes past Cora and toward the Green River Lakes. Once it crosses onto National Forest lands the road can be extremely washboarded and slow going. It is approximately 13 miles from the end of the pavement to the turnoff on Forest Road 680 (Moose Creek Road). Park vehicle after intersection or drive a 0.5 mile up the road to alternate parking areas.

HIGHLIGHTS

Little Sheep Mountain rises above the Green River near its headwaters. This sentinel to the awesomely beautiful Green River Lakes and Squaretop Mountain skirts the boundary of the Wind River Wilderness Area.

This route offers a challenging uphill ride and spectacular views. An old two-track road can be seen switchbacking to the summit of Little Sheep Mountain but its exit from the main Forest Road has been closed and reclaimed, making it difficult to locate and not suitable for biking. For the ambitious hiker a trek to the top of the mountain is possible by bushwhacking through a patch of forest and following a steep singletrack to the summit.

Instead of forking up the summit of Little Sheep Mountain, it branches off the other direction on an old logging road. It passes a secluded willow meadow.

Little Sheep Mountain

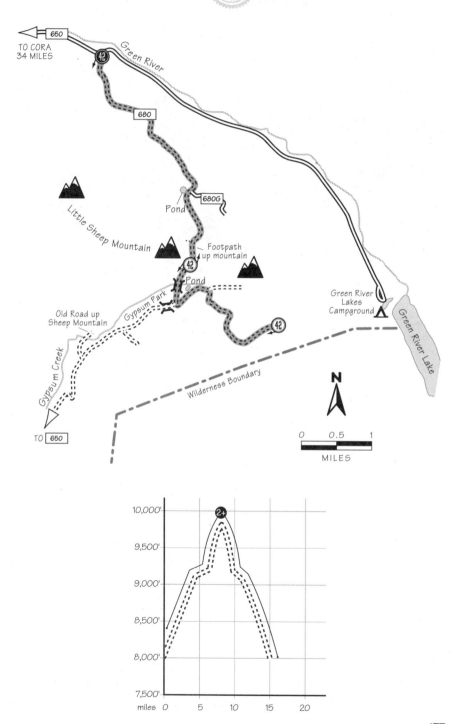

TO CORA
34 MILES

650

Green River

680

680G

Pond

Little Sheep Mountain

Pond

Footpath
up mountain

42

42

42

Gypsum Park

Old Road up
Sheep Mountain

Gypsum Creek

TO 650

Green River
Lakes
Campground

Green River Lake

Wilderness Boundary

N

0   0.5   1
MILES

The Little Sheep Mountain route continues to a ridge overlooking the granite cliffs along the border of the Wind River Wilderness Area.

A few tosses of a flyrod may be in order at the adjacent pond. The trail climbs a steep ridge offering a spectacular view of the peaks at the turnaround point.

THE RIDE

0.0 Head up FR 680 (going southwest).

1.9 Road forks. Stay right.

2.7 Cross cattleguard.

2.9 Doubletrack forks right. Stay straight on main road.

3.6 Pass by a little pond to the right.

4.5 Doubletrack goes right and down. Stay straight on main road.

4.6 At saddle. A footpath goes off to the right and looks as though it heads to the summit of Little Sheep Mountain. It is a cattle path that fades out after about 0.2 mile but it's a way to get started to the peak if you want a hike up.

5.2 Cross creek. Immediately after, road forks. Go left and start up hill on old logging road. Right goes along Gypsum Park, a nice willow meadow with some potential fishing in the creek. Eventually it goes all the way off the mountain and connects to FR 650.

5.8 Pass above a willow meadow with a pond.

6.1 Road forks. Go right and continue up the steep hill.

7.4 Road forks. Go left.

7.9 At end of road. View overlooks Green River Lakes. Return on same route (Now it's time for the downhill reward!).

15.8 Back at starting point.

Flat Lake

Location:	Near Union Pass in the Wind River Mountains, about halfway between Dubois and Pinedale.
Distance:	8.4 miles, out and back.
Time:	Two to three hours depending on how much time is spent ogling the amazing views.
Elevation gain:	1,250 feet.
Tread:	This ride is all on doubletrack road.
Season:	This ride goes up to over 10,000 feet and will not be snow-free until late spring or early summer. It is best in the summer, but it can be ridden in the fall until the snow flies. Even in the summer be prepared for cool temperatures.
Aerobic level:	Strenuous.
Technical difficulty:	The primary challenge with this ride is the aerobic challenge, but the road can be quite rocky, especially as it crosses a creek and wet meadow. The technical rating is 3+.
Hazards:	There are rocky areas and ruts along the road.
Land status:	U.S. Forest Service, Teton National Forest.
Maps:	USGS Union Peak.
Access:	From either Dubois or Pinedale, follow the Union Pass Road (Forest Road 600). Approximately 0.6 mile northeast of Union Pass, turn off gravel road onto doubletrack FR 699. Park vehicle near intersection.

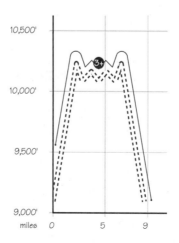

Flat Lake

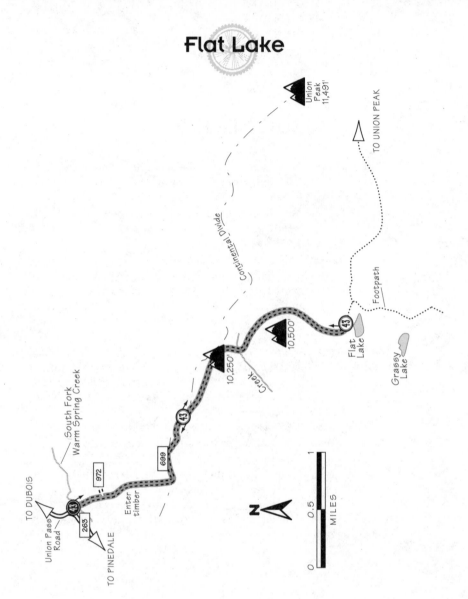

TO DUBOIS

Union Pass Road

South Fork Warm Spring Creek

TO PINEDALE

263

43

972

689

43

Enter timber

10,250'

Creek

10,500'

Continental Divide

Union Peak 11,491'

43

Flat Lake

Footpath

TO UNION PEAK

Grassy Lake

N

MILES

0   0.5   1

Treeless Flat Lake spreads across the high tundra beneath Union Peak.

Union Peak rises over 11,000 feet as a sentinel over Union Pass. This ride follows the Continental Divide for a couple of miles and then the Divide goes to the summit of Union Peak while the trail crosses open tundra to Flat Lake near the base of Union Peak.

This is a challenging ride as it climbs the mountain. The ride described climbs to Flat Lake. Along the way there is an awesome view to the northwest of the Teton Mountains over by Yellowstone. To the south are the peaks that make up the Continental Divide through the Wind River Wilderness Area; to the north are the Pinnacle Buttes near Togwotee Pass. The panoramic view seems to go a hundred miles in every direction. That breathtaking view is earned by making the steep ride to Flat Lake.

From Flat Lake the trail forks. One doubletrack fork continues up Union Peak and the other, a foot trail, drops down to Grassy Lake. Either optional ride may be easier on foot, hiding the bike in the timber near the trail fork. Or just have a picnic lunch at Flat Lake, fish for brook trout, and then enjoy the fun and fast ride back down to Union Pass.

THE RIDE

0.0   Head up FR 699.
0.1   Cross creek.

0.4 Go into timber.

0.6 Cross small creek.

2.0 End especially steep segment. Take a breather and look around at the amazing view. From here, you can see the Tetons, the Wyoming Range, the Gros Ventre Range, and the Wind River Mountains. Start short downhill.

2.2 Bottom of downhill. Now start back up for short segment.

2.6 At top of hill.

3.0 Cross small creek and willow area. Then go back uphill.

3.3 At next hill crest. Trail goes around side of hill.

4.0 Above Flat Lake and begin drop down to lake.

4.2 At the lake. This is the turnaround point. Go around the lake if you plan to continue on, either on the doubletrack road to Union Peak or the footpath to Grassy Lake and the other lakes below.

8.4 Back at beginning of ride.

Variation: At Flat Lake the trail forks. One fork goes up to Union Pass and the other drops down to several small lakes.

Strawberry Creek

Location:	Near Union Pass in the Wind River Mountains, about halfway between Dubois and Pinedale.
Distance:	9.5-mile loop.
Time:	Two to three hours.
Elevation gain:	550 feet.
Tread:	This ride is on good doubletrack road except for the final 2 miles, which follow a gravel forest road.
Season:	This ride is at 9,000 feet and will not be snow-free until late spring or early summer. It is best in the summer, but it can be ridden in the fall until the snow flies. Even in the summer be prepared for cool temperatures.
Aerobic level:	Easy.
Technical difficulty:	This ride is good for sightseeing and enjoying the mountain air. It has a technical rating of 2.
Hazards:	There are a few rocky and rutted areas, some pockets of gravel, and, after a rain, some mud holes.
Land status:	U.S. Forest Service, Teton National Forest.
Maps:	USGS Fish Creek Park.
Access:	From either Dubois or Pinedale, follow the Union Pass Road (Forest Road 600). Approximately 8.6 miles southwest of Union Pass, turn south onto doubletrack FR 640. Park vehicle near intersection.

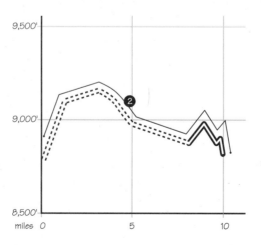

Strawberry Creek

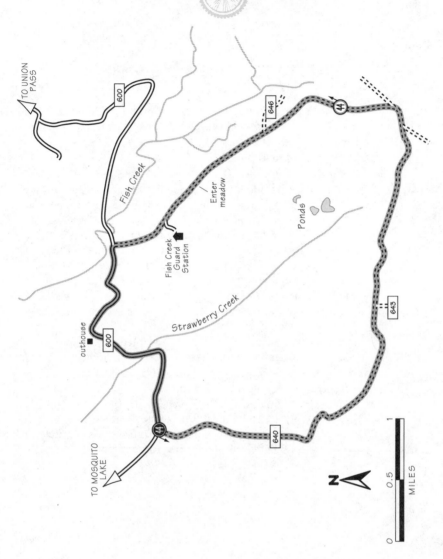

TO UNION PASS

600

Fish Creek

646

Enter meadow

Ponds

Fish Creek Guard Station

645

outhouse

600

Strawberry Creek

640

TO MOSQUITO LAKE

N

0   0.5   1

MILES

The Strawberry Creek loop passes along tree-lined doubletrack roads before passing into a large open alpine meadow.

Highlights

Strawberry Creek wanders through a big, wet meadow park surrounded by pine forests. The ride follows a good doubletrack road through the forests and past old logged areas that currently support young trees, 5 to 15 feet tall. Eventually, the road breaks out of the timber and wanders into the big, wet meadow park. This route is at high elevation and is prone to cooler temperatures and chilly winds. In early summer it can be buggy; bring insect repellent if you plan to stop for a picnic.

The Ride

0.0   Head south on FR 640.

0.5   FR 642 goes right; stay on FR 640.

0.7   FR 640A goes right; stay on FR 640.

2.8   FR 643 goes right. Continue on FR 640.

4.2   Unnumbered doubletrack goes right. Stay on main road.

4.6   FR 647 goes right. Stay on main road going downhill.

5.0   FR 646 goes right. Continue on main road as it becomes more level.

5.1   Pass by a lily pond on left.

5.6   Skirt along big sagebrush wetland park to the left.

6.4   Trail goes into the meadow.

6.9   Fish Creek Guard Station is on gravel road to the left.

7.4   Come to intersection with gravel FR 600. Go left and up hill.

8.1   End of uphill.

8.3   Outhouse (put there for use during the snowmobile season) is to the right. Start across big open meadow.

8.5   FR 672 forks right; stay on FR 600.

8.7   Cross creek and come up out of drainage.

9.5   Back at start of ride.

Mosquito Lake

Location:	Near Union Pass in the Wind River Mountains, about halfway between Dubois and Pinedale.
Distance:	7.3-mile loop.
Time:	One and one-half to two hours.
Elevation gain:	250 feet.
Tread:	This ride is on doubletrack road except for the final 3 miles, which follow a gravel forest road.
Season:	This ride is at 9,000 feet and will not be snow-free until late spring or early summer. It is best in the summer, but it can be ridden in the fall until the snow flies. Even in the summer be prepared for cool temperatures.
Aerobic level:	Easy.
Technical difficulty:	This ride is good for sightseeing and enjoying the mountain air. It has a technical rating of 2.
Hazards:	There are a few rocky and rutted areas, some pockets of gravel, and, after a rain, some mud holes.
Land status:	U.S. Forest Service, Bridger National Forest.
Maps:	USGS Mosquito Lake.
Access:	From either Dubois or Pinedale, follow the Union Pass Road (Forest Road 600). Three miles north of Mosquito Lake, turn east onto FR 630 and park vehicle just after intersection.

HIGHLIGHTS

This route wanders across a broad open plain, passing through small creeks and past cattail-filled ponds. This high-elevation wetland provides a specialized habitat that attracts a wide array of wildlife species. Ducks and shorebirds, including sandhill cranes, killdeer, and sanderlings are attracted to the area along with raptors such as the northern harrier and red-tailed hawk. As expected, elk and mule deer frequent this alpine muskeg, sharing it with the unexpected pronghorn that usually inhabit lower elevations.

There is dispersed camping in the area, both immediately adjacent to FR 600 and along nearby doubletracks. This route is at high elevation and is prone to cooler temperatures and chilly winds. Also, in early summer it can be buggy; bring insect repellent.

Mosquito Lake

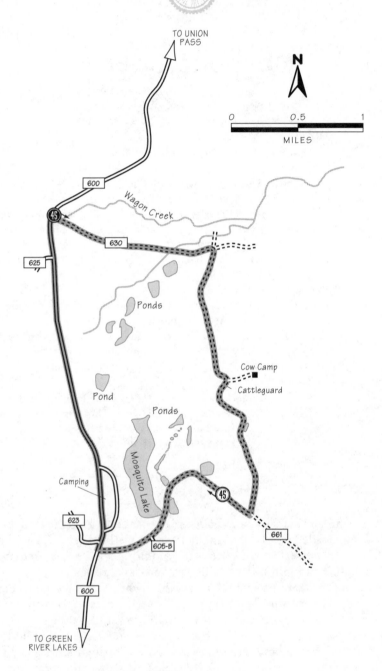

TO UNION
PASS

N

```
0          0.5          1
```
MILES

600

Wagon Creek

45

630

625

Ponds

Cow Camp

Cattleguard

Pond

Ponds

Mosquito Lake

Camping

45

623

661

605-B

600

TO GREEN
RIVER LAKES

0.0 Head east on FR 630.

1.0 Cross a creek.

1.2 Doubletrack goes left and another goes right. Stay right.

2.2 Doubletrack left goes to a cow camp. Stay right and go over raised cattleguard.

2.6 Pass by a little pond on the left.

2.8 Pass by "Road Closed" route to the left.

3.1 Road comes to a "T" intersection on FR 661. Go right.

3.4 Pass by a little pond on the right.

3.5 Road closed to the right.

3.9 Pass by Mosquito Lake on the right.

4.0 FR 605-B goes left. Stay right.

4.4 Come out onto main gravel road (FR 600). Go left.

6.4 FR 625 goes left. Go straight over cattleguard.

7.3 Return to start.

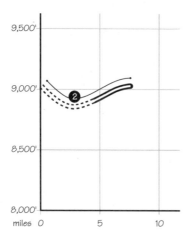

46

Elk Ridge

Location:	Along the Green River, immediately west of the Willow Grove Campground at the entrance to the Green River Lakes area.
Distance:	13.4-mile loop.
Time:	Four to five hours.
Elevation gain:	1,800 feet.
Tread:	This ride is all on doubletrack road.
Season:	This ride should be snow-free by mid-spring, with good riding through the fall.
Aerobic level:	Moderate to strenuous.
Technical difficulty:	This ride follows doubletrack with some steep and rocky segments and has an overall rating of 3.
Hazards:	There are steep, rocky, and rutted areas.
Land status:	U.S. Forest Service, Bridger National Forest.
Maps:	Klondike Hill Quad.
Access:	Follow Wyoming 352 past Cora and into the Shoshone National Forest. After passing Whiskey Grove Campground, road forks. Go left and cross Green River. At second left, turn onto doubletrack (the first left turn is right next to the Green River). This is 0.3 mile past the bridge. Park near intersection.

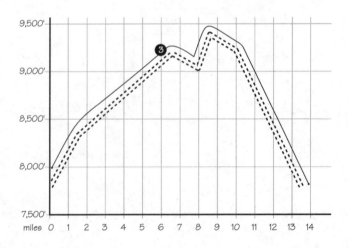

Elk Ridge

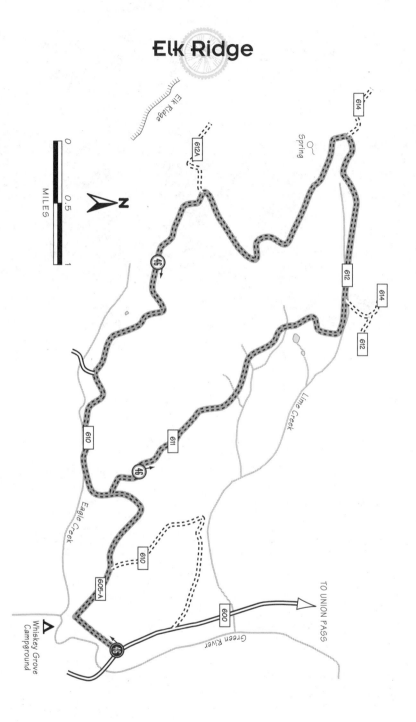

MILES

Elk Ridge

Spring

614

612A

612

614

612

46

610

611

46

Lime Creek

Eagle Creek

610

605-A

600

46

Whiskey Grove Campground

Green River

TO UNION PASS

The Elk Ridge loop passes through sagebrush grassland parks as well as dense timber and willow-lined creeks.

Highlights

This is a really enjoyable ride. It is challenging as it rises above the Green River valley but is not steep enough to require continual bike hiking. It wanders up the hillside, alternating between timber stands and sagebrush openings. Near the summit of the ride it approaches the stark rock cliffs of Elk Ridge. Although elk may not be present as you pedal by, it is easy to see how the area got its name, with the open grassy meadows and adjacent timber. This is certainly elk country. Surprisingly, it is also moose country. Be alert to these gangly animals, especially in the sagebrush-willow meadows.

The Ride

0.0 Ride begins at the first doubletrack past the Green River bridge, not counting the road that runs immediately adjacent to the river.

0.4 Doubletrack forks. Go right (Forest Road 605-A) and start up the hill.

0.8 Trail levels off a bit and becomes easier.

0.9 Road forks. Go left on FR 610 and cross the creek.

1.7 Road forks. Go right on doubletrack going directly up the hill (FR 611).

1.8 Cross creek twice.

4.0 Cross a little stream.

4.2 Cross another little stream (may not be flowing during dry weather).

4.5 Closed doubletrack forks right.

4.9 Come to "T" intersection with FR 612. Go left.

5.7 Cross dry creek bed.

6.1 At high point. Route heads down.

6.2 Faint doubletrack goes left across meadow. Stay straight on main road.

6.5 Cross a dry creekbed. Immediately after the crossing, the road forks. Go left. Right is FR 614 (an alternative route).

7.0 Cross little creek.

7.6 A faint doubletrack goes left. Stay straight on main road.

7.7 Another faint doubletrack goes left. Stay straight on main road.

7.9 At drainage bottom. Now head up steep hill.

8.2 Cross a little drainage and continue up the hill.

8.6 Near ridge summit. Road forks. Straight is FR 612A that goes to the wilderness boundary. Go left up a little ridge.

9.2 On little ridge overlooking the Green River Valley below and across to the Wind River Wilderness peaks. Awesome view!

9.9 A little livestock pond is off to the right.

10.5 Road forks. Go left. Sign may not be correct; this is FR 610.

11.6 At intersection with FR 611. Go right and continue on same route back to starting point.

13.4 Back at starting point.

Variation: There are a couple of alternatives. At mile 6.5, go right onto FR 614. This road continues uphill and eventually follows the base of Klondike Hill. Another alternative is to go right at mile 4.6 on FR 612.

Irish Canyon

Location:	22 miles southeast of Boulder, leading to the Wind River Mountains.
Distance:	7.4 miles, out and back.
Time:	Two to two and one-half hours.
Elevation gain:	475 feet.
Tread:	The trail follows a doubletrack road that has little vehicle traffic aside from ATV travel. After 3.4 miles the trail becomes a singletrack, but it fades after 0.6 mile near the turnaround point.
Season:	This ride begins at a lower elevation and, consequently, should be snow-free by mid-spring. It would be good riding through the fall.
Aerobic level:	Moderate.
Technical difficulty:	This doubletrack has some boulder fields and other rough segments, giving it a rating of 3.
Hazards:	There are boulder fields, rock, and ruts along the road. The singletrack fades and is difficult to follow after the turnaround point.
Land status:	U.S. Forest Service, Bridger National Forest.
Maps:	USGS Pocket Creek Lake, Big Sandy Opening. Most of this ride is on the wilderness map for the Southern Wind River Range.
Access:	From County Road 353, 18 miles east of Boulder, take the last left (east) exit before the pavement ends. There is a wooden sign at the intersection, although there may not be any information on the sign. If you want to add some distance to the ride, just park here and pedal on the gravel and doubletrack road going toward the Wind River Mountains. After 4.3 miles the road forks. Right goes over a saddle. Go left. Stay on main doubletrack and after nearly another 2 miles the road comes to a large sagebrush clearing followed by a timbered area that has been recently logged. Park on edge of timber.

Highlights

This trail parallels Irish Canyon Creek, on an old doubletrack road, and twists its way up toward the high country. It passes through timbered areas

Irish Canyon

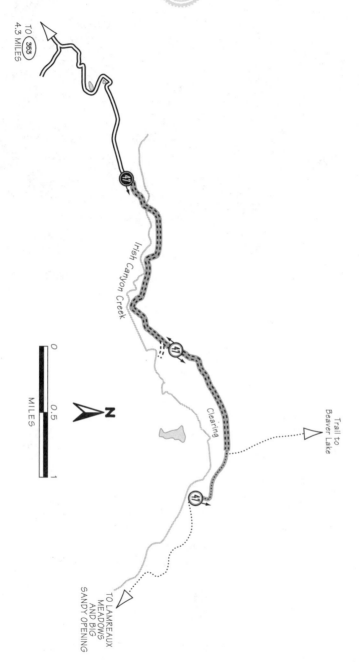

TO 353
4.3 MILES

Irish Canyon Creek

Clearing

Trail to
Beaver Lake

TO LAMREAUX
MEADOWS
AND BIG
SANDY OPENING

N

0   0.5   1
MILES

Irish Canyon Creek rises toward the high country, through sagebrush meadows and pine forests.

and into sagebrush and willow meadows. The uphill ride has a few stretches of tough climbing that will get the heart ticking, but the majority is a more gradual grade, allowing most riders to stay on the bike with minimal bike hiking. The more adventuresome, and those willing to bike hike when necessary, could explore the foottrail that connects this trail to Lamreaux Meadows or go north on the trail that goes to

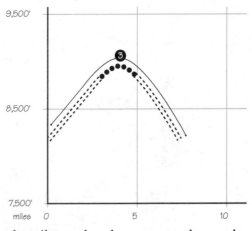

Beaver Lake. These trails are not heavily used and, consequently, can be difficult to follow. Expect rough singletrack on either of these trails.

THE RIDE

0.0 Take doubletrack that enters timber near the creek.
0.2 Road forks. Go left.
0.3 Go through gate.
0.4 Wade across creek.

0.5 Go past wooden fence (no gate).

1.9 Road forks. Go left.

2.5 Come out into big sagebrush meadow.

2.9 Trail forks. Left goes around meadow and then goes north. Go straight, crossing meadow.

3.4 As the meadow ends, the trail becomes a singletrack and starts uphill.

3.5 Cross creek.

3.7 Follow buck-rail fence and come to a gate. This is the turnaround point for this route. If you want to explore ahead, go through gate. The trail becomes especially difficult to locate but the map indicates it will connect to Lamreaux Meadows and Big Sandy Opening.

3.9 Recross creek and return on same route.

7.4 Back at starting point.

Variation: A trail connecting Irish Canyon Creek to Lamreaux Meadows is indicated on the topo map but was not located after the route's turnaround point. It may require some bushwhacking through the timber to an old road at the edge of Lamreaux Meadows. This road continues on to Big Sandy Opening.

Another option is to take the left fork at mile 2.9 and go to Beaver Lake. The trail is difficult to follow as it enters the timber from the meadow due to many livestock trails. But it becomes more distinct as it heads north.

Red Desert Area Rides

Mention the desert and visions of sand and sagebrush come to mind, endless flat country with nothing to see and nothing to do. The Interstate 80 corridor from Rawlins to Rock Springs is mentioned often by visitors and Wyoming natives alike as a boring stretch of highway. The goal of most motorists is to skedaddle through the area as fast as possible.

In reality this area holds many wonders and is a great place to explore. For those who like open space, expansive vistas, and solitude, the Red Desert is a paradise.

The Red Desert is part of the Great Divide Basin that covers approximately 3,500 square miles. Rainwater reaches neither ocean as the Continental Divide splits in two and encompasses the basin. The Red Desert derives its name from the red soil that covers the basin floor.

Much of the Red Desert looks the same as it did when emigrants on the Oregon Trail passed through the Great Divide Basin or when Pony Express riders braved the trails of the desert. The Red Desert still retains the tracks of the Oregon and Mormon Pioneer Trails and the infamous Outlaw Trails.

The Red Desert, with its scarce water and even scarcer trees, supports several unique wildlife habitats. Perhaps most unusual is the Red Desert elk herd. This herd numbers around 500 to 600 elk that wander the desert, using tree-like sagebrush for hiding and thermal cover.

Wild horses are also abundant in the Red Desert. Herds of horses gather at springs and watering holes as the summer progresses. The social interactions among individual members of a band of horses and the interactions between different bands are interesting to observe.

Three different road designations are present on the Red Desert. The majority of the area is designated as a Limited Use Area with motorized travel restricted to existing roads. These roads allow access to much of the region. Seven proposed wilderness areas lie in the Red Desert region and are designated as Wilderness Study Areas and allow only foot travel. One area, the Sand Dunes Off-Road Area, is an open area and allows dune buggy and four-wheel drive use anywhere in the area.

Steamboat Mountain

Location:	Red Desert, approximately 30 miles northeast of Rock Springs.
Distance:	6 miles, out and back.
Time:	One to two hours.
Elevation gain:	560 feet.
Tread:	The trail is all on doubletrack.
Season:	This route can be pedaled from mid-May through the fall. Muddy conditions, especially in the early spring, make the road across the desert nearly impassable; wait for the road to dry before making the trip. The route can be hot and dry in the summer; go in the early morning or after dinner when temperatures are cooler.
Aerobic level:	Moderate.
Technical difficulty:	The first mile has a rating of 4 due to rocks and boulders. On top, the trail is easier, with a rating of 2.
Hazards:	Watch for rocks and boulders as the trail passes through Split Rock Canyon. On top of the mountain the trail is easy, although with some rocky areas.
Land status:	Bureau of Land Management.
Maps:	Steamboat Mountain Quad.
Access:	The ride can be accessed from a number of routes, either coming from U.S. Highway 191, south of Eden, or Interstate 80 from Point of Rocks. Either route will bring you to the Tri-Territory Road. The route is well-marked from either direction. Follow the signs to the Tri-Territory Historic Site on County Road 83. On the eastern base of Steamboat Mountain, turn west on BLM Road 4102. This is a steep road and should be avoided when conditions are muddy. After 1.8 miles there is a four-way intersection. Go right onto doubletrack and park anywhere along the road.

Highlights

Steamboat Mountain rises just north of the Killpecker Sand Dunes and bears a faint resemblance to its namesakes, the great riverboat steamboats of the early 1900s. Motorized travel on Steamboat Mountain is prohibited from

Steamboat Mountain

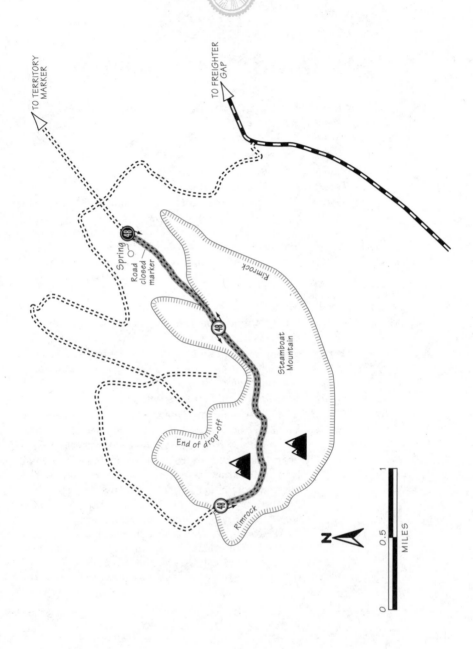

TO TERRITORY MARKER

TO FREIGHTER GAP

Spring

Road closed marker

Rimrock

Steamboat Mountain

End of drop-off

Rimrock

N

MILES
0   0.5   1

Steamboat Mountain, resembling the shape of the grand steamboats of yesteryear, rises from the surrounding Red Desert.

May 10 through July 1 to limit disturbance in elk calving areas. Bike, horse, and foot travel is allowed during this time period, but take care to avoid disturbing elk.

In early May the roads crossing the Red Desert can be especially slick and difficult to drive, making it a little scary to drive the switchbacks up the eastern side of Steamboat Mountain to the starting point. After crossing the starkness of the Red Desert, Steamboat Mountain is an unexpected delight. The starting point for this ride has an aspen grove next to a refreshing spring. The trail passes through the aspen and pine forests before opening up on top of Steamboat Mountain.

Even though this is a short ride, it offers a breathtaking view of the desert. Boar's Tusk, a distinct rock formation, can be viewed to the southwest; the Killpecker Sand Dunes skirt the base of the mountain. Table Top and Black Rock mesas can be seen to the southeast, and the snow-capped peaks of the Wind River Mountains rise above the desert to the north.

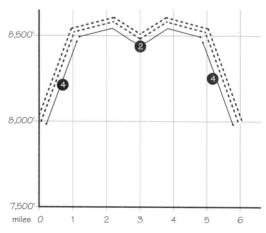

THE RIDE

0.0 Begin ride on doubletrack road going up Split Rock Canyon.

1.4 Come to top of canyon.

1.6 Road forks; go right.

1.9 Faint doubletrack goes to the right (north). Continue straight on main doubletrack.

2.3 Another faint doubletrack forks to left. Stay on main road.

3.0 Come to western rim of the mountain. Boar's Tusk and the Killpecker Sand Dunes can be seen to the west. A short climb and hike across the boulder field that rises to the southwest is worth the time, providing an unobstructed view of the expanse of the Red Desert. Return on the same trail.

6.0 Back at parking site.

Pinnacle Buttes

Location:	Red Desert, approximately 30 miles northeast of Rock Springs.
Distance:	29.1-mile loop.
Time:	Four to five hours.
Elevation gain:	1,065 feet.
Tread:	The trail begins on a gravel road for 7 miles and then follows doubletrack for the next 4 miles before following another gravel road for 4.5 miles. The final 13.5 miles follow doubletrack.
Season:	This route can be pedaled from mid-May through the fall. Muddy conditions, especially in the early spring, make the road across the desert nearly impassable; wait for the road to dry before making the trip. The route can be hot and dry in the summer and this is better as a spring or fall ride.
Aerobic level:	Moderate.
Technical difficulty:	This is a non-technical ride with a rating of 2 for the entire route.
Hazards:	Watch for sand traps, especially on the doubletrack as you pass by The Pinnacles and go toward Freighter Gap.
Land status:	Bureau of Land Management.
Maps:	USGS The Pinnacles, Freighter Gap, Monument Ridge.
Access:	The ride can be accessed from a number of routes, either coming from U.S. Highway 181, south of Eden, or Interstate 80 at Point of Rocks. Either route will bring you to the Tri-Territory Road (County Road 83). The route is well-marked from either direction. Follow the signs to Freighter Gap. After passing the fork going to the Tri-Territory Historical Site, continue straight for 2 miles to a fork in road where a doubletrack branches right. Park here.

HIGHLIGHTS

The Pinnacles is a group of rugged clay escarpments that rise above the desert floor. A 27,000-acre area, which includes the pinnacles, is currently a Wilderness Study Area; the proposed area is well-marked with BLM signs.

Pinnacle Buttes

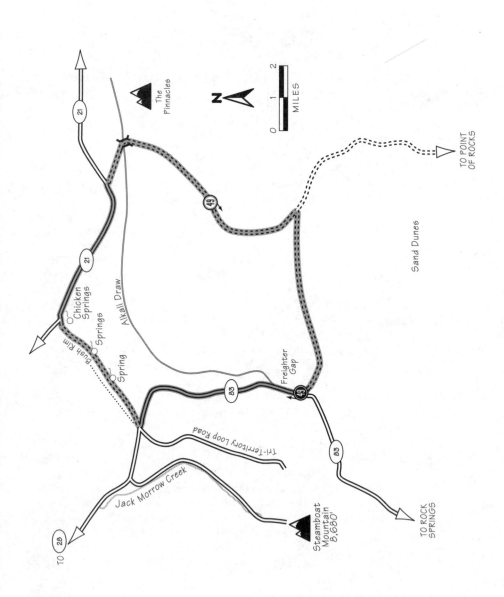

The Pinnacles

N

MILES
0 1 2

21

49

TO POINT OF ROCKS

Sand Dunes

Chicken Springs

Springs

Alkali Draw

Bush Rim

Spring

Freighter Gap

49

83

Tri-Territory Loop Road

83

Jack Morrow Creek

TO ROCK SPRINGS

Steamboat Mountain 8,680'

TO 28

Rainbow-colored mud cliffs rise above the surrounding sagebrush prairie along the Pinnacles Loop.

If you leave the designated route to explore the unusual wind-carved rocks, travel only on foot and take special care to "leave no trace."

The first part of this route passes by several springs. These serve as attractants to a number of species of wildlife. Most unusual is the Red Desert elk herd. This herd numbers around 500 to 600 elk that wander the desert, using tree-sized sagebrush for hiding and thermal cover.

Wild horses also gather at springs and watering holes on the Red Desert. Many of these animals are descendants of those that escaped from emigrants, ranchers, and the like many years ago.

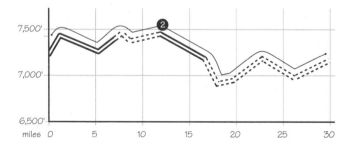

THE RIDE

0.0 Continue north on main Freighter Gap Road (CR 83).

0.2 Begin uphill.

1.6 Road levels off and then goes down into basin.

5.6 At bottom of basin. Now road begins uphill.

7.4 At a four-way intersection, take doubletrack road going right, below Bush Rim.

7.7 Take fainter doubletrack to the right. The main road switchbacks up the rim.

9.0 Come to a spring that is surrounded by fencing to protect it from erosion (primarily livestock trampling).

9.3 Pass by an unfenced spring.

10.4 Pass by another unfenced spring.

10.5 A faint doubletrack forks to the left. Continue straight on main doubletrack.

11.8 Pass by fenced Chicken Springs on the right. Immediately after, the road forks with a doubletrack going to the northeast (left); stay on main doubletrack heading southeast.

12.0 Intercept a good developed road (CR 21). Turn right, heading down into the basin.

12.3 End downhill into basin. Begin easy, flat ride across basin floor.

16.5 Turn right onto doubletrack going southeast.

16.9 Begin downhill into Alkali Draw.

17.8 Cross old wooden bridge going over Alkali Draw. The Pinnacles, to the southeast, rise up from the desert floor.

19.2 Cross a gully and then trail forks. Stay right on main doubletrack.

23.9 Trail comes into a more substantial doubletrack.

28.4 Drill site goes off to the right. As oil and gas exploration continues in the Red Desert, additional roads leading to drill sites can be expected. Continue on main road.

29.1 Back at starting point.

Oregon Buttes

Location:	The Red Desert, approximately 20 miles south of South Pass.
Distance:	22.5-mile loop.
Time:	Four to five hours.
Elevation gain:	1,950 feet.
Tread:	The trail begins on a gravel county road for 7.7 miles and then follows doubletrack roads for the remainder of the route until it rejoins the county road for the final 0.4 mile.
Season:	This route can be pedaled from mid-May through the fall. Muddy conditions, especially in the early spring, make the road across the desert nearly impassable; wait for the road to dry before making the trip. The route can be hot and dry in the summer and is better as a spring or fall ride.
Aerobic level:	Moderate.
Technical difficulty:	The roads on this route are primarily in good condition, resulting in a rating of 2 for the entire route, although sandy areas create stretches with a rating of 3.
Hazards:	Watch for sand traps on the doubletracks.
Land status:	Bureau of Land Management. A short segment near the end of the ride crosses private land. The landowner has given permission to cross his property, but take special care to stay only on the road in this segment.
Maps:	USGS Dickie Springs, Joe Hay Rim, Rock Cabin Spring, Pacific Springs. The entire route is on the BLM 1:100,000 scale South Pass map.
Access:	The ride can be accessed from Wyoming 28, between Farson and South Pass. Approximately 1 mile south of the rest station, turn south onto County Road 446. On the opposite side of the highway is the turnoff to the Big Sandy Entrance. Continue down dirt road for 9.3 miles. At start of CR 74 (it is the same road, just a different county), park on flat area on the left side of the road.

Oregon Buttes

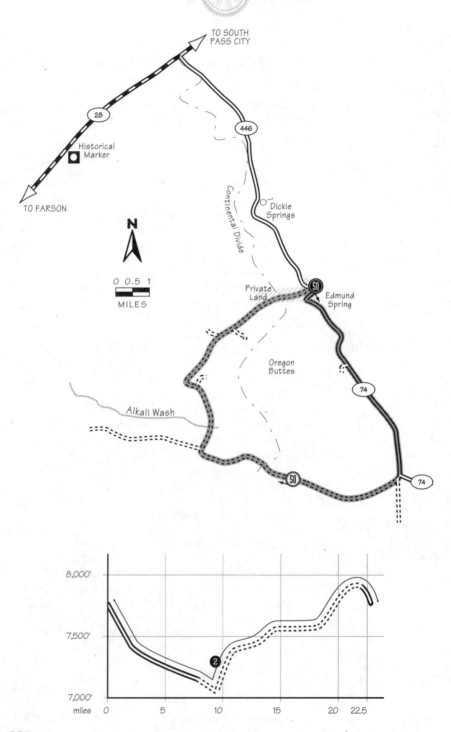

TO SOUTH
PASS CITY

28

Historical
Marker

TO FARSON

N

0 0.5 1
MILES

446

Continental Divide

Dickie
Springs

50

Private
Land

Edmund
Spring

Oregon
Buttes

74

Alkali Wash

50

74

8,000'

7,500'

②

7,000'

miles   0   5   10   15   20   22.5

The Oregon Buttes were once a welcome landscape marker for pioneers crossing on the nearby Oregon Trail. It was the half-way point on their trek to California.

HIGHLIGHTS

The Oregon Buttes are made up of steep cliffs surrounded by sagebrush prairie. Named by settlers traveling the Oregon Trail, this desert sentinel was a welcome landmark to pioneers because it marked the halfway point on their journey to the West Coast. Petrified wood is abundant here, indicating that the area wasn't always just sagebrush and greasewood.

This ride begins on a county road and then heads across the desert on doubletrack roads. Alternate roads criss-cross the desert, offering exploration opportunities.

This route has mostly rolling and easy terrain until the northwest and northern segments, where the route climbs along the edge of Oregon Buttes. Be sure to carry enough water to last the entire trip. There are a couple of sources of water on the route but their reliability as the summer progresses is difficult to predict.

As the route passes near Oregon Buttes it follows the border of the Wilderness Study Area. Although not yet an actual wilderness area, this area is under review by the Bureau of Land Management and is currently managed as if it were wilderness. If you leave the designated route to explore the unusual wind-carved rocks, travel only on foot and take special care to "leave no trace."

THE RIDE

0.0 Begin on Sweetwater CR 74 going south.

0.9 Pass by ponds on the left.

1.7 Cross over an earthen bridge.

3.1 Doubletrack forks right. Continue straight on main road.

7.7 Come to a three-way fork in the road. Go right. Another doubletrack continues straight and main CR 74 goes left.

8.1 A doubletrack joins the route from behind.

9.6 Start up a hill.

10.1 Over steep part of the hill.

10.6 Doubletrack forks. Stay left.

11.6 Doubletrack forks. Stay left.

12.2 Doubletrack joins in from the left. Stay right.

13.1 Another faint doubletrack joins from left.

13.5 Trail forks. Stay right.

13.8 Come to a spring area. Water is available; be sure to bring a filter or other water purification system.

14.3 Pass by a stock pond.

14.5 Doubletrack road joins from the right.

14.7 Trail forks. Stay right on grassy trail (old pipeline route).

15.2 Doubletrack goes right. Stay straight.

15.5 Steep gully down-and-up.

16.8 Doubletrack comes in from the right. Stay left.

17.2 Cross gully on earthen bridge. After crossing, stay right.

18.1 Doubletrack goes left. Stay right on main route. Route becomes more difficult.

18.9 At ridge top, come to an intersection. Continue on main doubletrack to the right.

19.3 Cross by a spring.

19.5 Cross by another spring.

20.8 Old mine debris is to the left. The route now crosses private land from here until returning to the start of the route. The property owner allows bike travel across his property; be sure to respect private property rights. Stay on the road for the remaining 2.3 miles.

21.0 Pass by a dense patch of aspen trees with a spring area below.

21.2 Pass by a reservoir to the right.

21.7 Road forks. Stay right.

22.2 Return to main gravel county road. Turn right.

22.5 Back at start of route.

Wyoming Range
Area Rides

The Wyoming Range is probably the least known of all Wyoming's mountain ranges. Even if you ask long-time Wyoming residents if they've been to the Wyoming Range, they may give you a quizzical look, not knowing what you are talking about. This range, which parallels the Wyoming-Idaho border in extreme western Wyoming, is a delight for mountain bikers. There are no designated wilderness areas within the range and there are no areas where bikes are restricted.

This is a great place to bike for the adventurer seeking solitude and an opportunity to explore. However, some of the trails are not well-marked and can be easily confused with livestock paths.

McDougal Ridge

Location:	The Wyoming Range, between Daniel and Alpine.
Distance:	10 miles, out and back.
Time:	Three and one-half to four and one-half hours.
Elevation gain:	1,440 feet.
Tread:	The first and final 3.3 miles are on good doubletrack. The route follows singletrack for 3.4 miles.
Season:	This route is clear of snow in late spring to early summer and it can be ridden until snowfall in the autumn.
Aerobic level:	Moderate to strenuous.
Technical difficulty:	The doubletrack has a rating of 2. Once the trail changes to singletrack it has a rating of 3+ with some short segments rated 4.
Hazards:	There are a few rough and rutted areas on the doubletrack, but it is a good road that has been closed for a few years. When it ends, the route can be a little difficult to locate as it changes to singletrack and heads toward McDougal Ridge. The singletrack has rough areas due to livestock trampling, and some rocky and steep segments.
Land status:	U.S. Forest Service, Bridger National Forest.
Maps:	USGS Triple Peak, Lookout Mountain.
Access:	One mile south of Daniel, turn west on County Road 117 (Cottonwood Ryegrass Road). Continue on this road and follow the signs to the North Cottonwood Creek entrance to the Wyoming Range. Once in the National Forest, continue on the McDougal Gap Road (Forest Road 10125) to the intersection with FR 10346 (Sjhoberg Creek Road). Park vehicle near intersection.

HIGHLIGHTS

McDougal Ridge is a vertical cliff rising majestically along the crest of the Wyoming Range. This ride follows a doubletrack road as it rises from the Sjhoberg Creek drainage toward the ridge. The road once led to a drill site but is now closed to motorized traffic. It is popular with horseback riders but few hikers or mountain bikers have yet to discover this area. After pass-

McDougal Ridge

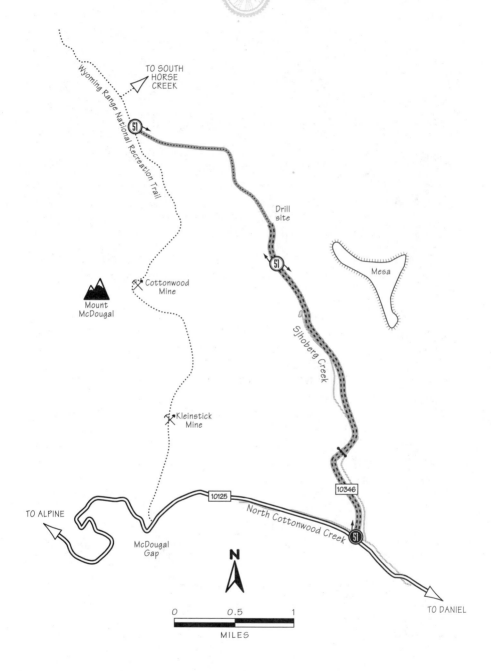

TO SOUTH
HORSE
CREEK

Wyoming Range National Recreation Trail

51

Drill
site

51

Mesa

Cottonwood
Mine

Mount
McDougal

Sjhoberg Creek

Kleinstick
Mine

10346

TO ALPINE

10125

North Cottonwood Creek

51

McDougal
Gap

N

TO DANIEL

0   0.5   1

MILES

McDougal Ridge rises above the Wyoming Range National Recreational Trail in the Wyoming Range.

ing the old drill pad, now just a flat grassy clearing, the route follows a singletrack that can be easily mistaken for a livestock path. It begins a steep and rocky uphill climb, crossing several small creeks and, eventually, Dead Cow Creek. The turnaround point is at a "T" intersection with the Wyoming Range National Recreation Trail.

This ride is an example of a trail that is difficult to locate and where livestock trails greatly confuse the issue. It was intended to be a loop that connects with the Wyoming Range National Recreation Trail to McDougal Gap, returning on FR 10125. Unfortunately, at the time of the ride for this book, the Wyoming Range Trail became indistinct within a half-mile after the "T" intersection with the Sjhoberg Creek Trail. Many cattle trails create false trails and a confusing maze of tracks. If you feel adventurous or if the trail is clearly marked by the Forest Service in the future, this would make a nice loop route.

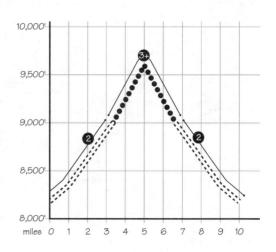

THE RIDE

0.0 From intersection of FR 10125 (McDougal Gap Road) and FR 10346 (Sjhoberg Creek Road), head north on the Sjhoberg Trail.

1.0 Cross creek on earthen bridge. Immediately after, road goes left. Go around "Road Closed" gate and continue up the hill.

2.9 Road levels out a bit and becomes easier riding.

3.3 At old drill site. Road ends here. The trail is a little difficult to locate. Go left (west) through an opening in the sagebrush where trail becomes a singletrack.

3.6 Skirt around a wet meadow and re-enter the timber to the west.

4.1 Cross over a little stream (it may not be running).

4.3 Cross over another little stream. Dead Cow Creek can be heard flowing below.

4.4 Cross Dead Cow Creek.

4.8 Cross a little stream. Trail rises steeply for final stretch.

5.0 Meet the Wyoming Range National Recreational Trail. Turnaround point. Trail continues north to a saddle where it forks. At saddle, the Wyoming Range National Recreational Trail continues straight; right trail goes to South Horse Creek; and left deadends a short distance farther on. The Wyoming Range National Recreational Trail going south should go past the Cottonwood and Kleinstick mines and intercept the McDougal Gap Road. (At the time of route exploration, the recreational trail faded out after a quarter mile. There are many false trails that are actually livestock paths that deadend at salt licks and stock ponds.) Try this route if you're feeling adventurous or if the Forest Service marks the trail and provides some directional signage. Continue back down the trail, returning on same route.

10.0 Back at starting point.

Variation: The loop route to McDougal Gap has already been mentioned. Another option is to continue north on the Wyoming Range National Recreational Trail, either going all the way to Hoback Canyon or going to Bull Creek and west to the Grey's River.

Cliff Creek Falls

Location:	The Wyoming Range, south of the Hoback River.
Distance:	12.8 miles, out and back.
Time:	Four to five hours.
Elevation gain:	1,300 feet.
Tread:	This ride is all on singletrack.
Season:	This route is clear of snow in late spring to early summer and it can be ridden until snowfall in the autumn.
Aerobic level:	Moderate.
Technical difficulty:	The doubletrack has a rating of 4. The segment between the two crossings of Cliff Creek (miles 4.2 to 4.8) is rougher and rockier than the rest of the trail.
Hazards:	Watch for rocks, logs, waterbars, and other obstacles on and next to the trail.
Land status:	U.S. Forest Service, Bridger National Forest.
Maps:	USGS Triple Peak, Lookout Mountain.
Access:	Six miles west of Bondurant, exit from U.S. Highway 189-191 (Hoback Canyon Road) at Forest Road 30530. Continue south on gravel road for 7 miles to the end of the road and trailhead. There is camping and parking available at the trailhead.

HIGHLIGHTS

Hang onto your handlebars on this route. Sudden twists and turns are necessary to avoid rocks, logs, and low-hanging tree branches. The trail occasionally breaks out into open meadows with dense vegetation obscuring the trail. To ogle the steep canyon walls you'll have to stop riding to look up long enough to enjoy the scenery.

This is one of the most fun and most challenging singletrack routes in this book. Only short portions of the trail are steep enough to require bike hiking; most is rideable but your heart rate will be soaring. The technical level of this ride does not allow for much sightseeing.

The turnaround point is at the Cliff Creek Falls. This is a narrow band of water, cascading down sheer cliffs. The sight is worth the climb. Actually, the climb is worth getting the opportunity for the adventure to ride back down the trail.

Cliff Creek Falls

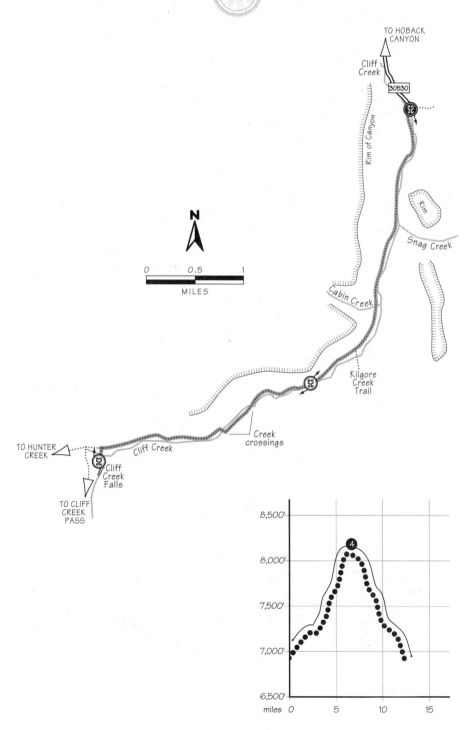

TO HOBACK
CANYON

Cliff
Creek

30530

52

Rim of Canyon

Rim

Snag Creek

Cabin Creek

Kilgore
Creek
Trail

N

0   0.5   1

MILES

52

Creek
crossings

TO HUNTER
CREEK

Cliff Creek

52

Cliff
Creek
Falls

TO CLIFF
CREEK
PASS

8,500'

4

8,000'

7,500'

7,000'

6,500'

miles 0   5   10   15

Cliff Creek Falls marks the turnaround point for the singletrack route along Cliff Creek.

THE RIDE

0.0 From trailhead, cross bridge to start of route.

2.3 Cross small creek.

2.7 Trail forks. Go right. Kilgore Creek Trail goes left.

3.8 Cross small creek.

4.2 Cross Cliff Creek. This is a wet crossing and requires wading across the creek.

4.8 Cross back across Cliff Creek.

4.9 Cross little creek (it may not be flowing).

5.2 Cross little creek.

5.3 Cross little creek (only 18 inches across).

5.4 Skirt around a little pond.

5.6 Cross little creek and canyon opens up. Vegetation is dense and may hide the trail.

6.3 Cross creek to the falls.

6.4 At the falls. Turnaround point. Return on same route.

12.8 Back at starting point.

Variation: From the falls, the trail continues another 2 miles to Cliff Creek Pass.

Jackson and Grand Teton Area Rides

Jackson is surrounded by national forest and national park lands. This provides considerable opportunity for mountain biking through some of the most spectacular scenery on the planet. Cycling in both Grand Teton and Yellowstone National Parks is limited to existing roads, but a few gravel roads have been closed to motorized travel and are ideal for mountain biking. Mountain bikes are not allowed on the park's hiking trails.

The Gros Ventre Wilderness Area, Teton Wilderness Area, and Jedediah Smith Wilderness Area are all off-limits to mountain bikes, but plenty of non-wilderness remains to be explored. A good area to investigate is the Gros Ventre National Forest north of Lower Slide Lake and the Gros Ventre River and extending toward and past Togwotee and Union passes.

This is grizzly and black bear country; care must be taken to ensure safety. Read the introduction of this book for some general directions and check with park and forest rangers for additional information.

Snow comes to this part of the state early in the fall and stays well into spring and even summer at the higher elevations. To prevent damage to trails, be sure to wait until the routes are clear of snow and are mostly dry before venturing out. Also, take along some bug repellent if you plan to stop for a picnic. One of the best times of years to bike this area is late August and into September, when many of the bugs are gone. Take care if you bike during the hunting season, though, and wear plenty of hunter orange clothing. This is a very popular hunting area.

Granite Creek

Location:	The Gros Ventre Mountains, north of the Hoback River.
Distance:	18.9-mile loop.
Time:	Two to three hours.
Elevation gain:	650 feet.
Tread:	This ride follows a gravel road for 9.3 miles and then continues for 1.7 miles on a singletrack hiking trail. The final 7.7 miles return on gravel road.
Season:	This route is clear of snow in late spring to early summer and it can be ridden until snowfall in the autumn.
Aerobic level:	Moderate.
Technical difficulty:	The gravel road has a rating of 2 due to washboarding and some dense gravel pockets. If this road is newly graded and graveled, it could be difficult to ride due to the soft gravel base. The singletrack trail on the east side of Granite Creek has some steep and rocky areas with a technical rating of 4, but the majority has a rating of 3.
Hazards:	Watch for traffic on the gravel road. Most vehicles are slow moving but drivers may be looking at the scenery more than the road. This road can be washboarded and a bit rutted. The singletrack has some steep segments that are safer to bike hike than to ride.
Land status:	U.S. Forest Service, Bridger National Forest.
Maps:	USGS Bull Creek, Granite Falls.
Access:	Approximately 11 miles east of Hoback Junction on U.S. Highway 189-191, exit just before the bridge crossing of the Hoback River, onto Forest Road 30530 leading to Granite Recreation Area. Go 0.1 mile up the road and park in wide gravel area near the creek.

HIGHLIGHTS

Granite Creek is bordered along its length by cliffs rising abruptly from the timbered hillsides. The cliffs west of the creek mark the boundary of the Gros Ventre Wilderness Area and effectively limit any mountain biking in

Granite Creek

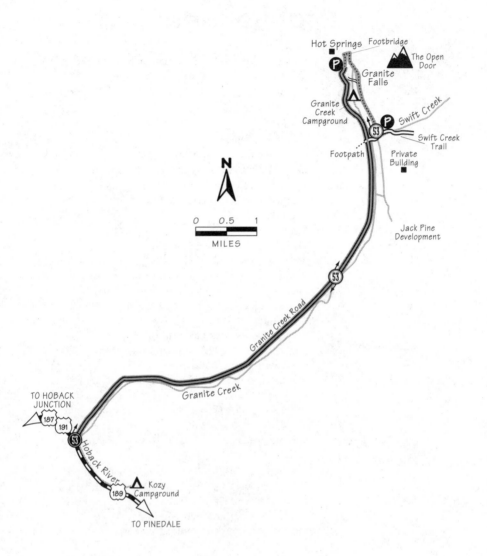

N

0   0.5   1

MILES

Hot Springs   Footbridge

The Open
Door

Granite
Falls

Granite
Creek
Campground

Swift Creek

Swift Creek
Trail

Footpath

Private
Building

Jack Pine
Development

53

Granite Creek Road

Granite Creek

TO HOBACK
JUNCTION

187

191

53

Hoback River

189   Kozy
Campground

TO PINEDALE

The Granite Creek route provides a sightseeing tour of Granite Creek, offering views into the Gros Ventre Wilderness Area.

that direction. To the west, a 10-mile-wide swath extending north from the Hoback River has numerous footpaths and a few forest roads that are available to mountain bikes and worth exploring.

Granite Creek is a major tributary to the Hoback River. Its headwaters are in the Gros Ventre Wilderness Area. This route follows a good gravel road, paralleling Granite Creek. It leads to Granite Recreation Area and, consequently, has some tourist traffic. Near the halfway point of this ride, and at the end of the gravel road, is Granite Hot Springs, complete with a swimming pool. The route crosses a footbridge and begins a 2-mile technical ride down a hiking trail before reconnecting with the main gravel road.

An optional shorter version of this ride is to begin at Granite Creek Campground, going north on the gravel road, crossing to the singletrack, and then returning on the gravel road, back to the campground.

THE RIDE

0.0   Head up main gravel road, going toward the hot springs.
0.3   Pass by a couple of portable outhouses. (They may be moved in the future but are there primarily for use during the snowmobile season.)
1.3   Road forks. Go right and over bridge.
3.7   Start steeper climb.
4.0   At top of tough hill.
4.7   Doubletrack goes right. Stay on main road.

6.7   Road forks. Stay straight. Right is FR 30519.

7.7   Footpaths go left and a gravel road forks right. Stay straight on main road.

8.5   Pass by Granite Creek Campground.

8.7   Road forks. Right goes to Granite Falls. Stay straight.

9.2   At end of main road. Continue straight.

9.3   Cross footbridge and go right onto singletrack to begin fun, and sometimes challenging, downhill.

11.0 Trail comes to a trailhead parking area. Go through parking area and onto gravel road, turning right and over bridge.

11.2 Rejoin Granite Creek Road (FR 30530); turn left and return to start of ride.

18.9 Back at start.

Variation: For a short and fun 3.5-mile loop, begin at Granite Creek Campground, going up road to hot springs, crossing to singletrack, and looping back below the campground before returning to the starting point.

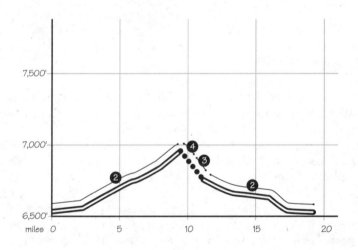

Falls Creek to Wilson Shuttle

Location:	Immediately west of Hoback Junction and ending in the town of Wilson.
Distance:	18 miles one way.
Time:	Three to four hours.
Elevation gain:	1,225 feet.
Tread:	This ride is on a gravel road until it joins a paved road for the final 4.5 miles.
Season:	This route is best in late spring through the fall.
Aerobic level:	Moderate.
Technical difficulty:	The first 13.5 miles are on gravel road with a rating of 2+. The final 4.5 miles are paved but are also a rating of 2+ because of the lack of shoulder.
Hazards:	The gravel road can become washboarded and could have potholes and ruts. The paved road has no shoulder yet has heavy traffic; be especially cautious on this segment or end the ride just before the pavement begins.
Land status:	U.S. Forest Service, Teton National Forest.
Maps:	USGS Jackson, Munger Mountain, and Teton Pass Quads.
Access:	From Hoback Junction, turn west on U.S. Highway 26-89. Continue past Astoria Hot Springs. About 4.5 miles from junction, turn right onto Falls Creek Road, Forest Road 31000.

HIGHLIGHTS

This route begins near the entrance of Snake River Canyon, just west of Hoback Junction. It follows a wide gravel road for its entire length, initially passing next to Pritchard Creek before climbing up to Pritchard Pass. The route descends slightly and runs adjacent to the thick willow corridor of Falls Creek. It leaves the national forest but continues on a public road as it passes by subdivisions and housing developments that have spread across the Snake River Valley from Jackson. The road winds along the gravel road until it turns to pavement at milepost 13.5. This is a good end point for those not wanting to battle traffic the final 4.5 miles to Wilson. Traffic increases after this point; the road remains narrow and does not have a shoulder.

Falls Creek to Wilson Shuttle

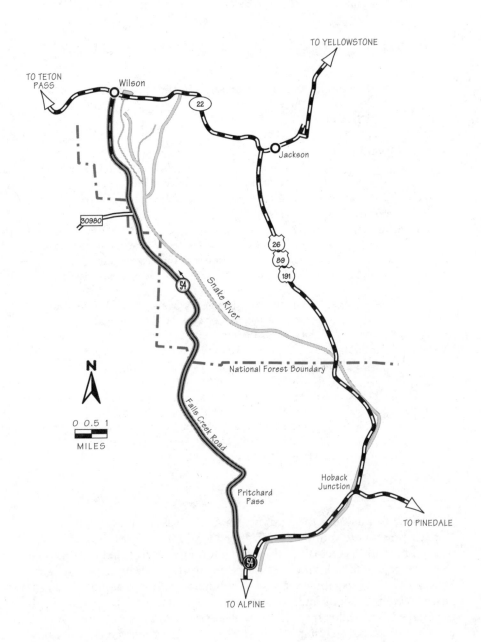

TO YELLOWSTONE

TO TETON PASS

Wilson

22

Jackson

30980

54

Snake River

26

89

191

National Forest Boundary

N

0 0.5 1
MILES

Falls Creek Road

Pritchard Pass

Hoback Junction

TO PINEDALE

54

TO ALPINE

THE RIDE

0.0 From intersection with US26-89, go north on Falls Creek Road.

0.1 Pavement ends. Continue straight. Forest Service Work Station is on the right.

1.0 Cross cattleguard.

2.2 At top of long uphill.

3.1 Cross creek.

3.2 Road forks. Continue straight.

5.1 Road forks with a doubletrack going right. Continue on main road.

5.4 Cross cattleguard.

7.7 Cross cattleguard.

9.3 Cross cattleguard.

11.8 Start uphill climb.

12.1 Cross cattleguard as route levels out.

13.5 Cross creek. Road is paved on other side. This is a good ending point if you don't like riding in traffic on a narrow road.

18.0 At Wilson.

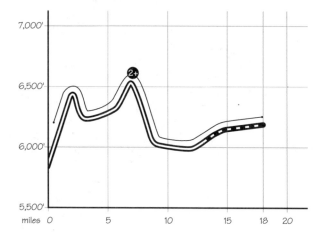

Cache Creek to Game Creek Loop

Location:	Immediately southeast of the town of Jackson.
Distance:	18-mile loop.
Time:	Three to four hours.
Elevation gain:	1,625 feet.
Tread:	This ride follows a dirt road for about 2 miles and then goes to a wide singletrack for another 2 miles before becoming a narrow trail. After 2.5 miles, the route follows a dirt road again and the final 8 miles are on pavement.
Season:	This route is best in late spring through the fall.
Aerobic level:	Moderate.
Technical difficulty:	The first 4 miles have a rating of 2. The climb out of Cache Creek has a rating of 4 but eases to a rating of 3 until meeting the Game Creek Road, with a rating of 2. The paved highway is a rating of 1.
Hazards:	The first 4 miles have few hazards. Game Creek Trail has steep and rocky segments. Watch for traffic on the U.S. highway. The tourist traffic in and around Jackson can be quite heavy.
Land status:	U.S. Forest Service, Teton National Forest and U.S. highway.
Maps:	USGS Jackson, Cache Creek.
Access:	In Jackson, from U.S. Highway 26-89-191 on west end of town, turn south at intersection with Maple Way. At "T" intersection, turn left onto Scott and then an immediate right onto Snow King Avenue. Turn left onto Vine and, at a stop sign, turn right onto Kelly Avenue. Turn right onto Redmond and immediately left on Cache Creek Drive. Pavement ends at Forest Service boundary and the road is Forest Road 30450. After about a half mile, road ends at parking area. Park here.

Cache Creek to Game Creek Loop

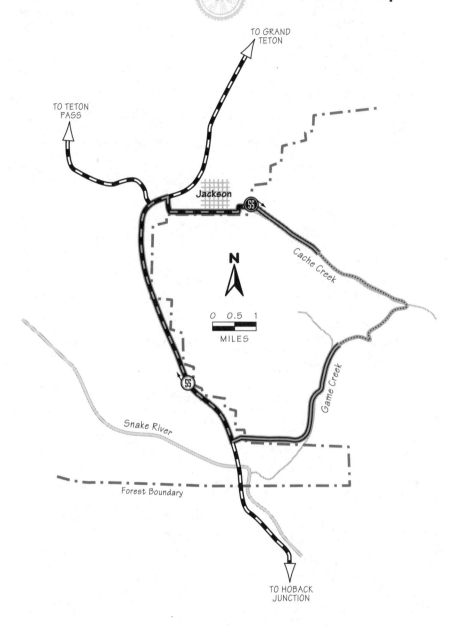

TO GRAND
TETON

TO TETON
PASS

Jackson

Cache Creek

N

0   0.5   1

MILES

Game Creek

Snake River

Forest Boundary

TO HOBACK
JUNCTION

The Cache Creek to Game Creek Loop begins on a tree-lined trail adjacent to Cache Creek.

HIGHLIGHTS

This is a really entertaining ride as it heads up Cache Creek on a wide singletrack. After crossing Cache Creek, the route heads up out of the drainage on a rocky trail that may require a bit of bike hiking. The steep segment is over quickly and the exciting downhill begins. Everything about the Jackson area is scenic and this ride is no exception. The views of the Gros Ventre Range and into the Snake River Valley are striking. If you want to avoid the pavement and traffic hassles on the U.S. highway and into Jackson, make this ride a shuttle with a pickup point at the intersection with the highway.

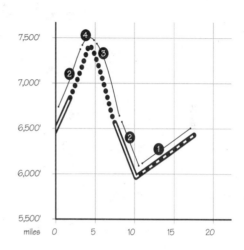

THE RIDE

0.0 From parking area, go to east side and onto road following Cache Creek.

0.4 Road forks. Stay left. Right goes to a private site.

1.9 At trailhead. Gate over trail may, or may not, be closed. Go past or around it. Trail goes to singletrack.

3.7 Cross creek on a good wooden bridge.

3.9 Trail forks. Go right across good bridge onto Game Creek Trail and start up steep and rocky hill.

4.6 Come to saddle and start downhill.

7.3 Pass by pond to the right.

7.5 Trail joins Game Creek Road.

9.6 Road forks. Go right onto dirt road and downhill.

10.6 Come to intersection with paved US189-191. Shuttle route ends here and avoids pavement and heavy traffic. To continue on loop, turn right and return to start via the highway.

18.0 Back at start of ride.

Putt-Putt

Location:	Immediately southeast of the town of Jackson.
Distance:	4.7-mile loop.
Time:	Forty-five minutes to one hour.
Elevation gain:	550 feet.
Tread:	This ride follows a dirt road for 1.4 miles and then is on singletrack for the remainder of the route.
Season:	This route is best in late spring through the fall but it can be ridden whenever there isn't snow on the ground.
Aerobic level:	Easy to moderate.
Technical difficulty:	The first 1.5 miles have a rating of 2. The actual Putt-Putt Trail has a rating of 3 due to deep ruts, and some steep and rocky areas.
Hazards:	The first 1.5 miles have few hazards. Putt-Putt Trail is deeply rutted, making for little room to maneuver. There are a few steep rocky segments and some wet crossings through washes with little streams running through them.
Land status:	U.S. Forest Service, Teton National Forest.
Maps:	USGS Cache Creek.
Access:	In Jackson, from U.S. Highway 26-89-191, on the west end of town, turn south at intersection with Maple Way. At "T" intersection, turn left onto Scott and then an immediate right onto Snow King Avenue. Turn left onto Vine and at a stop sign turn right onto Kelly Avenue. Turn right onto Redmond and immediately left on to Cache Creek Drive. Pavement ends at Forest Service boundary and the road is Forest Road 30450. After about a half mile, road ends at parking area. Park here.

HIGHLIGHTS

Imagine combining a roller-coaster ride and a bobsled run. The result is this Putt-Putt loop. It begins by heading up the Cache Creek Trail for 1.5 miles and then turns onto the singletrack Putt-Putt trail. The trail is deeply rutted

Putt-Putt

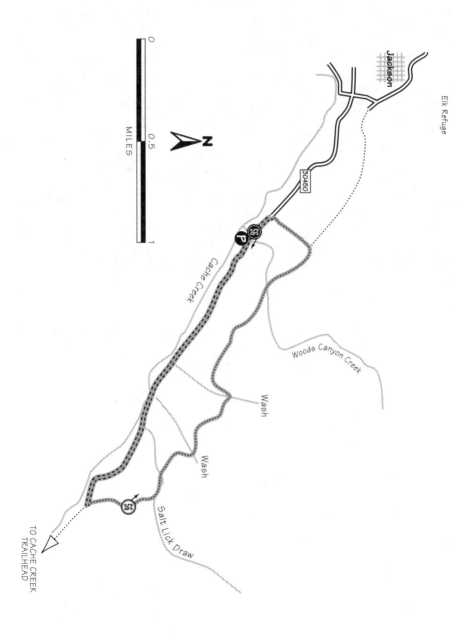

MILES

N

Jackson

Elk Refuge

30450

56

P

Cache Creek

Woods Canyon Creek

Wash

Wash

Salt Lick Draw

56

TO CACHE CREEK
TRAILHEAD

The Putt-Putt loop cuts across steep hillsides as it overlooks Jackson Hole and the National Elk Refuge.

in places and seems like a dash down a bobsled run. The downhill runs are short as the trail hits the bottom of a wash and then goes up the other side, roller-coastering across the hillside. The only disappointment with this trial is that it's so short, but it makes a fun little ride before or after work.

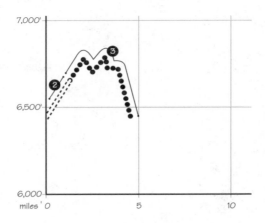

The Ride

0.0 From parking area, go to east side and onto road following Cache Creek.

0.4 Road forks. Stay left. Right goes to a private site.

1.4 Trail forks. Go left on steep uphill trail, marked with Putt-Putt trail sign. Straight continues up Cache Creek Trail.

1.6 At top of steep segment. Trail becomes a series of up-and-down runs from one wash to the next.

4.0 Start steep downhill.

4.3 Trail forks. Go left. Right continues route on into town.

4.4 Trail forks. Go right.

4.5 Come out onto gravel FR 30450. Turn left.

4.7 Back at parking area.

Variation: At mile 4.3, continue on trail into town.

Antelope Flats

Location:	Grand Teton National Park.
Distance:	13.6-mile loop.
Time:	One and one-half to two and one-half hours.
Elevation gain:	350 feet.
Tread:	This ride follows a paved road for nearly 9 miles before following a doubletrack for 3 miles. The final 2 miles return to pavement.
Season:	This route is best in late spring through the fall, but it can be ridden whenever there isn't snow on the ground.
Aerobic level:	Easy.
Technical difficulty:	The paved road is a rating 1 +, while the doubletrack has a rating of 2 +.
Hazards:	The paved road has some rough pavement. Watch for traffic on the road, especially on U.S. Highway 26-89-191. The doubletrack can be rutted and it has a segment that has washed out and must be bike hiked.
Land status:	National Park Service, Grand Teton National Park.
Maps:	USGS Moose, Shadow Mountain.
Access:	From Jackson, go north on US26-89-191 into Grand Teton National Park. One mile past the Moose intersection, park in the small parking area on right side of highway. This parking area is popular with local climbers going up a rock face on Blacktail Butte.

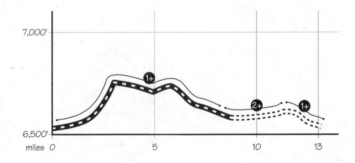

Antelope Flats

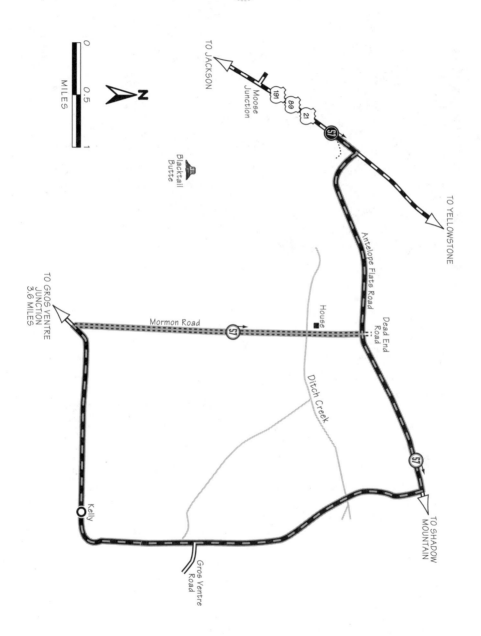

N

MILES
0   0.5   1

TO JACKSON

Moose Junction

191

89

21

57

TO YELLOWSTONE

Blacktail Butte

Antelope Flats Road

Dead End Road

House

57

Mormon Road

Ditch Creek

TO GROS VENTRE JUNCTION
3.6 MILES

Kelly

Gros Ventre Road

57

TO SHADOW MOUNTAIN

The Antelope Flats loop offers a sightseeing tour with an unobstructed view of the Teton Mountains.

HIGHLIGHTS

Both Grand Teton and Yellowstone National Parks restrict where bicycles are allowed. Off-road travel is not allowed and bikes are not allowed on hiking trails. There are a few old roads that are closed to motorized travel but remain open to bicycles. Check with the rangers at the park entrances to find additional biking opportunities in the parks.

For this ride, forget highly technical and aerobic challenges. This is a sightseeing ride. The flat terrain and gravel roads provide plenty of opportunity to look up from the trail and gaze at Grand Teton, Mount Moran, and the other peaks that make up the Tetons.

As you follow the dirt road near Blacktail Butte, watch for bison ranging the prairie. Remember, these are wild animals and care must be taken to avoid them if they come close to the road.

THE RIDE

0.0 From parking area, go north on US26-89-191. Be cautious of heavy traffic.

0.3 At Antelope Flats Road, turn right onto rough pavement.

2.1 Pass by Mormon Road. This will be the return route.

3.3 At four-way intersection. Go right. Left goes to Shadow Mountain.

4.9 Paved road goes left to Teton Science Camp. Continue straight.

5.8 Gros Ventre Road goes left. Continue straight to Kelly.

7.0 At Kelly. Turn left if you want to go into the little town. Continue straight and past a small store next to the road.

8.8 Turn right onto gravel Mormon Road. Straight goes past the Gros Ventre Campground.

8.9 Gravel road becomes rougher doubletrack. A sign may still be present that states the road is closed ahead. Don't worry, it is still passable to bicyclists.

9.9 Doubletrack goes right. Stay straight.

11.0 Come to "Road Closed" sign. Continue around it.

11.1 Walk across area where road is damaged.

11.2 Pass by residential home on the left.

11.5 Rejoin paved road. Turn left and return to starting point.

13.6 Back at starting area.

Shadow Mountain

Location:	Immediately east of Grand Teton National Park, approximately 10 miles northeast of Moose.
Distance:	9-mile loop.
Time:	Two to three hours.
Elevation gain:	1,450 feet.
Tread:	This ride follows a gravel road for all but the final 1.4 miles, where it follows a doubletrack road.
Season:	This route is best in late spring through the fall.
Aerobic level:	Moderate.
Technical difficulty:	The entire route is a rating of 2. There are rougher patches and some rutted areas, but most of the road is easy riding.
Hazards:	The gravel road has some steep and rocky areas with ruts, but these are not very numerous. The doubletrack around the base of the mountain is rutted with muddy potholes.
Land status:	U.S. Forest Service, Teton National Forest and National Park Service, Grand Teton National Park.
Maps:	USGS Moose, Shadow Mountain.
Access:	From Jackson, go north on U.S. Highway 26-89-191 into Grand Teton National Park. A little over a mile past the Moose intersection, turn right onto the Antelope Flats road. Continue straight for 3 miles to a four-way intersection. Turn left onto forest access road. After about 1.5 miles, the road enters national forest. Park near forest sign in one of the dispersed camping areas.

HIGHLIGHTS

Shadow Mountain rises along the eastern border of Antelope Flats. It is within Teton National Forest, but a short segment of this ride passes through Grand Teton National Park. The mountain seems to be lying in the shadow of the Tetons, whose stark craggy peaks rise to the west across the flat grassland of Antelope Flats. There is dispersed camping on Shadow Mountain plus some additional roads and trails worth exploring. The route described here rises to the summit of Shadow Mountain before dropping back down to the flat plains that skirt the base of the mountain. Another alternative is to come down the face of the mountain on a singletrack path.

Shadow Mountain

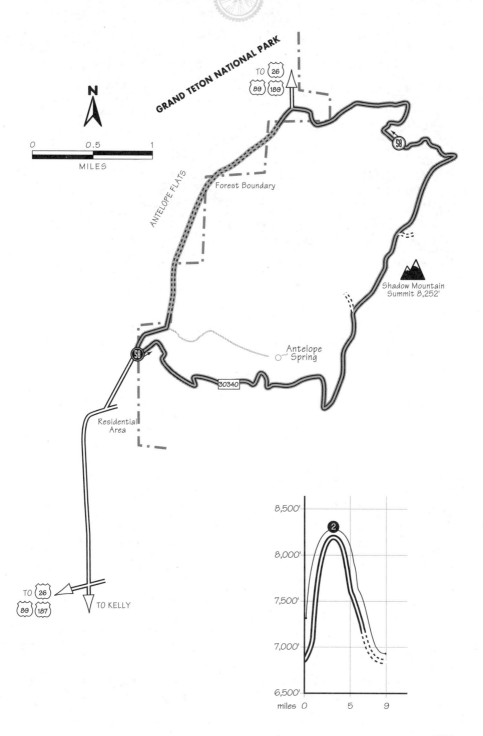

N

0   0.5   1
MILES

GRAND TETON NATIONAL PARK

TO 26
89 189

58

ANTELOPE FLATS

Forest Boundary

Shadow Mountain
Summit 8,252'

Antelope
Spring

58

30340

Residential
Area

TO 26
89 187

TO KELLY

8,500'

2

8,000'

7,500'

7,000'

6,500'

miles 0   5   9

Shadow Mountain rises above Antelope Flats and numerous overlook openings provide breathtaking views of the Tetons.

THE RIDE

0.0 From parking area, go to the southeast on Forest Road 30340.

0.2 Begin steep uphill.

3.3 At summit.

3.7 Road forks. Stay left. Road becomes rougher and winds through pine and aspen woods.

5.6 Road forks. Go left.

6.2 Exit National Forest and enter Grand Teton National Park.

6.6 Road forks. Go left onto rougher doubletrack and past buck-rail gate/fence. Right returns to highway.

8.8 Go past buck-rail fence.

9.0 Back at starting point.

Variation: Start ride at four-way intersection, parking vehicle in good parking site near intersection. This adds 1.6 miles to the ride. Another alternative is to park at the same site as the Antelope Flats Loop route. This adds 6.6 miles to the ride.

A singletrack trail forks west from the summit of Shadow Mountain and winds through the forest for a more challenging ride to the base of the mountain.

Additional doubletrack and hiking trails are worth exploring on Shadow Mountain and in the Gros Ventre Mountains to the east.

The Great Divide Mountain Bike Route

You've heard of the Continental Divide Trail. That is the backpacking trail that is being developed to extend from Mexico to Canada. Fewer people have heard of the Great Divide Mountain Bike Route. It is the world's longest mountain bike route, covering 2,465 miles from Canada to Mexico, paralleling the Continental Divide.

Adventure Cycling, a non-profit bicycle organization based out of Missoula, Montana, developed the route beginning in 1994, and completed it in 1997. It crosses Montana, Idaho, Wyoming, Colorado, and New Mexico and is designed specifically for backroad bicycle touring.

The route enters Wyoming along the Idaho border, just south of Yellowstone National Park. After passing through Grand Teton National Park, the route goes over two mountain passes, first on pavement over Togwotee Pass and then on a dirt road over Union Pass in the Wind River Mountains.

As the Continental Divide crosses Wyoming, it isn't relegated to just mountain ranges. As it comes to the southern end of the Wind River Mountains, it drops down to the desert and the Great Divide Basin before rising back into the Sierra Madre Mountains. It exits Wyoming at the Colorado border near the small town of Baggs.

The route is described here in six different sections. Each section can be an independent one- or two-day ride, or the entire route can be pedaled in a seven- to nine-day stretch. Adventure Cycling publishes maps of the entire Great Divide Mountain Bike Route.

Idaho Border to Moran Junction

Location:	Grand Teton National Park.
Distance:	51.7 miles one way.
Time:	One day.
Elevation gain:	1,980 feet.
Tread:	This ride follows a rough dirt road for the first 25 miles and then joins the main paved road through Grand Teton National Park.
Season:	This route can be taken in late spring through the fall, but it is best from July through mid-September.
Aerobic level:	Moderate.
Technical difficulty:	The dirt road is a rating 2+ due to potholes and rocky areas. The paved road is a rating 1+.
Hazards:	The dirt road has potholes and rough areas. The paved road has a narrow shoulder and heavy traffic.
Land status:	U.S. Forest Service, Targhee National Forest and National Park Service, Grand Teton National Park.
Maps:	USGS Sheep Falls, Hominy Peak, Grassy Lake Reservoir, Survey Peak, Flagg Ranch, Colter Bay, Two Ocean Lake, Moran. Other suitable maps in 1:100,000 scale include BLM surface ownership maps for Yellowstone National Park South and Jackson Lake. Also, the National Park Service has a Grand Teton National Park map and the U.S. Forest Service has a Bridger-Teton National Forest map.
Access:	From Jackson, go north on U.S. Highway 26-89-191 into Grand Teton National Park. At Flagg Ranch, turn west on Grassy Lake Road. Continue to the Idaho-Wyoming border.

HIGHLIGHTS

The route starts at the Idaho border and follows a tree-lined dirt road into Targhee National Forest and past Grassy Lake. This road would be annoying in a car due to the numerous, deep potholes; it is well-suited for biking.

Overnight camping is possible at Grassy Lake or, upon entering Grand Teton National Park, at several developed campsites adjacent to the road. In the national park, camping is allowed only in designated campsites; no dispersed camping is allowed. Each campsite is equipped with a cast-iron bear-

Idaho Border to Moran Junction

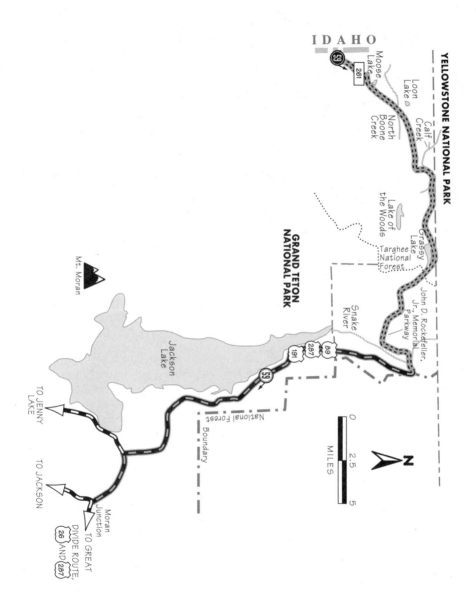

The author takes a photo break at the entrance to Grand Teton National Park while riding the Wyoming segment of the Great Divide Mountain Bike Route.

proof box to store food and other belongings. Eat and prepare food well away from your tent and store all food and equipment in the box. Pepper spray is recommended to deter an attacking bear. Carry a canister when you camp and as you pedal through the park.

The dirt Grassy Lake Road connects with the paved Rockefeller Parkway as it passes by the lodge and restaurant at Flagg Ranch. The remainder of this segment is on pavement as it passes before Jackson Lake and the Teton Mountains before reaching Moran Junction. Moran Junction is little more than a post office and has no overnight lodging or other services.

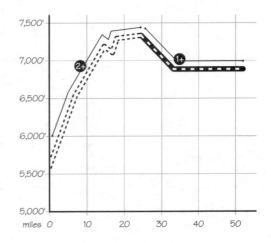

THE RIDE

0.0 From Idaho border, go east on Forest Road 261 toward Grassy Lake.

7.2 Cross Boone Creek.

15.1 Pass by Grassy Lake. Dispersed camping is available around the lake with bear-proof storage boxes provided.

17.2 Enter John D. Rockefeller, Jr., Memorial Parkway.

18.8 Pass by first of eight individual campsites. Each campsite includes an outhouse, picnic table, and bear-proof storage box. The sites are free of charge (at least at the time of this writing) but it is difficult to predict their availability.

24.9 Pass by the last campsite.

25.2 Pavement begins.

26.3 Pass by Flagg Ranch. Lodging and restaurant available. After ranch, turn right on US89-191-287.

27.0 Cross the Snake River.

34.7 Begin long passing of Jackson Lake.

46.6 Pass by Jackson Lake Lodge. Lodging and restaurant available.

47.7 At intersection. Continue straight.

51.5 Grand Teton National Park Station.

51.7 At Moran Junction. To continue Great Divide Bike Route, turn left on US26-287-191.

Moran Junction to Union Pass Road

Location:	Northwest Wyoming, between Moran Junction and Dubois.
Distance:	51.4 miles one way.
Time:	One day.
Elevation gain:	3,100 feet.
Tread:	This ride follows pavement for all but the 8 miles leading from Turpin Meadows Resort to Cowboy Village Resort. In that segment, for 4 miles the route follows a gravel road and for 4 miles it follows a doubletrack road.
Season:	This route is rideable in late spring through the fall but is best from July through mid-September.
Aerobic level:	Moderate.
Technical difficulty:	The paved roads have a technical rating of 1+. The gravel road has a technical rating of 2 and the doubletrack has a rating of 3.
Hazards:	The doubletrack has ruts and potholes. Watch for traffic on the shoulderless paved road through the Buffalo Valley.
Land status:	U.S. highway right-of-way, U.S. Forest Service, Shoshone National Forest.
Maps:	USGS Moran, Davis Hill, Rosies Ridge, Angle Mountain, Togwotee Pass, Lava Mountain, Kisinger Lakes, Esmond Park, Warm Spring Mountain. The route is also on the Jackson Lake and Ramshorn BLM land status maps and the Bridger-Teton National Forest travel map.
Access:	From Jackson, go north on U.S. Highway 26-89-191 to Moran Junction, where the route begins.

HIGHLIGHTS

At Moran Junction, the Great Divide Mountain Bike Route goes east on US26-287 toward Dubois. After just a few miles the route leaves the highway and goes into the Buffalo Valley. This paved road has no shoulder but the traffic is light. It is a lovely valley and the road climbs gradually, offering plenty of sightseeing opportunities.

Moran Junction to Union Pass Road

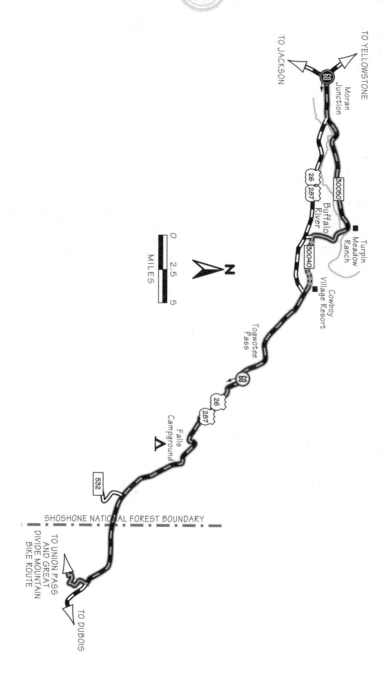

TO YELLOWSTONE

TO JACKSON

Moran Junction

26 287

30050

Buffalo River

Turpin Meadow Ranch

30040

Cowboy Village Resort

Togwotee Pass

26 287

Falls Campground

532

SHOSHONE NATIONAL FOREST BOUNDARY

TO UNION PASS AND GREAT DIVIDE MOUNTAIN BIKE ROUTE

TO DUBOIS

0 2.5 5

MILES

N

The Palisades rise above Togwotee Pass on the Great Divide Mountain Bike Route.

At the east end of the valley, the route passes by a dude ranch and then heads uphill on a doubletrack road. Camping opportunities are available along the doubletrack road with dispersed camping sites. Be wary, though, and give special consideration to food preparation and storage because this is still bear country.

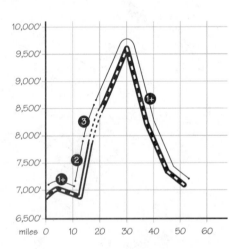

The route passes by Cowboy Village Resort before rejoining US26-287 and continuing up toward Togwotee Pass. The route drops down toward Dubois, but 9 miles before reaching town, it turns south onto the Union Pass Road.

THE RIDE

0.0   At Moran Junction, turn east on US26-287.
2.1   Leave Grand Teton National Park.
3.6   At intersection turn left onto paved Forest Road 30050 (Buffalo Valley Road).
4.9   Pass by Buffalo Valley Café.

13.2 Cross the Buffalo River where pavement ends. Road goes in front of the Turpin Meadow Ranch. This is a dude ranch and generally provides lodging for extended stays, not overnight stays. After the ranch, the road is good gravel. Begin tough uphill.

17.3 Turn left onto doubletrack FR 30040.

18.0 At fork in road, go right.

20.5 Pass by beaver ponds. US26-287 can be seen on the other side.

20.7 Go through gate.

21.2 Pass onto and through Cowboy Village Resort with lodging, restaurant, and a convenience store. Just past resort, turn left onto US26-287.

30.4 At Togwotee Pass (pronounced toag-a-tee), elevation 9,658 feet. Start downhill.

37.5 Pass by Falls Campground.

37.9 Pass by Brooks Lake Recreation Area on left side of highway. Camping is available in the recreation area.

42.8 Pass Tie Hack Historical Monument.

45.8 Leave Shoshone National Forest.

51.4 Just past a convenience store, the Union Pass Road forks off to the south. The Great Divide Bicycle Route turns here. The town of Dubois is 9 miles farther down the highway.

Union Pass Road to Pinedale

Location:	Northwest Wyoming, between Dubois and Pinedale.
Distance:	81.2 miles one way.
Time:	One and one-half to two days.
Elevation gain:	2,550 feet.
Tread:	This route follows a gravel road for 48 miles. When it leaves national forest lands, the route is paved all the way to Pinedale except for 4.2 miles of gravel along a county road.
Season:	This route is rideable in late spring through the fall but is best from July through mid-September.
Aerobic level:	Strenuous, and actually "killer" would be more appropriate on Union Pass.
Technical difficulty:	The gravel road has a technical rating of 3 due to coarse gravel that seems more like rocks and boulders than gravel. There are also rocky segments, and dense gravel. The paved road has a technical rating of 1.
Hazards:	The gravel road has ruts and washboarded areas. The quality of the road varies: some segments have rocks instead of gravel, some areas have pockets of dense gravel, and some are obnoxiously rough. If the road has been recently graded, it becomes especially difficult to pedal. Also, heavy rains can soften the road surface, making it somewhat treacherous, causing a bike to fishtail.
Land status:	Public access roads, U.S. Forest Service, Shoshone National Forest and Bridger-Teton National Forest, county roads, and U.S. highways.
Maps:	Warm Spring Mountain, Fish Creek Park, Klondike Hill, Dodge Butte, Kendall Mountain, Warren Bridge, Cora, and Pinedale Quads. The route is on BLM 1:100,000 scale Ramshorn, Gannet Peak, and Pinedale maps. The Forest Service has good travel maps of the route, too.
Access:	Begin this route 9 miles west of Dubois on U.S. Highway 26-287.

Union Pass Road to Pinedale

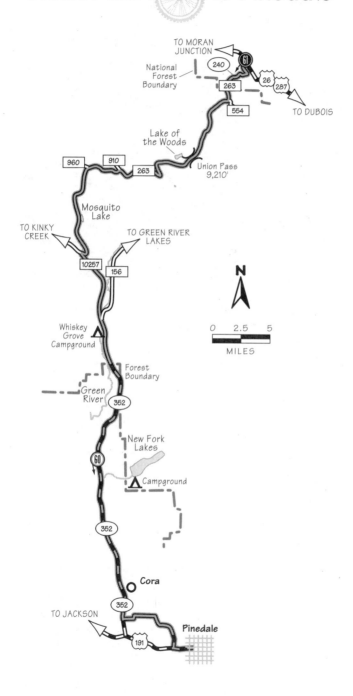

TO MORAN JUNCTION

240

61

National Forest Boundary

263

26

287

554

TO DUBOIS

Lake of the Woods

960

910

263

Union Pass 9,210'

Mosquito Lake

TO KINKY CREEK

TO GREEN RIVER LAKES

10257

156

N

0   2.5   5
MILES

Whiskey Grove Campground

Forest Boundary

Green River

352

New Fork Lakes

60

Campground

352

Cora

352

TO JACKSON

Pinedale

191

The author takes a photo break at the summit of Union Pass as the Great Divide Mountain Bike Route crosses over the Wind River Mountains.

Highlights

This segment of the Great Divide Mountain Bike Route begins on a wide gravel road as it rises toward Union Pass. The road passes through a housing development, with the fancy houses perched on the steep hillside having panoramic views of the distant Pinnacle Buttes.

    The steep road, combined with the depth of the gravel and the added weight of a loaded bike, makes it difficult to get enough traction to make hasty headway up the mountain. Bike hiking may be the only solution at times. But the

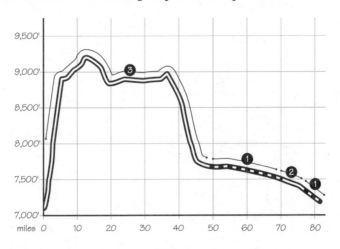

steep switchbacks are eventually left behind, giving way to rolling grasslands and pine forests crossing Union Pass. Dispersed camping sites can be found at Lake of the Woods, along Fish Creek, and adjacent to Mosquito Lake. The route continues on a gravel road off the mountain, dropping into the spectacular Green River Valley. Whiskey Grove Campground is the last public camping area on national forest lands on this ride. Once the road leaves the national forest, it is bordered by private land for the remaining 33 miles to Pinedale.

THE RIDE

0.0 From US26-287, turn south on the Union Pass Road (County Road 240 that becomes Forest Road 263).

0.6 Cross cattleguard and begin steep uphill climb.

4.3 Grade eases.

4.8 Pass by a restaurant and lodge (currently called Lake's Lodge) that has camping and showers, in addition to food and lodging.

5.4 At fork, go straight on FR 263.

6.5 At intersection stay straight. FR 554 is left.

10.3 Cross cattleguard and route levels out.

14.1 Cross a creek.

14.2 Cross Union Pass. Elevation 9,210 feet.

14.5 Road forks; stay straight. Right goes to Lake of the Woods, with some nice dispersed camping sites.

15.7 Pass by a spring next to the road. There is a pipe that allows the water to flow and is especially good for filling water bottles.

20.7 Cross South Fork of Fish Creek. Road forks right after the creek. Go right. Left goes to Forest Service Guard Station.

22.2 Cross Strawberry Creek.

27.7 At fork, stay straight. Right goes to Park Creek Meadows.

31.0 Cross cattleguard.

32.9 Pass by Mosquito Lake. Dispersed camping is available near the lake.

37.1 Road forks. Go left on FR 10257. Right goes to Kinky Creek.

38.0 Cross cattleguard.

39.1 Road forks. Stay left on FR 10015.

39.7 Cross cattleguard.

41.6 Come to "T" intersection. Go right on FR 10156. Road improves.

45.0 Cross the Green River. Immediately after, road forks. Go right. Left goes to Green River Lakes.

45.6 Pass by entrance to Whiskey Grove Campground.

48.0 Exit national forest lands and pass Forest Service Guard Station. Road becomes paved.

69.4 Pass by Cora. The post office is up the road.

72.2 Turn left onto gravel CR 23-144.

76.4 Pavement begins.

79.2 Turn left onto US191.

81.2 Enter Pinedale.

Pinedale to Atlantic City

Location:	West central Wyoming, between Pinedale and Atlantic City.
Distance:	87.7 miles one way.
Time:	One and one-half to two and one-half days.
Elevation gain:	2,670 feet.
Tread:	This route follows doubletrack roads between Pinedale and Boulder (or, if you prefer, just take the paved highway between the two towns). At Boulder, it follows a paved county road that eventually turns to gravel. After the Big Sandy entrance road forks off, the road deteriorates but is still a wide dirt/gravel road until it follows a paved state highway. The final 10 miles to South Pass City and Atlantic City are on wide gravel roads.
Season:	This route is open in late spring through the fall but it is best from July through mid-September.
Aerobic level:	Moderate.
Technical difficulty:	The doubletrack roads have a technical rating of 3 due to rocky and steep segments. The paved road has a rating of 1, while the gravel road has a technical rating of 2 as long as the road has not been recently graded. If the road has been recently graded, the technical rating can go as high as 4.
Hazards:	The doubletrack has ruts and rocky segments. The gravel road has ruts and washboarded areas. If the road has been recently graded, it becomes especially difficult to pedal. Also, heavy rains can soften the road surface, making it somewhat treacherous and causing a bike to fishtail. After passing the Big Sandy opening route, the road deteriorates and becomes more washboarded.
Land status:	Public access roads, county road, and state highways, Bureau of Land Management.
Maps:	USGS Pinedale, Boulder Lake, Boulder, Fremont Butte, Pocket Creek Lake, Leckie SW, Leckie, Jensen Meadows, Prospect Mountains, Halls Meadow Spring, Anderson Ridge, South Pass City, Atlantic City. 1:100,000 scale BLM maps: Pinedale, Farson, South Pass.

Pinedale to Atlantic City

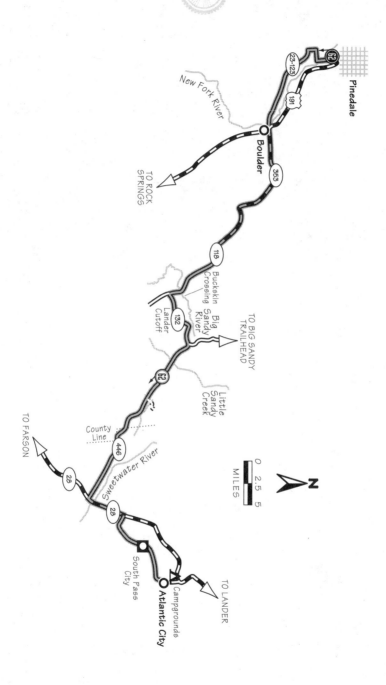

The Great Divide Mountain Bike Route drops into South Pass City, where cyclists can take a break and wander through the restored mining town.

Access: Begin this route in the town of Pinedale. In town, take U.S. Highway 191 over Pine Creek. Turn right onto Tyler Street; this turns into County Road 23-123. On the edge of town, the road turns to gravel.

HIGHLIGHTS

A paved 12-mile road connects Pinedale to Boulder, but the Great Divide Mountain Bike Route follows a more interesting 17-mile route. This route meanders across sagebrush prairie, between mesas, and along the New Fork River. This area may undergo a significant change in the future if plans materialize for an oil and gas development. New roads have already been constructed since the initial mapping of the Great Divide Route.

After passing through Boulder, which consists of a motel and a gas station/convenience store, the route follows a paved county road for 18 miles until the road turns to good gravel. Some traffic is present because the road leads to the Big Sandy Recreation Area, a popular backpacking trailhead. After Big Sandy, there is very little traffic as the route passes along the foothills of the Wind River Mountains, on the edge of the Red Desert. Water is scarce, as are trees. Four miles before the road intersects with Wyoming 28 a few doubletrack roads branch left. Follow one of these if you're looking for a place to camp. The roads drop down to the Sweetwater River, where trees line the river and make an excellent camping site.

At South Pass City, take the time to walk through the delightfully reconstructed buildings. For a $1 entry fee, you can step back into the mining days of yesteryear.

The last few miles to Atlantic City are tough, with steep up-and-down hills. This Atlantic City lacks casinos and gambling halls; it is a charming little town with a couple of restaurants and a convenience store.

THE RIDE

0.0 From Tyler Street, go south on County Road 23-123.

1.1 Pavement ends and road becomes a good gravel road.

2.2 Cross New Fork River and go straight.

3.2 Go left onto doubletrack road immediately after crossing a cattleguard.

4.3 Come to intersection of five doubletracks. Go straight.

4.6 At ridge top.

4.7 Stay left at fork.

5.1 Come to a main new road leading to a drilling rig. Cross over road and continue on doubletrack on other side.

5.3 Come to fenceline. Go sharp right.

5.9 Road forks away from the fence.

6.8 Road curves left around fenceline corner.

7.1 Road veers to the right. A faint doubletrack continues along fenceline.

8.2 Begin up steep slickrock.

8.5 At top of slickrock.

8.6 Go through gate.

9.5 Road forks. Stay right. Faint doubletrack goes left.

10.9 Stay left as road forks.

12.9 Meet gravel county road. Turn left.

14.1 Cross the New Fork River.

14.3 Turn right on US191.

14.9 At Boulder. Turn left onto paved WY 353.

21.8 Cross Silver Creek. Right after, come to historical marker for Fremont Butte.

33.0 Pavement ends and gravel road begins. Continue on main CR 118.

41.5 Cross the Big Sandy River at the historic Buckskin Crossing.

42.5 Come to a four-way intersection. Go left onto CR 132 (Lander Cutoff-Emigrant Trail to Big Sandy Campground). Straight is CR 23-118.

47.1 Continue right on main road toward Big Sandy Recreation Area.

49.6 Come to "T" intersection. Go right toward Sweetwater Guard Station. Left goes to Big Sandy Campground.

52.9 Cross Little Sandy Creek and Continental Divide. This would be a nice camping site.

57.5 Road forks. Continue straight. Left goes to Sweetwater Gap Ranch and Sweetwater Guard Station and Campground.

61.9 Cross county line.

68.4 Watch for various doubletracks going left as potential routes to drop down to the Sweetwater River if you are looking for a campsite.

72.4 Come to WY 28. Turn left.

73.2 Cross the Sweetwater River and, right after, pass by rest area.

76.6 Pass by Oregon Trail-Lander Cutoff-South Pass historical marker.

77.8 Turn right onto gravel road (no signs).

79.2 Continue left on main road.

80.0 Cross Pine Creek.

83.3 Drop into South Pass City with an historical site that is open from May 15 through September 30. Continue through town on main gravel road.

83.8 Road forks. Stay right.

85.8 At four-way intersection, continue straight.

86.2 At stop sign, turn right.

87.7 Enter Atlantic City.

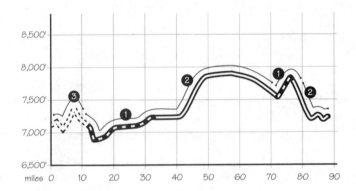

63

Atlantic City to Rawlins

Location:	Central Wyoming, between Atlantic City and Rawlins.
Distance:	131.9 miles one way.
Time:	One and one-half to two and one-half days.
Elevation gain:	2,230 feet.
Tread:	This route follows doubletrack roads out of Atlantic City for 92 miles. The final 40 miles are on pavement.
Season:	This route is rideable in late spring through the fall. Avoid it, if possible, after heavy rains.
Aerobic level:	Moderate.
Technical difficulty:	The doubletracks have a technical rating of 3 due to scattered rocky segments and numerous sand traps. The final 40 miles of pavement have a rating of 1.
Hazards:	The doubletracks have ruts and rocky segments, but the greatest hazards are the sand pockets and washboarding that seem to pop up without warning. The 26 miles of pavement on county road have some deep potholes. Watch for heavy traffic when joining U.S. Highway 287.
Land status:	Public access roads, county road, and U.S. highways, Bureau of Land Management lands across the basin.
Maps:	USGS Atlantic City, Radium Springs, Circle Bar Lake, Picket Lake, Sulphur Bar Spring, Olson Springs, Lost Creek Reservoir, Brenton Springs, Antelope Reservoir, Battle Spring, Sooner Reservoir, Hansen Lake, Hansen Lake NE, Larsen Knoll, Buck Draw, Separation Rim, Shamrock Hills, Rendle Hill, Rawlins Peak, Rawlins. 1:100,000 scale BLM maps: South Pass, Bairoil, Rawlins.
Access:	Begin this route in the town of Atlantic City, 2 miles east of Wyoming 28. In Atlantic City, exit on main road going south out of town. Go south on BLM Road 512, leading to Willie's HandCart.

HIGHLIGHTS

When the Continental Divide emerges from the Wind River Mountains, it splits in two and forms the Great Divide Basin. Rainwater falling in the

Atlantic City to Rawlins

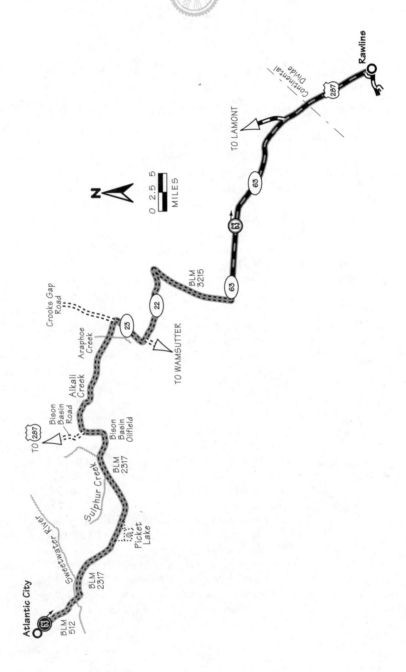

Rawlins

Continental Divide

287

TO LAMONT

63

63

N

0 2.5 5
MILES

63

63

BLM
3215

Crooks Gap
Road

22

23

Araphoe
Creek

TO WAMSUTTER

Alkali
Creek

Bison
Basin
Road

TO 287

Bison
Basin
Oilfield

BLM
2317

Sulphur Creek

Picket
Lake

Sweetwater River

BLM
2317

Atlantic City

63

BLM
512

The Great Divide Mountain Bike Route crosses the vast Great Divide Basin with seemingly endless miles of sagebrush prairie.

basin reaches neither ocean but either sits in one of the few playa lakes or evaporates in the heat of the day.

The critical factor in crossing the 130 miles of the basin is carrying enough water. It is best to load up in Atlantic City and be sure to bring along a water purifier in case you need to get water from one of those playa lakes. When you cross over the Sweetwater River, fill any empty water bottles; the next reliable water source is on the other side of the basin at A&M Reservoir.

If you like vast open spaces, you are in for a treat as you cross the basin. It is huge. Few people venture through the area, but you won't be alone: prong-horn, wild horses, coyotes, and prairie dogs will be your companions. The weather can be a critical factor on this segment; winds whip across the unbroken terrain. Wind direction is somewhat unpredictable. This high-elevation desert can also have surprisingly chilly temperatures and sudden rainstorms can turn the roads into tire-grabbing muck. On the other hand, it is possible to have sunny, warm, and dry days—with a tail wind. Just be prepared.

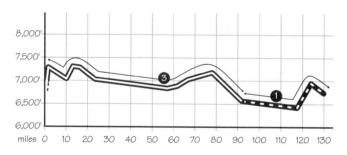

THE RIDE

0.0 Go south on BLM Road 512. Begin steep climb out of the town.

0.7 At top of hill. Note "Goat Crossing" sign.

0.9 Road curves left.

3.9 Road forks. Continue straight toward Sweetwater River (6 miles away).

6.9 Concrete post marks junction of Oregon Trail and Pony Express Trail.

10.3 Cross the Sweetwater River. This would be a good camping area.

12.5 Cross cattleguard.

12.7 Road forks. Stay on main road, called the California Trail-Seminoe Cutoff.

15.9 Road forks. Go left on BLM Road 2317. The California Trail-Seminoe Cutoff goes left. A number of faint doubletracks fork from, and cross, the main BLM road. Continue on main road at each of these.

23.4 Road forks. Continue straight. Right goes to Picket Lake, a playa lake that can be used as a water source (2 miles away).

38.8 Good road joins the route. Continue on main road as it veers left.

40.4 Road forks. Curve left on BLM Road 2317. BLM Road 3221 goes right.

43.0 Road intersection. Go right onto less-developed road. Left is the Bison Basin Road; Sweetwater Station on US287, is 18 miles north.

50.9 Road intersection. Stay straight on main road.

57.6 Cross Arapahoe Creek. Warning! It may not have any water.

58.4 Another road joins in from behind. Stay straight. Road improves.

60.6 Pass under powerline.

61.6 Follow Crooks Gap Road as it curves right.

65.2 Enter Sweetwater County. Road becomes County Road 23.

67.9 Road forks. Turn left onto CR 22 to Bairoil.

78.9 Road forks. Turn right onto Sooner Road (BLM Road 3215). A&M Reservoir, 1 mile straight ahead, is a good emergency water source.

92.6 Come to intersection with paved CR 63. Turn left.

118.4 Come to intersection. Go right on US287 and start up the hill.

124.4 Cross Continental Divide as route levels off.

131.9 Enter Rawlins.

Rawlins to the Colorado Border

Location:	South-central Wyoming, between Rawlins and the Wyoming-Colorado border at Slater, Colorado.
Distance:	71.1 miles one way.
Time:	One and one-half to two days.
Elevation gain:	3,200 feet.
Tread:	This route follows a paved road as it leaves Rawlins. After 23 miles, the pavement ends and becomes a wide gravel road. It narrows and becomes less developed when it enters Medicine Bow National Forest. It joins the paved Wyoming 70 for the final 16 miles to the Colorado border.
Season:	This route is best in late spring through the fall.
Aerobic level:	Moderate.
Technical difficulty:	The gravel roads have a technical rating of 2+ due to scattered rocky and rutted segments. The final 16 miles of pavement have a rating of 1.
Hazards:	The gravel roads have ruts and rocky segments with some pockets of dense gravel and washboarding. Watch for traffic all along the route.
Land status:	Public access county roads, state highways, U.S. Forest Service, Medicine Bow National Forest.
Maps:	USGS Rawlins, Coal Mine Ridge, LA Marsh Creek West, LA Marsh Creek East, Middlewood Hill, Divide Peak, Tullis, Singer Peak, Cottonwood Rim, Grieve Reservoir, Savery. Use the 1:100,000 scale BLM maps: Rawlins and Baggs.
Access:	Begin this route on the southwest edge of the town of Rawlins at the start of paved WY 71.

HIGHLIGHTS

The Great Divide Mountain Bike Route continues from Rawlins, south across the high prairie. The terrain rolls past sagebrush-covered mesas with aspen-filled drainages. Elk and mule deer reside year-round in this mosaic of habitats, while pronghorn occupy the open sagebrush prairie.

The route makes its seventh Wyoming crossing of the Continental Divide as it passes over Middlewood Hill. Fifteen miles farther along the road narrows as it crosses into the Sierra Madre Mountains and the Medicine Bow

Rawlins to the Colorado Border

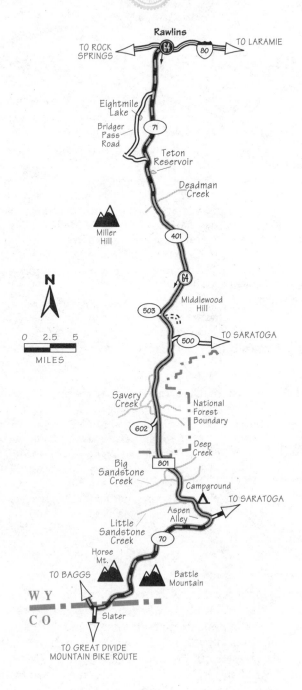

Rawlins

TO ROCK SPRINGS

TO LARAMIE

Eightmile Lake

Bridger Pass Road

Teton Reservoir

Deadman Creek

Miller Hill

Middlewood Hill

TO SARATOGA

N

0   2.5   5
MILES

Savery Creek

National Forest Boundary

Deep Creek

Big Sandstone Creek

Campground

TO SARATOGA

Little Sandstone Creek

Aspen Alley

Horse Mt.

Battle Mountain

TO BAGGS

WY
CO

Slater

TO GREAT DIVIDE MOUNTAIN BIKE ROUTE

The Great Divide Mountain Bike Route passes along Aspen Alley while going through the Sierra Madre Mountains.

National Forest. These mountains are not heavily used by recreationists except during the hunting season. Logging is a prime use of the forest; many clearcut areas can be inspected as you pass through the timbered habitats.

One mile before the intersection with WY 70, the road narrows as it passes "Aspen Alley," a delightful and unexpected mile where the road tunnels through dense aspen. At the intersection, the gravel road meets the newly paved WY 70 to provide an exhilarating dash down the mountain to the end of the Wyoming segment of the Great Divide Mountain Bike Route as it crosses over the Colorado border.

THE RIDE

0.0 Go south on WY 71.

0.7 Pass under Interstate 80.

12.8 At intersection, go straight. Bridger Pass Road (County Road 3301) goes right.

23.2 Road forks. Continue straight. Left goes to Teton Reservoir. Dispersed camping sites are available at the reservoir (but no trees!).

24.1 Pavement ends.

29.5 CR 503 forks to the right. Stay on WY 71.

29.7 Cross the Continental Divide at the top of Middlewood Hill. BLM Road 3422 forks to the left. Stay straight.

32.4 CR 500 to Saratoga forks left. This is a good optional ride as it rolls along the foothills of the Sierra Madre Mountains to Saratoga.

40.4 Cross over creek.

40.8 CR 602 forks to the right. Stay straight.

44.6 Enter Medicine Bow National Forest. The road narrows and becomes rougher.

46.6 Cross over creek.

48.3 Steep down-and-up to cross over Big Sandstone Creek.

51.9 Another steep down-and-up to cross over Little Sandstone Creek.

52.2 Pass by an older, more primitive campground site to the left.

53.6 Road narrows at entrance to Aspen Alley.

54.7 Come to "T" intersection. Go right on paved WY 70.

71.1 Enter Colorado near small settlement of Slater, Colorado. This is the end of the Wyoming section of the Great Divide Mountain Bike Route.

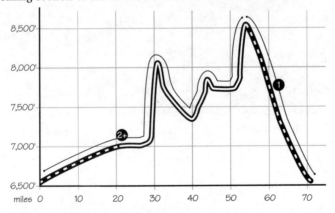

Appendix A: Resources

Bureau of Land Management Offices

Bighorn Basin Resource Area, 101 South 23rd, P.O. Box 119, Worland, WY 82401-0119; (307) 347-5100.

Buffalo Resource Area, 1425 Fort Street, Buffalo, WY 82834-2436; (307) 684-1100.

Casper District Office, 1701 East E Street, Casper, WY 82601-2167; (307) 261-7600.

Cody Resource Area, 1002 Blackburn, P.O. Box 518, Cody, WY 82414-0518; (307) 587-2216.

Great Divide Resource Area, 1300 North 3rd, Rawlins, WY 82301-4376; (307) 328-4200

Green River Resource Area, 280 Highway 191 North, Rock Springs, WY 82901-3448; (307) 352-0256.

Kemmerer Resource Area, 312 Highway 189 N., Kemmerer, WY 83101-9710; (307) 877-3933.

Lander Resource Area, 1335 Main, P.O. Box 589, Lander, WY 82520-0589; (307) 332-8400.

Newcastle Resource Area, 1101 Washington Boulevard, Newcastle, WY 82701-2972; (307) 746-4453.

Pinedale Resource Area, 432 East Mill Street, P.O. Box 768, Pinedale, WY 82941-0768, (307) 367-4358.

Platte River Resource Area, 815 Connie Street, P.O. Drawer 2420, Mills, WY 82644-2420; (307) 261-7500.

Rawlins District Office, 1300 North Third, Rawlins, WY 82301-4376; (307) 328-4200.

Rock Springs District Office, 280 Highway 191 North, Rock Springs, WY 82901-3448; (307) 352-0256

Worland District Office, 101 South 23rd, P.O. Box 119, Worland, WY 82401-0119; (307) 347-5100.

Wyoming State Office, P.O. Box 1828, Cheyenne, WY 82003-1828; 5353 Yellowstone Road, Cheyenne, WY 82009-4137; (307) 775-6256.

National Forest Service Offices

Big Piney Ranger District, Highway 189, P.O. Box 218, Big Piney, WY 83113; (307) 276-3375.

Bighorn National Forest, 1969 South Sheridan Avenue, Sheridan, WY 82801; (307) 672-0751.

Black Hills National Forest Headquarters, RR 2, Box 200, Custer, SD 57730; (605) 673-2251.

Bridger-Teton National Forest, P.O. Box 1888, Jackson, WY 83001; (307) 739-5500.

Brush Creek/Hayden Ranger District, South Highway 130/230, P.O. Box 249, Saratoga, WY 82331; (307) 326-5258.

Buffalo Ranger District, P.O. Box 278, Moran, WY 83013; (307) 543-2386.

Buffalo Ranger District, 1425 Fort Street, Buffalo, WY 82834; (307) 684-1100.

Clarks Fork Ranger District, 1002 Road 11, Powell, WY 82435; (307) 754-7207.

District Ranger Stations, Bearlodge Ranger District, P.O. Box 680, Sundance, WY 82729; (307) 283-1361.

Douglas Ranger District, 2250 East Richards, Douglas, WY 82633; (307) 358-4690.

Greybull Ranger District, 2044 State, P.O. Box 158, Meeteetse, WY 82433; (307) 868-2536.

Greys River Ranger District, 125 Washington, P.O. Box 338, Afton, WY 83110; (307) 886-3166.

Jackson Ranger District, P.O. Box 1689, Jackson, WY 83001; (307) 739-5400.

Kemmerer Ranger District, Highway 189, P.O. Box 31, Kemmerer, WY 83101; (307) 877-4415.

Medicine Bow National Forest, 2468 Jackson Street, Laramie, WY 82070; (307) 745-2300.

Pinedale Ranger District, P.O. Box 220, Pinedale, WY 82941; (307) 367-4326.

Shoshone National Forest, 808 Meadow Lane, Cody, WY 82414; (307)527-6241, TDD: (307)578-1294.

Tongue Ranger District, 1969 South Sheridan Avenue, Sheridan, WY 82801; (307) 672-0751.

Wapiti Ranger District, 203A Yellowstone Avenue, Cody, WY 82414; (307) 527-6921.

Washakie Ranger District, 333 Highway 789, South Lander, WY 82520; (307) 332-5460.

Wind River Ranger District, 1403 West Ramshorn, P.O. Box 186, Dubois, WY 82513; (307) 455-2466.

National Park Service

Grand Teton National Park, P.O. Drawer 170, Moose, WY 83012; (307) 739-3300, (307) 739-3399 Visitor Information.

Yellowstone National Park, P.O. Box 168, Yellowstone National Park, WY 82190; (307) 344-7381, TDD (307) 344-2386. Old Faithful Visitor Center; (307) 545-2750. Yellowstone National Park Lodges; (307) 344-7311.

Appendix B: Wyoming Bicycle Shops

All Terrain Sports, 412 Grand Avenue, Laramie, WY 82070; (307) 721-8036.

Back Country Bicycles, 334 North Main, Sheridan, WY 82801; (307) 672-2453.

BackCountry Mountain Works, LC, 4120 South Poplar, Sunrise Center, Casper, WY 82601; (307) 234-5330.

The Bicycle Shop, 1211 South Douglas Highway, Gillette, WY 82716.

Bicycle Station, 2634 Dell Range, Cheyenne, WY 82001; (307) 634-4268.

Bob's Bike Corral, P.O. Box 673, Dubois, WY 82513.

Coast-to-Coast Store, 777 West Pine, Pinedale, WY 82941; (307) 367-2116.

Dr. Spokes Cyclery, 240 South Center, Casper, WY 82601; (307) 265-7740.

Fine Edge, 1660-E North 4th, Laramie, WY 82072; (307) 745-4499.

Freewheel Ski and Cycle, 160 South 4th Street, Lander, WY 82520; (307) 332-6616.

High Desert Cyclery, 520 Wilkes Number 1, Green River, WY 82935.

Highland Cycles, 513 West Cedar Street, Rawlins, WY 82301.

Hoback Sports, Inc., 40 South Millward, Jackson, WY 83001.

Hot Steel, 624 West Cheyenne Drive, Evanston, WY 82930.

King's Cyclery, 1123 South Beverly, Casper, WY 82601; (307) 237-8602.

Larsen's Bicycles, 255 East Second Street, Powell, WY 82435; (307) 745-5481.

Larsen's Bicycles, 610 South 12th, Worland, WY 82401.

Mike's Bikes, 1937 Yucca Court, Douglas, WY 82633.

Mountain Sports, Center and 6th Street, Casper, WY 82601; (307) 266-1136.

Murray's, 1602 East Marray Street, Rawlins, WY 82301; (307) 324-4767.

Old Faithful Bicycles, 1362 Sheridan Avenue, Cody, WY 82414.

Out Sportin', 310 East Main, Riverton, WY 82501.

The Pedal Grinder, 513 Broadway, Thermopolis, WY 82443.

Pedal House, 207 South 1st, Laramie, WY 82070; (307) 742-5533.

Spoke and Edge Sports, 900 Camel Drive, Gillette, WY 82716.

The Sport Stop and Bike Shop, 208 North Main, 198 North Main, Sheridan, WY 82801; (307) 672-5356.

The Sports Lure, 66 South Main, Buffalo, WY 82834; (800) 684-7682.

Sports Tech, 303 Elk Street, Rock Springs, WY 82902.

Teton Cyclery, 175 North Glenwood, Jackson, WY 83001.

Well Spoken Bike Shop, 218 N. 1st, Saratoga, WY 82331; (307) 326-8038.

Appendix C: Index of Rides

Glossary of Mountain Biking Terms

ATB: All-terrain bicycle; a.k.a. mountain bike.

ATV: All-terrain vehicle; in this book ATV refers to motorbikes along with three- and four-wheelers designed for off-road use.

Bail: Getting off the bike, usually in a hurry, and whether or not you mean to. Often a last resort.

Bar ends: Extensions added to the ends of the handlebars, shaped similar to bull horns, that are especially helpful during uphill climbs.

Bike hike: Walking the bike. Usually done when the trail gets too rough and rocky or the slope too steep.

Blaze: Mark on a tree, usually a dot-dash pattern, marking a trail.

Bunny hop: Leaping up, while riding, and lifting both wheels off the ground to jump over an obstacle (or just for the fun of it).

Cairn: Pile of rocks used to mark a trail, especially when it crosses open terrain.

Clean: To ride without touching a foot, or other body part, to the ground; to ride a tough section successfully.

Clipless: A type of pedal with a binding that accepts a special cleat on the soles of bike shoes. The cleat clicks in for more control and efficient pedaling and pops out for a quick release.

Contour: A line on a topographic map showing a continuous elevation level over uneven ground. Also used as a verb to indicate a fairly easy or moderate grade: "The trail contours around the canyon rim before the final grunt to the top."

Dab: To put a foot or hand down (or hold onto or lean on a tree or other support) while riding. If you have to dab, then you haven't ridden that piece of trail clean.

Derailleur: Bicycle parts that move the chain from one chainring to another. There is a front derailleur at the crank and a rear derailleur near the back axle.

Dot-dash: Typical blaze marking on a tree to indicate a trail's path. The two marks are placed vertically with a circular dot placed above a rectangular dash.

Downfall: Trees that have fallen on the ground.

Doubletrack: A trail, jeep road, ATV route, or other track with two distinct ribbons of tread, typically with grass growing in between. Also known as two-track. No matter which side you ride on, the other side looks smoother.

Endo: Lifting the rear wheel off the ground and riding (or abruptly not riding) on the front wheel only. Also known, at various degrees of control and finality, as a nose wheelie, "going over the handlebars," and a face plant.

Fall line: The angle and direction of a slope. If a ball were placed on the hill, the fall line is the direction the ball would go as it rolled to the bottom.

Fishtail: When the back end of the bike sways from side to side, typically when going through deep sand.

Gnarly: A term describing a difficult and technical trail.

Graded: When a gravel road is scraped level to smooth out the washboards and potholes, it has been graded. A newly graded road can be especially difficult on a mountain bike due to the lack of a solid, hard surface.

Granny gear: The lowest (easiest) gear; a combination of the smallest of the three chainrings on the bottom bracket spindle (spindle is where the pedals and crank arms attach to the bike's frame), and the largest cog on the rear cluster. The granny gear is used for serious climbing.

Hammer: To ride hard; derived from how it feels afterward: "I'm hammered."

Hammerhead: Someone who actually enjoys feeling hammered. Usually a Type-A personality rider who goes hard and fast all the time.

Hardtail: Refers to a bike that has front suspension only but no rear suspension.

Line: The route (or trajectory) between or over obstacles or through turns. Tread or trail refers to the ground you're riding on; the line is the path you choose within the tread (and exists mostly in the eye of the beholder).

Off-the-seat: Moving your seat behind the bike saddle and over the rear tire: used for control on extremely steep descents. This position increases braking power, helps prevent endos, and reduces skidding.

Out-and-back: Ride that returns on the same trail as first half of the ride.

Panniers: Special bike packs attached to the bike for carrying equipment and supplies. Panniers can be attached at both the front and rear tires.

Portage: To carry the bike, usually up a steep hill, across unrideable obstacles, or through a stream.

Quads: Thigh muscles (short for quadriceps); also refers to U.S. Geological Survey topographic maps (short for quadrangles). Good quads—both legs and maps—can help get you out of trouble in the backcountry.

Ratcheting: Also known as backpedaling; pedaling backward to avoid hitting rocks or logs with the pedals.

Sidehill: Where the trail crosses a slope. If the tread is narrow, keep your inside (uphill) pedal up to avoid hitting the ground. If the tread tilts downhill, you may have to use some body language to keep the bike straight or vertical to avoid slipping out.

Singletrack: A trail, game run, cow path, or other track with only one ribbon of tread. Width can vary from as wide as 4 feet to as narrow as 6 inches.

Stile: A series of steps over a fence or wall. Usually these are wooden steps, often constructed on national forest lands when a trail crosses a fence without a gate.

Spur: A side road or trail that splits off from the main route.

Surfing: Riding through loose gravel or sand, when the wheels sway from side to side.

Suspension: A bike with front suspension has a shock absorbing fork or stem. Rear suspension absorbs shock between the rear wheel and frame. A bike with both is said to be fully suspended.

Switchbacks: When a trail goes up a steep slope, it zigzags or switchbacks across the fall line to ease the gradient of the climb. It is important not to take shortcuts down a slope, rather than following the switchback. The shortcuts only increase erosion problems.

Toe clips: Attachment to the pedal where the toe of the shoe is held in place on the pedal. Most toe clips have a strap that can be tightened around the shoe to increase attachment of the shoe to the pedal. Toe clips increase pedaling efficiency, allowing continued force even during the upstroke.

Track stand: Balancing on a bike in one place, without rolling forward appreciably. To do this maneuver, turn the front wheel to one side and bring that pedal up to the one- or two-o'clock position. Control your side-to-side balance by applying pressure on the pedals and brakes and changing the angle of the front wheel as needed.

Trashed: A trail that has been chopped, pitted, and rutted to the point of being unrideable.

Tread: The riding surfaces; includes singletrack, doubletrack, dirt, gravel, and pavement.

Waterbar: A log, dirt berm, or other barrier placed on the trail or tread to divert water off the road and prevent erosion. Peeled logs can be especially slippery; cross with caution.

Water bladder: Hydration system that uses a flexible plastic bag carried in a special pack on the back. A plastic tube passes over the cyclists' shoulder and is held in place near the shoulder to allow for convenient sipping of water during a ride.

Wilderness area: Land that is federally designated to be set aside and undeveloped. These areas are closed to mountain bike travel.

Wilderness study area: Area currently under review by the federal government as a future wilderness area. These areas are closed to mountain bike travel and should be treated the same as wilderness areas.

Wind chill: A reference to the wind's cooling effect on the skin, which can greatly reduce the perception of the temperature.

About the Author

Amber Travsky is a life-long resident of Wyoming and has spent over two decades exploring the backcountry as a wildlife biologist. Her passion for fitness combines with her love of the outdoors in the sport of mountain biking. She lives in Laramie with her husband and is self-employed as a biologist, fitness specialist, and freelance writer.

FALCONGUIDES® Leading the Way™

FALCONGUIDES® are available for where-to-go hiking, mountain biking, rock climbing, walking, scenic driving, fishing, rockhounding, paddling, birding, wildlife viewing, and camping. We also have FalconGuides on essential outdoor skills and subjects and field identification. The following titles are currently available, but this list grows every year. For a free catalog with a complete list of titles, call FALCON toll-free at 1-800-582-2665.

MOUNTAIN BIKING GUIDES
Mountain Biking Arizona
Mountain Biking Colorado
Mountain Biking Georgia
Mountain Biking New Mexico
Mountain Biking New York
Mountain Biking Northern New England
Mountain Biking Oregon
Mountain Biking South Carolina
Mountain Biking Southern California
Mountain Biking Southern New England
Mountain Biking Utah
Mountain Biking Wisconsin
Mountain Biking Wyoming

LOCAL CYCLING SERIES
Fat Trax Bozeman
Mountain Biking Bend
Mountain Biking Boise
Mountain Biking Chequamegon
Mountain Biking Chico
Mountain Biking Colorado Springs
Mountain Biking Denver/Boulder
Mountain Biking Durango
Mountain Biking Flagstaff and Sedona
Mountain Biking Helena
Mountain Biking Moab
Mountain Biking Utah's St. George/Cedar City Area
Mountain Biking the White Mountains (West)

■ *To order any of these books, check with your local bookseller or call FALCON® at **1-800-582-2665**. Visit us on the world wide web at: www.FalconOutdoors.com*

FALCON®

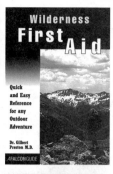

WILDERNESS FIRST AID

By Dr. Gilbert Preston M.D.

Enjoy the outdoors and face the inherent risks with confidence. By reading this easy-to-follow first-aid text, all outdoor enthusiasts can pack a little extra peace of mind on their next adventure. *Wilderness First Aid* offers expert medical advice for dealing with outdoor emergencies beyond the reach of 911. It easily fits in most backcountry first-aid kits.

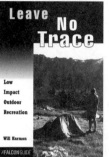

LEAVE NO TRACE

By Will Harmon

The concept of "leave no trace" seems simple, but it actually gets fairly complicated. This handy quick-reference guidebook includes all the newest information on this growing and all-important subject. This book is written to help the outdoor enthusiast make the hundreds of decisions necessary to protect the natural landscape and still have an enjoyable wilderness experience. Part of the proceeds from the sale of this book go to continue leave-no-trace education efforts. The Official Manual of American Hiking Society.

BEAR AWARE

By Bill Schneider

Hiking in bear country can be very safe if hikers follow the guidelines summarized in this small, "packable" book. Extensively reviewed by bear experts, the book contains the latest information on the intriguing science of bear-human interactions. *Bear Aware* can not only make your hike safer, but it can help you avoid the fear of bears that can take the edge off your trip.

MOUNTAIN LION ALERT

By Steve Torres

Recent mountain lion attacks have received national attention. Although infrequent, lion attacks raise concern for public safety. *Mountain Lion Alert* contains helpful advice for mountain bikers, trail runners, horse riders, pet owners, and suburban landowners on how to reduce the chances of mountain lion-human conflicts.

Also Available

Wilderness Survival • Reading Weather • Backpacking Tips • Climbing Safely • Avalanche Aware • Desert Hiking Tips • Hiking with Dogs • Using GPS • Route Finding • Wild Country Companion

To order check with your local bookseller or
call FALCON® at **1-800-582-2665.**
www.FalconOutdoors.com

FALCONGUIDES ® Leading the Way™

WILDLIFE VIEWING GUIDES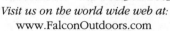

Alaska Wildlife Viewing Guide
Arizona Wildlife Viewing Guide
California Wildlife Viewing Guide
Colorado Wildlife Viewing Guide
Florida Wildlife Viewing Guide
Indiana Wildlife Vewing Guide
Iowa Wildlife Viewing Guide
Kentucky Wildlife Viewing Guide
Massachusetts Wildlife Viewing Guide
Montana Wildlife Viewing Guide
Nebraska Wildlife Viewing Guide
Nevada Wildlife Viewing Guide
New Hampshire Wildlife Viewing Guide
New Jersey Wildlife Viewing Guide
New Mexico Wildlife Viewing Guide
New York Wildlife Viewing Guide
North Carolina Wildlife Viewing Guide
North Dakota Wildlife Viewing Guide
Ohio Wildlife Viewing Guide
Oregon Wildlife Viewing Guide
Puerto Rico and the Virgin Islands WVG
Tennessee Wildlife Viewing Guide
Texas Wildlife Viewing Guide
Utah Wildlife Viewing Guide
Vermont Wildlife Viewing Guide
Virginia Wildlife Viewing Guide
Washington Wildlife Viewing Guide
West Virginia Wildlife Viewing Guide
Wisconsin Wildlife Viewing Guide

HISTORIC TRAIL GUIDES

Traveling California's Gold Rush Country
Traveling the Lewis & Clark Trail
Traveling the Oregon Trail
Traveler's Guide to the Pony Express Trail

SCENIC DRIVING GUIDES

Scenic Driving Alaska and the Yukon
Scenic Driving Arizona
Scenic Driving the Beartooth Highway
Scenic Driving California
Scenic Driving Colorado
Scenic Driving Florida
Scenic Driving Georgia
Scenic Driving Hawaii
Scenic Driving Idaho
Scenic Driving Michigan
Scenic Driving Minnesota
Scenic Driving Montana
Scenic Driving New England
Scenic Driving New Mexico
Scenic Driving North Carolina
Scenic Driving Oregon
Scenic Driving the Ozarks including the
    Ouchita Mountains
Scenic Driving Pennsylvania
Scenic Driving Texas
Scenic Driving Utah
Scenic Driving Washington
Scenic Driving Wisconsin
Scenic Driving Wyoming
Scenic Driving Yellowstone & Grand Teton
    National Parks
Back Country Byways
Scenic Byways East
Scenic Byways Farwest
Scenic Byways Rocky Mountains

■ *To order any of these books, check with your local bookseller
or call FALCON ® at **1-800-582-2665**.
Visit us on the world wide web at:
www.FalconOutdoors.com*

FALCON®

FALCON GUIDES® Leading the Way

FIELD GUIDES
Bitterroot: Montana State Flower
Canyon Country Wildflowers
Central Rocky Mountains
  Wildflowers
Great Lakes Berry Book
New England Berry Book
Ozark Wildflowers
Pacific Northwest Berry Book
Plants of Arizona
Rare Plants of Colorado
Rocky Mountain Berry Book
Scats & Tracks of the Pacific
  Coast States
Scats & Tracks of the
  Rocky Mountains
Southern Rocky Mountain
  Wildflowers
Tallgrass Prairie Wildflowers
Western Trees
Wildflowers of Southwestern
  Utah
Willow Bark and Rosehips

FISHING GUIDES
Fishing Alaska
Fishing the Beartooths
Fishing Florida
Fishing Glacier National Park
Fishing Maine
Fishing Montana
Fishing Wyoming
Fishing Yellowstone
  National Park

ROCKHOUNDING GUIDES
Rockhounding Arizona
Rockhounding California
Rockhounding Colorado
Rockhounding Montana
Rockhounding Nevada
Rockhound's Guide to New
  Mexico
Rockhounding Texas
Rockhounding Utah
Rockhounding Wyoming

MORE GUIDEBOOKS
Backcountry Horseman's
  Guide to Washington
Camping California's
  National Forests
Exploring Canyonlands &
  Arches National Parks
Exploring Hawaii's Parklands
Exploring Mount Helena
Exploring Southern California
  Beaches
Recreation Guide to WA
  National Forests
Touring California & Nevada
  Hot Springs
Touring Colorado Hot Springs
Touring Montana & Wyoming
  Hot Springs
Trail Riding Western
  Montana
Wild Country Companion
Wilderness Directory
Wild Montana
Wild Utah

BIRDING GUIDES
Birding Minnesota
Birding Montana
Birding Northern California
Birding Texas
Birding Utah

PADDLING GUIDES
Floater's Guide to Colorado
Paddling Minnesota
Paddling Montana
Paddling Okefenokee
Paddling Oregon
Paddling Yellowstone & Grand
  Teton National Parks

HOW-TO GUIDES
Avalanche Aware
Backpacking Tips
Bear Aware
Desert Hiking Tips
Hiking with Dogs
Leave No Trace
Mountain Lion Alert
Reading Weather
Route Finding
Using GPS
Wilderness First Aid
Wilderness Survival

WALKING
Walking Colorado Springs
Walking Denver
Walking Portland
Walking St. Louis
Walking Virginia Beach

■ *To order any of these books, check with your local bookseller*
*or call FALCON® at **1-800-582-2665***.
Visit us on the world wide web at:
www.FalconOutdoors.com

FALCON®

FALCON GUIDES® Leading the Way™

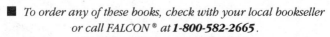